# Modern Critical Interpretations

Adventures of Huckleberry Finn
All Quiet on the Western Front
Animal Farm
Beloved
Beowulf
Billy Budd, Benito Cereno, Bartleby
    the Scrivener, and Other Tales
The Bluest Eye
The Catcher in the Rye
Catch-22
The Color Purple
Crime and Punishment
The Crucible
Daisy Miller, The Turn of the Screw,
    and Other Tales
David Copperfield
Death of a Salesman
The Divine Comedy
Don Quixote
Dubliners
Emma
Fahrenheit 451
A Farewell to Arms
Frankenstein
The General Prologue to the
    Canterbury Tales
The Glass Menagerie
The Grapes of Wrath
Great Expectations
The Great Gatsby
Gulliver's Travels
Hamlet
The Handmaid's Tale
Heart of Darkness
I Know Why the Caged Bird Sings
The Iliad
The Interpretation of Dreams
Invisible Man
Jane Eyre
Julius Caesar
King Lear
Long Day's Journey into Night
Lord Jim
Lord of the Flies
The Lord of the Rings

Macbeth
The Merchant of Venice
The Metamorphosis
A Midsummer Night's Dream
Moby-Dick
My Ántonia
Native Son
Night
1984
The Odyssey
Oedipus Rex
The Old Man and the Sea
Othello
Paradise Lost
The Pardoner's Tale
A Portrait of the Artist as a Young
    Man
Pride and Prejudice
The Red Badge of Courage
The Rime of the Ancient Mariner
Romeo and Juliet
The Scarlet Letter
A Scholarly Look at the Diary of
    Anne Frank
A Separate Peace
Slaughterhouse Five
Song of Solomon
The Sonnets
The Sound and the Fury
The Stranger
A Streetcar Named Desire
Sula
The Sun Also Rises
A Tale of Two Cities
The Tales of Poe
The Tempest
Tess of the D'Urbervilles
Their Eyes Were Watching God
To Kill a Mockingbird
Ulysses
Waiting for Godot
Walden
The Waste Land
Wuthering Heights

*Modern Critical Interpretations*

Margaret Atwood's
*The Handmaid's Tale*

*Edited and with an introduction by*
Harold Bloom
Sterling Professor of the Humanities
Yale University

CHELSEA HOUSE PUBLISHERS
Philadelphia

Library of Congress Cataloging-in-Publication Data

The handmaid's tale / Harold Bloom, editor.
    p.cm. — (Modern critical interpretations)
  Includes bibliographical references(p. ) and index.
  ISBN 0-7910-5926-X (alk. paper)
    1. Atwood, Margaret Eleanor, 1939–     . Handmaid's tale.
  2. Fantasy fiction, Canadian—History and criticism.
  I. Bloom, Harold.   II. Series.
  PR9199.3.A8  H3165  2001
    813'.54—dc21                              00-065839

Chelsea House Publishers
1974 Sproul Road, Suite 400
Broomall, PA 19008-0914

The Chelsea House World Wide Web address is
http://www.chelseahouse.com

Contributing Editor: Pamela Loos

Produced by: Robert Gerson Publisher's Services, Santa Barbara, CA

# Contents

Editor's Note     vii

Introduction     1
   *Harold Bloom*

Margaret Atwood's *The Handmaid's Tale* and
the Dystopian Tradition     3
   *Amin Malak*

Nature and Nurture in Dystopia: *The Handmaid's Tale*     11
   *Roberta Rubenstein*

"Trust Me": Reading the Romance Plot in Margaret Atwood's
*The Handmaid's Tale*     21
   *Madonne Miner*

The Misogyny of Patriarchal Culture in *The Handmaid's Tale*     41
   *J. Brooks Bouson*

Off the Path to Grandma's House in *The Handmaid's Tale*     63
   *Sharon Rose Wilson*

"The Missionary Position": Feminism and Nationalism in
Margaret Atwood's *The Handmaid's Tale*     81
   *Sandra Tomc*

*The Handmaid's Tale*: Dystopia and the Paradoxes of Power     93
   *Glenn Deer*

Margaret Atwood's *The Handmaid's Tale*:
Resistance through Narrating     113
   *Hilde Staels*

Margaret Atwood's Modest Proposal: *The Handmaid's Tale*     127
   *Karen Stein*

What Is Real/Reel? Margaret Atwood's "Rearrangement of
Shapes on a Flat Surface," or Narrative as Collage     141
   *Marta Dvorak*

*The Handmaid's Tale*: "Historical Notes" and
Documentary Subversion     155
   *Dominick M. Grace*

Chronology     167

Contributors     171

Bibliography     173

Acknowledgments     177

Index     179

# Editor's Note

My Introduction admires the literary skill and grim humor of *The Handmaid's Tale*.

In the first two essays, Amin Malak and Roberta Rubenstein each discuss *The Handmaid's Tale* in the tradition of Dystopian fiction, after which Madonne Miner reads the romance plot in the work and J. Brooks Bouson comments on the patriarchal culture described in the book.

Sharon Rose Wilson reads *The Handmaid's Tale* as a fairy tale about fairy tales, and Sandra Tomc asserts that the novel fails as feminist doctrine. Glenn Deer emphasizes Atwood's cunningly firm authorial control, after which Atwoodian Gothic is seen by Hilde Staels as a turning-inside-out of the genre.

Karen Stein explains how the epigraphs chosen as framing texts prepare the reader of *The Handmaid's Tale*, and Marta Dvorak discusses Atwood's use of visual images in the novel.

In the volume's final essay, Dominick M. Grace parses the "Historical Notes" that close *The Handmaid's Tale*.

# Introduction

Literary survival, as such, was not my overt subject when I started out as a critic, nearly a half-century ago, but I have aged into an exegete who rarely moves far from a concern with the question: Will it last? I have little regard for the ideologies—feminist, Marxist, historicist, deconstructive that now tend to dominate both literary study and literary journalism. Margaret Atwood seems to me vastly superior as a critic of Atwood to the ideologues she attracts. My brief comments upon *The Handmaid's Tale* will be indebted to Atwood's own published observations, and if I take any issue with her, it is with diffidence, as she herself is an authentic authority upon literary survival.

I first read *The Handmaid's Tale* in 1986, shortly after it was published. Rereading it in 1999 remains a frightening experience, even if one lives in New Haven and New York City, and not in Cambridge, Massachusetts, where the Handmaid Offred suffers the humiliations and torments afflicted upon much of womankind in the Fascist Republic of Gilead, which has taken over the Northeastern United States. Atwood, in describing her novel as a dystopia, called it a cognate of *A Clockwork Orange*, *Brave New World*, and *Nineteen Eighty-Four*. All of these, in 1999, are now period pieces. Anthony Burgess's *A Clockwork Orange*, despite its Joycean wordplay, is a much weaker book than his memorable *Inside Enderby*, or his superb *Nothing Like the Sun*, persuasively spoken by Shakespeare-as-narrator. Aldous Huxley's *Brave New World* now seems genial but thin to the point of transparency, while George Orwell's *Nineteen Eighty-Four* is just a rather bad fiction. Approaching Millennium, these prophecies do not caution us. London's thugs, like New York City's, are not an enormous menace; Henry Ford does not seem to be the God of the American Religion; Big Brother is not yet watching us, in our realm of virtual reality. But theocracy is a live menace: in Iran and Afghanistan, in the influence of the Christian Coalition upon the Republican Party, and on a much smaller scale, in the tyranny over English-speaking universities of our New Puritans, the academic feminists. *The Handmaid's*

*Tale*, even if it did not have authentic aesthetic value (and it does), is not at all a period piece under our current circumstances. The Right-to-Life demagogues rant on, urging that the Constitution be amended, and while contemporary Mormonism maintains its repudiation of plural marriage, the Old Faith of Joseph Smith and Brigham Young is practiced by tens of thousands of polygamists in Utah and adjacent states.

Atwood says of *The Handmaid's Tale*: "It is an imagined account of what happens when not uncommon pronouncements about women are taken to their logical conclusions." Unless there is a Swiftian irony in that sentence, which I cannot quite hear, I am moved to murmur: just when and where, in the world of Atwood and her readers, are those not uncommon pronouncements being made? There are a certain number of Southern Republican senators, and there is the leadership of the Southern Baptist convention, and some other clerical Fascists, who perhaps would dare to make such pronouncements, but "pronouncements" presumably have to be public, and in 1999 you don't get very far by saying that a woman's place is in the home. Doubtless we still have millions of men (and some women) who in private endorse the Bismarckian formula for women: *Kinder, Kirche, und Kuchen*, but they do not proclaim these sentiments to the voters.

Atwood makes a less disputable point when she warns us about the history of American Puritanism, which is long and dangerous. Its tendencies are always with us, and speculative fictions from Hawthorne to Atwood legitimately play upon its darkest aspects. *The Handmaid's Tale* emerges from the strongest strain in Atwood's imaginative sensibility, which is Gothic. A Gothic dystopia is an oddly mixed genre, but Atwood makes it work. Offred's tone is consistent, cautious, and finally quite frightening. Atwood, in much, if not most, of her best poetry and prose, writes Northern Gothic in the tradition of the Brontës and of Mary Shelley. Though acclaimed by so many Post-Modernist ideologues, Atwood is a kind of late Victorian novelist, and all the better for it. Her Gilead, at bottom, is a vampiric realm, a society sick with blood. *The Handmaid's Tale* is a brilliant Gothic achievement, and a salutary warning to keep our Puritanism mostly in the past.

AMIN MALAK

# Margaret Atwood's The Handmaid's Tale and the Dystopian Tradition

In *The History of Sexuality*, Michel Foucault impressively articulates the complex, formidably paradoxical relationship between sexuality and power, arguing how power dictates its law to sex:

> To deal with sex, power employs nothing more than a law of prohibition. Its objective: that sex renounce itself. Its instrument: the threat of a punishment that is nothing other than the suppression of sex. Renounce yourself or suffer the penalty of being suppressed; do not appear if you do not want to disappear. Your existence will be maintained only at the cost of your nullification. Power constrains sex only through a taboo that plays on the alternative between two nonexistences.

Any reader of Margaret Atwood's *The Handmaid's Tale* needs to recall Foucault's observation to contextualize the agonies of the narrator-protagonist, Offred, the victim of such a prohibition ordinance. By focusing the narrative on one central character, Atwood reveals the indignity and terror of living under a futuristic regime controlled by Christian fundamentalists. The heroine is one of several "handmaids" who, because of their "viable ovaries," are confined to a prison-like compound in order to be

From *Canadian Literature* 112 (Spring 1987). © 1996 by the University of British Columbia, Vancouver.

available for periodically programmed sexual intercourse with their "Commanders of the Faith." This church-state regime, called Gilead, condones such an unorthodox practice out of necessity to overcome a fertility crisis amongst the dwindling Caucasian population; as one of the novel's epigrams suggests, the polygamy of the Old Testament provides the sanction. True to the precedent set in Genesis, the Commander's Wife arranges and supervises these sex sessions, in which the handmaid, desexed and dehumanized, is obliged to participate. The dire alternative for the handmaid is banishment to the colonies, where women clean up radioactive waste as slave labourers. The dictates of state policy in Gilead thus relegate sex to a saleable commodity exchanged for mere minimal survival.

One of the novel's successful aspects concerns the skilful portrayal of a state that in theory claims to be founded on Christian principles, yet in practice miserably lacks spirituality and benevolence. The state in Gilead prescribes a pattern of life based on frugality, conformity, censorship, corruption, fear, and terror—in short, the usual terms of existence enforced by totalitarian states, instance of which can be found in such dystopian works as Zamyatin's *We*, Huxley's *Brave New World*, and Orwell's *1984*.

In order to situate Atwood's novel within the relevant context of dystopia, I wish to articulate the salient dystopian features those three classics reveal. The ensuing discussion will be an elaboration on Atwood's rendition and redefinition of those features.

1. *Power, Totalitarianism, War:*

Dystopias essentially deal with power: power as the prohibition or perversion of human potential; power in its absolute form that, to quote from *1984*, tolerates no flaws in the pattern it imposes on society. Dystopias thus show, in extreme terms, power functioning efficiently and mercilessly to its optimal totalitarian limit. Interestingly, war or foreign threats often loom in the background, providing the pretext to join external tension with internal terror.

2. *Dream-Nightmare: Fantasy: Reality:*

While dystopias may be fear-laden horror fiction (how the dream turns into a nightmare), the emphasis of the work is not on horror for its own sake, but on forewarning. Similarly, while dystopias contain elements of the fantastic with a "touch of excess" carrying the narrative "one step [or more] beyond our reality," the aim is neither to distort reality beyond recognition, nor to provide an escapist world for the reader, but "to allow certain tendencies in modern society to spin forward without the brake of sentiment and humaneness."

3. *Binary Oppositions:*

Dystopias dramatize the eternal conflict between individual choice and social necessity: the individual resenting the replacement of his private volition by compulsory uniformitarian decisions made by an impersonal bureaucratic machinery; Zamyatin's heroine poignantly sums up the conflict: "I do not want anyone to want for me. I want to want for myself." The sphere of the binary opposition expands further to cover such dialectical dualities as emotion and reason, creative imagination and mathematical logic, intuition and science, tolerance and judgment, kindness and cruelty, spirituality and materialism, love and power, good and evil. The list can go on.

4. *Characterization:*

Dystopias often tend to offer two-dimensional character types; this tendency is possibly due to the pressure of the metaphorical and ideological thrust of these works. Moreover, the nightmarish atmosphere of dystopias seems to preclude advancing positive, assertive characters that might provide the reader with consoling hope. If such positive characters do exist, they usually prove miserably ineffectual when contending with ruthless overwhelming powers.

5. *Change and Time:*

Dystopian societies, consumed and controlled by regressive dogmas, appear constantly static: founded on coercion and rigid structures, the system resists change and becomes arrested in paralysis. Such a static life "shorn of dynamic possibility," becomes for the underprivileged members of society mediocre, monotonous and predictable: "a given and measured quantity that can neither rise to tragedy nor tumble to comedy." Accordingly, dystopias are not associated with innovation and progress, but with fear of the future. They use, however, the present as an instructive referent, offering a tacit alternative to the dystopian configuration.

## 6. *Roman à These:*

To varying degrees, dystopias are quintessentially ideological novels: they engage the reader in what Fredrick Jameson calls a "theoretical discourse," whereby a range of thematic possibilities are posited and polarized against each other, yet the novels eventually reveal a definite philosophical and socio-political outlook for which fiction proves to be a convenient medium.

What distinguishes Atwood's novel from those dystopian classics is its obvious feminist focus. Gilead is openly misogynistic, in both its theocracy and practice. The state reduces the handmaids to the slavery status of being mere "breeders" (a term bearing Swift's satirical coinage):

> We are all for breeding purposes: We aren't concubines, geisha girls, courtesans. On the contrary: everything possible has been done to remove us from that category. There is supposed to be nothing entertaining about us. . . . We are two-legged wombs, that's all: sacred vessels, ambulatory chalices.

In addition to the handmaids, Gilead offers its own state-sponsored brand of prostitutes called the Jezebels: dolled-up women whose sole function is to entertain foreign delegations. In order to erase the former identity of the handmaids, the state, moreover, cancels their original names and labels them according to the names of their Commanders, hence the names Offred, Ofglen, Ofwayne, Ofwarren. The women then become possessed articles, mere appendages to those men who exercise sexual mastery over them. The handmaid's situation lucidly illustrates Simone de Beauvoir's assertion in *The Second Sex* about man defining woman not as an autonomous being but as simply what he decrees to be relative to him: "For him she is sex—absolute sex, no less. She is defined and differentiated with reference to man and not with reference to her; she is the incidental, as opposed to the essential. He is the Subject, he is the Absolute—she is the Other." This view of man's marginalization of woman corroborates Foucault's earlier observation about the power-sex correlative; since man holds the sanctified reigns of power in society, he rules, assigns roles, and decrees after social, religious, and cosmic concepts convenient to his interests and desires.

However, not all the female characters in Atwood's novel are sympathetic, nor all the male ones demonic. The Aunts, a vicious élite of collaborators who conduct torture lectures, are among the church-state's staunchest supporters; these renegades turn into zealous converts, appropriating male values at the expense of their feminine instincts. One of them, Aunt Lydia, functions, ironically, as the spokesperson of antifeminism; she urges the handmaids to renounce themselves and become non-persons: "Modesty is invisibility, said Aunt Lydia. Never forget it. To be seen—to be *seen*—is to be—her voice trembled—penetrated. What you must be, girls, is impenetrable. She called us girls." On the other hand, Nick, the Commander's chauffeur, is involved with the underground network, of men and women, that aims at rescuing women and conducting sabotage. Besides, Atwood's heroine constantly yearns for her former marriage life with Luke, presently presumed dead. Accordingly, while Atwood poignantly condemns the misogynous mentality that can cause a heavy toll of human suffering, she refrains from convicting a gender in its entirety as the perpetrator of the nightmare that is Gilead. Indeed, we witness very few of the male characters acting with stark cruelty: the narrative reports most of the violent acts after the fact, sparing the reader gory scenes. Even the Commander appears more pathetic than sinister, baffled than manipulative, almost, at times, a Fool.

Some may interpret Atwood's position here as a non-feminist stance, approving of women's status-quo. In a review for the *Times Literary Supplement*, Lorna Sage describes *The Handmaid's Tale* as Atwood's "revisionist look at her more visionary self," and as "a novel in praise of the present, for which, perhaps, you have to have the perspective of dystopia." It is really difficult to conceive Atwood's praising the present, because, like Orwell who in *1984* extrapolated specific ominous events and tendencies in twentieth-century politics, she tries to caution against right-wing fundamentalism, rigid dogmas, and misogynous theosophies that may be currently gaining a deceptive popularity. The novel's mimetic impulse then aims at wresting an imperfect present from a horror-ridden future: it appeals for vigilance, and an appreciation of the mature values of tolerance, compassion, and, above all, for women's unique identity.

The novel's thematics operate by posting polarized extremes: a decadent present, which Aunt Lydia cynically describes as "a society dying . . . of too much choice," and a totalitarian future that prohibits choice. Naturally, while rejecting the indulgent decadence and chaos of an anarchic society, the reader condemns the Gilead regime for its intolerant, prescriptive set of values that projects a tunnel vision on reality and eliminates human volition: "There is more than one kind of freedom, said Aunt Lydia. Freedom to and freedom from. In the days of anarchy, it was freedom to. Now you are being given freedom from. Don't underrate it." As illustrated by the fears and agonies that Offred endures, when human beings are not free to aspire toward whatever they wish, when choices become so severely constrained that, to quote from Dostoyevsky's *The Possessed*, "only the necessary is necessary," life turns into a painfully prolonged prison term. Interestingly, the victimization process does not involve Offred and the handmaids alone, but extends to the oppressors as well. Everyone ruled by the Gilead regime suffers the deprivation of having no choice, except what the church-state decrees; even the Commander is compelled to perform his sexual assignment with Offred as a matter of obligation: "This is no recreation, even for the Commander. This is serious business. The Commander, too, is doing his duty."

Since the inhabitants of Gilead lead the precarious existence befitting victims, most try in varied ways to cope, endure, and survive. This situation of being a victim and trying to survive dramatizes Atwood's major thesis in her critical work *Survival: A Thematic Guide to Canadian Literature*, in which she suggests that Canada, metaphorically still a colony or an oppressed minority, is "a collective victim," and that "the central symbol for Canada . . . is undoubtedly Survival, *la Survivance.*" Atwood, furthermore, enumerates what she labels "basic victim positions," whereby a victim may choose any of four possible options, one of which is to acknowledge being a victim but refuse "to accept the assumption that the role is inevitable." This position fully explains Offred's role as the protagonist-narrator of *The Handmaid's Tale.* Offred's progress as a maturing consciousness is indexed by an evolving awareness of herself as a victimized woman, and then a gradual development toward initiating risky but assertive schemes that break the slavery syndrome. Her double-crossing the Commander and his Wife, her choice to hazard a sexual affair with Nick, and her association with the underground network, all point to the shift from being a helpless victim to being a sly, subversive survivor. This impulse to survive, together with the occasional flashes of warmth and concern among the handmaids, transmits reassuring signs of hope and humanity in an otherwise chilling and depressing tale.

What makes Atwood's book such a moving tale is its clever technique in presenting the heroine initially as a voice, almost like a sleepwalker conceiving disjointed perceptions of its surroundings, as well as flashing reminiscences about a bygone life. As the scenes gather more details, the heroine's voice is steadily and imperceptively, yet convincingly, transfigured into a full-roundedness, that parallels her maturing comprehension of what is happening around her. Thus the victim, manipulated and coerced, is metamorphosed into a determined conniver who daringly violates the perverted canons of Gilead. Moreover, Atwood skilfully manipulates the time sequence between the heroine's past (pre-Gilead life) and the present: those shifting reminiscences offer glimpses of a life, though not ideal, still filled with energy, creativity, humaneness and a sense of selfhood, a life that sharply contrasts with the alienation, slavery, and suffering under totalitarianism. By the end of the novel, the reader is effectively and conclusively shown how the misogynous regime functions on the basis of power, not choice; coercion, not volition; fear, not desire. In other words, Atwood administers in doses the assaulting shocks to our sensibilities of a grim dystopian nightmare: initially, the narrative voice, distant and almost diffidently void of any emotions, emphasizes those aspects of frugality and solemnity imposed by the state, then progressively tyranny and corruption begin to unfold piecemeal. As the novel concludes, as the horror reaches a climax, the narrative voice assumes a fully engaged emotional tone that cleverly keeps us in suspense about the heroine's fate. This method of measured, well-punctuated revelations about Gilead connects symbolically with the novel's central meaning: misogynous dogmas, no matter how seemingly innocuous and trustworthy they may appear at their initial conception, are bound, when allowed access to power, to reveal their ruthlessly tyrannical nature.

Regardless of the novel's dystopian essence, it nevertheless avoids being solemn; on the contrary, it sustains an ironic texture throughout. We do not find too many frightening images that may compare with Oceana's torture chambers: the few graphic horror scenes are crisply and snappily presented, sparing us a blood-curdling impact. (Some may criticize this restraint as undermining the novel's integrity and emotional validity.) As in all dystopias, Atwood's aim is to encourage the reader to adopt a rational stance that avoids *total* "suspension of disbelief." This rational stance dislocates full emotional involvement in order to create a Brechtian type of alienation that, in turn, generates an ironic charge. This rational stance too should not be total, because Atwood does want us to care sympathetically about her heroine's fate; hence the emotional distance between reader and character must allow for closeness, but up to a point. Furthermore, Atwood is equally keen on preserving the ironic flair intact. No wonder then that she concludes *The Handmaid's Tale* with a climactic moment of irony: she exposes, in a hilarious epilogue, the absurdity and futility of certain academic writings that engage in dull, clinically sceptic analysis of irrelevancies and inanities, yet miss the vital issues. "If I may be permitted an editorial aside," blabbers the keynote speaker at a twenty-second century anthropological conference,

> allow me to say that in my opinion we must be cautious about passing moral judgement upon the Gileadeans. Surely we have learned by now that such judgements are of necessity culture-specific. Also, Gileadean society was under a good deal of pressure, demographic and otherwise, and was subject to factors from which we ourselves are happily more free. Our job is not to censure but to understand. (Applause.)

The entire "Historical Notes" at the end of the novel represents a satire on critics who spin out theories about literary or historical texts without genuinely recognizing or experiencing the pathos expressed in them: they circumvent issues, classify data, construct clever hypotheses garbed in ritualistic, fashionable jargon, but no spirited illumination ever comes out of their endeavours. Atwood soberly demonstrates that when a critic or scholar (and by extension a reader) avoids, under the guise of scholarly objectivity, taking a moral or political stand about an issue of crucial magnitude such as totalitarianism, he or she will necessarily become an apologist for evil; more significantly, the applause the speaker receives gives us a further compelling glimpse into a distant future that still harbours strong misogynous tendencies.

While the major dystopian features can clearly be located in *The Handmaid's Tale*, the novel offers two distinct additional features: feminism and irony. Dramatizing the interrelationship between power and sex, the book's feminism, despite condemning male misogynous mentality, upholds and cherishes a man-woman axis; here, feminism functions inclusively rather than exclusively, poignantly rather than stridently, humanely rather than cynically. The novel's ironic tone, on the other hand, betokens a confident narrative strategy that aims at treating a depressing material gently and gradually, yet firmly, openly, and conclusively, thus skilfully succeeding in securing the reader's sympathy and interest. The novel shows Atwood's strengths both as an engaging story-teller and a creator of a sympathetic heroine, and as an articulate crafts-woman of a theme that is both current and controversial. As the novel signifies a landmark in the maturing process of Atwood's creative career, her self-assured depiction of the grim dystopian world gives an energetic and meaningful impetus to the genre.

ROBERTA RUBENSTEIN

# Nature and Nurture in Dystopia:
# The Handmaid's Tale

One might say that Margaret Atwood has always been concerned with issues of survival—first as a condition of Canadian experience and, more recently, as a condition of female experience. In her latest fiction and poetry, she connects the personal and political dimensions of victimization and survival in explicitly female and feminist terms. Moreover, in the course of her fiction the terms of survival have become increasingly problematic. In her fablelike *The Handmaid's Tale*, she stunningly extends, recasts, and inverts two of the most persistent clusters of theme and imagery that originate in her earlier concern with survival: *nature* and *nurture*.

As a number of her commentators have pointed out, Atwood uses the imagery of nature in her poetry and fiction in complex ways, delineating the terms of survival and growth as well as oppression and death. Concurrently, from the beginning of her fictional oeuvre in particular, *nurture*—I use the term here as ironic shorthand for motherhood and procreation—is viewed in problematic terms. In *The Edible Woman*, Marian MacAlpin's female friends dramatize extreme attitudes toward procreation as a "natural" function of female identity: Ainsley is obsessed with becoming pregnant while Clara is virtually engulfed by maternity. Marian views both women with scepticism and anxiety. A central problem for the narrator of *Surfacing* is the necessity to come to terms with her denied abortion; the somewhat ambiguous sign of

From *Margaret Atwood: Vision and Forms*. © 1988 by the Board of Trustees, Southern Illinois University.

11

her psychological recovery is her desire to be impregnated by her primitive lover, Joe.

Joan Foster of *Lady Oracle* also feels anxiety about motherhood, principally because for much of her life (as revealed in her story) she has remained psychologically merged with her destructive mother. Her childhood obesity and her adult fantasies of the sideshow "Fat Lady" are grotesque exaggerations of anxieties about maternity. In *Life Before Man* Elizabeth Schoenhof and Lesje Green represent complementary views of motherhood. Elizabeth has appreciative but rather remote relationships with her two daughters; Lesje, unmarried but perhaps pregnant (by Elizabeth's husband, Nate) by the end of the narrative, seeks maternity to confirm her fragile female identity. Rennie Wilford of *Bodily Harm* worries that the cancer in her body, which has already resulted in the loss of part of a breast, will fundamentally alter her reproductive capacity.

In *The Handmaid's Tale*, female anxieties associated with fertility, procreation, and maternity are projected as feminist nightmare and cultural catastrophe. Atwood demonstrates the way in which the profound and irreconcilable split between "pro-life" and "pro-choice" ideologies of reproduction in contemporary social experience corroborate female ambivalence about childbearing in patriarchy. She imagines a world in which women are explicitly defined by their potential fertility (or its absence); procreation and maternity are simultaneously idealized and dehumanized.

Atwood has recently acknowledged her increasingly explicit ideological focus, noting that there is a vital connection between the function of the novel as a "moral instrument," the responsibility of the writer to "bear witness," and politics. As she elaborates, "By 'political' I mean having to do with power: who's got it, who wants it, how it operates; in a word, who's allowed to do what to whom, who gets away with it and how." In her most recent novel to date, the correspondences between "personal" and "political" find brilliant and disturbing expression. Both public and private worlds are radically altered, exaggerating the unresolved cultural and ideological controversy over the circumstances of procreation.

In the Republic of Gilead the "natural" world is utterly denatured. Pollution of the environment has resulted in adult sterility and genetic mutation and deformity of offspring; generativity itself is at risk. Hence, fertile females are made vessels for procreation; anatomy is indeed destiny. The physically confining rooms, walls, and other actual boundaries of the Republic of Gilead corroborate the condition of reproductive "confinement" to which the handmaids are subject. Maternity is both wish (handmaids are discarded after three unsuccessful attempts at pregnancy) and fear (the baby, unless deformed and declared an "Unbaby," becomes the property of the handmaid's Commander and his wife). The surrogate mother's function ceases after a brief lactation period following delivery of a healthy child.

The handmaid Offred (the narrator), subjected to sexual exploitation masquerading as religious fervor and worship of procreation, experiences herself as utterly subordinated to the procreative function. In her former life she had regarded her body as an "instrument" under her own control—with "limits . . . but nevertheless lithe, single, solid, one with me." In Gilead, her body, like that of her coequal "handmaids," exists literally to be used against her: "Now the flesh rearranges itself differently. I'm a cloud, congealed around a central object, the shape of a pear, which is hard and more real than I am and glows red within its translucent wrapping. Inside it is a space, huge as the sky at night. . . ." Under the pressure of terrifying alternatives, Offred (whose name encodes her indentured sexuality: both "offered" and the property "Of-Fred") "resign[s her] body freely, to the uses of others. They can do what they like with me. I am abject"—and object.

## II

From the central issue of procreation to the language and imagery that form the substructure of Offred's narrative, *The Handmaid's Tale* demonstrates multiple inversions and violations of *nature* and *natural*. Not only is the female body used as a tool for reproduction, but bodies in general are objectified and described in terms of parts rather than as wholes. In *Bodily Harm* Atwood implied that the reduction of the body to a "thing" is connected to its violation; in *The Handmaid's Tale* torture and mutilation as well as less extreme forms of manipulation underscore the ruthless and repressive values that shape Gilead. Both men and women who are identified as political "enemies" of the state—guilty of such crimes as "gender treachery"—are sacrificed at public ceremonies called "Salvagings" (the word resonates ironically with *salvage, salvation,* and *savaging*) in which they are mutilated and hanged in public view.

Other images throughout the narrative reinforce the symbolism of disembodiment and dismemberment. When Offred tries to recall her visceral connections to the husband and daughter from whom she has been so abruptly separated, she mourns, "Nobody dies from lack of sex. It's lack of love we die from. There's nobody here I can love. . . . Who knows where they are or what their names are now? They might as well be nowhere, as I am for them. I too am a missing person. . . . Can I be blamed for wanting a real body, to put my arms around? Without it I too am disembodied." Most obviously, Offred and other handmaids are, to those in power in Gilead, merely parts of bodies: "two-legged wombs." The doctor who examines them periodically for signs of pregnancy never even sees their faces; he "deals with a torso only." The ceiling ornament in Offred's room resembles "the place in a face where the eye has been taken out"; in fact, there are Eyes—the network of informants (C-Eye-A?)—everywhere. The grappling hooks on the large Berlin Wall–like structure where criminals are hanged look like "appliances for the armless." An image of people with "no legs" resonates with the unknown but terrible torture to which the rebel handmaid Moira is subjected and with Offred's first intimation of the changing dispensation that has culminated in the Republic of Gilead. When she and other women were fired from their jobs and summarily stripped of political and legal rights, she felt as if someone had "cut off [her] feet." In these latter instances of literal or symbolic mutilation of female feet, the image of Chinese footbinding— another form of social control of women—comes to mind.

In Gilead, Aunt Lydia (one of the "Aunts," who retain power in the puritanical state through their role as indoctrinators of the handmaids) speaks distastefully of women in the recent past who cultivated suntans, "oiling themselves like roast meat on a spit. . . ." In her former life, Offred had been aware of the self-mutilations practiced by women who, desperate to attract men, had "starved themselves thin or pumped their breasts full of silicone, had their noses cut off." She also recalls more violent crimes against the (implicitly female) body, as expressed in newspaper stories of "corpses in ditches or the woods, bludgeoned to death or mutilated, interfered with as they used to say. . . ." In Gilead the handmaids, as part of their "re-education" in submission, are made to watch old pornographic films from the seventies and eighties in which women appear in various attitudes of submission, brutalization, and grotesque mutilation. Extrapolating from these contemporary realities, Atwood extends into the future her critique of female brutalization articulated in *Bodily Harm* and in recent essays.

The imagery of mutilation and dismemberment permeates the narrator's own language. Offred struggles to "reconstruct" her fragmented selfhood and to justify the choices she has made (or which have been imposed on her) under the circumstances she describes. Her past experiences, apparently severed from the "present" time of Gileadean tyranny, are in fact linked by these very images of female brutalization. The terse words she exchanges with other handmaids, who may or may not be trustworthy confidantes, are "amputated speech." Late in her story Offred apologizes to an unknown audience in whom she must believe for her own survival; her story is an act of self-generation that opposes the oppressive obligations of procreation. She describes her narrative as if it were herself, "a body caught in crossfire or pulled apart by force . . . this sad and hungry and sordid, this limping and mutilated story."

## III

Among the multiple inversions of normalcy in *The Handmaid's Tale* are frequent references to animals, plants, smells, and other objects or experiences typically associated with "nature." In Gilead the changing seasons bring no solace; spring is "undergone." The month of May, however, is linked with the one possibility of freedom: the password of the resistance movement, "Mayday," with its coded message of "*M'aidez*."

Flowers are among the few objects of the natural world whose symbolic associations have not been entirely corrupted. Offred frequently describes them in terms of color and variety and, late in her narrative, confesses that they are among the "good things" she has tried to put in her sordid story. More often, flowers and plants suggest the confining circumstances of sexuality and reproduction. Offred struggles to keep the image of crimson tulips (also the color of the nunlike robes worn by the handmaids) free from association with blood. The blossoms worn by Serena Joy (the ironic name of Offred's Commander's wife) are withered, like her sexuality; flowers are, Offred reminds herself, merely "the genital organs of plants." Elsewhere she describes the reeking "stink" of "pollen thrown into the wind in handfuls, like oyster spawn into the sea. All this prodigal breeding." Handmaids are told to think of themselves as seeds; their password to each other is "Blessed be the fruit"—yet seeds and fruit are associated with manipulated, not natural, reproduction.

The narrative is studded with such references to plant and animal life—generally primitive or lower forms—which are often juxtaposed with aspects of the human body and/or sexuality. The animals in Gilead are, for the most part, repugnant. A virtual menagerie of insects, fish, fowl, and beasts parades, figuratively, through the narrative: ant, beetle, spider, fly, worm, oyster, mollusk, rat, mouse, fish, frog, snake, pigeon, hawk, vulture, chicken, turkey, pig, sheep, horse, cat, dog, elephant. The handmaids are treated like brood livestock: tattooed with "cattle brands," they are kept in line by women called Aunts who wield electric cattleprods.

The "livestock" of the narrative is partly of the zoo, partly of the barnyard—the latter figures recalling Orwell's satiric *Animal Farm*. Offred thinks of herself, in the eyes of the powers of Gilead, as a "prize pig"; another handmaid takes mincing steps like a "trained pig." Both usages resonate ironically with the other-gendered "chauvinist pig[s]" and "fucking pigs" of Offred's mother's generation. A number of the animal images are associated with confinement: caged rats in mazes, "held birds" or birds with wings clipped or "stopped in flight," and the predatory relationship of spider to fly. Handmaids are both sexual "bait" and "baited," as in the sense of "fishbait" or "throwing peanuts at elephants."

Often, the animal references suggest the debased, denatured, dismembered human body as mere flesh. Offred, walking after a rainy night on a path through the back lawn that suggests "a hair parting," observes half-dead worms, "flexible and pink, like lips." In the dehumanized sexual act (a ménage à trois in the service of insemination: the Commander, his Wife, and the Handmaid), the penis is disembodied: the male "tentacle, his delicate stalked slug's eye, which extrudes, expands, winces, and shrivels back into himself when touched wrongly, grows big again, bulging a little at the tip, travelling forward as if along a leaf, into [the women], avid for vision." Elsewhere Offred imagines sexual encounters between "Angels" and their brides (insipid young men and women of Gilead who actually marry) as "furry encounters . . . cocks like three-week-old carrots, anguished fumblings upon flesh cold and unresponding as uncooked fish." Similarly, she imagines a balding Commander with his wife and handmaid, "fertilizing away like mad, like a rutting salmon. . . ."

Thus, in the perverse relations of Gilead, the distinctions between "natural" and "unnatural," between human and nonhuman, are grotesquely inverted or reduced. In a central passage Atwood suggestively links these levels of imagery and theme, clustering the ideas of institutionalized reproduction, environmental pollution, and the inversions between animal, vermin, and human that result from these perversions of normalcy. As Offred explains,

> The air got too full, once, of chemicals, rays, radiation, the water swarmed with toxic molecules, all of that takes years to clean up, and meanwhile they creep into your body, camp out in your fatty cells. Who knows, your very flesh may be polluted, dirty as an oily beach, sure death to shore birds and unborn babies. Maybe a vulture would die of eating you. Maybe you light up in the dark, like an old-fashioned watch. Death watch. That's a kind of beetle, it buries carrion.
>
> I can't think of myself, my body, sometimes, without seeing the skeleton: how I must appear to an electron. A cradle of life made of bones; and within, hazards, warped proteins, bad crystal jagged as glass. Women took medicines, pills, men sprayed trees, cows ate grass, all that souped-up piss flowed into the rivers. Not to mention the exploding atomic power plants, along the San Andreas fault, nobody's fault, during the earthquakes, and the mutant strain of syphilis no mould could touch. Some did it themselves, had themselves tied shut with catgut or scarred with chemicals.

The chances of giving birth to a deformed infant are, the handmaids learn during their indoctrination, one in four. Yet Gileadean ideology prohibits birth control and abortion under any circumstances as "unnatural" and obliges the handmaids to submit to "natural" childbirth without medication. The pregnancy that culminates in birth during Offred's narrative is a manifestation of this revolt by nature, the blurring of categories of living forms. Before the handmaid Janine delivers, Offred speculates on whether the baby will be normal or "an Unbaby, with a pinhead or a snout like a dog's, or two bodies, or a hole in its heart or no arms, or webbed hands and feet." In fact the baby initially seems normal, but is later discovered to be deformed and is mysteriously disposed of. Despite the obsessive focus on procreation, actual children are notably absent from Gilead. The only child described in the narrative is the young daughter from whom Offred has been painfully separated.

As part of the inversion of "natural" in the unnatural Republic of Gilead, Atwood demonstrates the assault on the senses as well as the body and the psyche. In keeping with the implicit barnyard references, Gilead *stinks*. The stench of rotting flesh from the corpses of executed political enemies—including doctors who practiced abortion—masks the equally humanmade but relatively less repugnant odors of "Pine and Floral" deodorizing sprays. As Offred phrases it, "people retain the taste" for these artificial scents as the expression of "purity"—embodying the false connection between cleanliness and godliness.

Conversely, uncleanliness is associated with sin and—since sex is evil in Gilead apart from procreation—sexuality. The servant Martha's express distaste toward the handmaids, objecting to their smell; the handmaids, to whom baths are permitted as a luxury rather than as a hygienic routine, are regarded as unclean not only in the literal but in the moral sense. Nuns who are forced to renounce celibacy and become reproductive objects have "an odour of witch about them, something mysterious and exotic. . . ." When Offred first observes Nick, her Commander's chauffeur who later becomes her lover, she wonders whether or not he supports the status quo arrangements between the sexes. As she expresses her doubts, "Smells fishy, they used to say; or, I smell a rat. Misfit as odour." Yet, instead, she thinks of "how he might smell. Not fish or decaying rat: tanned skin, moist in the sun, filmed with smoke. I sigh, inhaling." When Offred tries to (and tries not to) imagine what might have happened to her husband, Luke, she thinks of him "surrounded by a smell, his own, the smell of a cooped-up animal in a dirty cage." Later the rebel handmaid Moira describes her contact with the underground resistance movement in similar terms. "'I almost made it out. They got me up as far as Salem, then in a truck full of chickens into Maine. I almost puked from the smell.'"

The air of Gilead is stagnant, suffocating, oppressive: literally, the polluted atmosphere; symbolically, the claustrophobia and oppression experienced by its unwilling female captives. Offred describes the atmosphere of a "birthing"—a collective ceremony, attended by both handmaids and wives who coach the delivering handmaid—in language that reverberates with other images derived from animals and nature: "the smell is of our own flesh, an organic smell, sweat and a tinge of iron, from the blood on the sheet, and another smell, more animal, that's coming, it must be, from Janine: a smell of dens, of inhabited caves. . . . Smell of matrix."

As the sense of smell is more typically assaulted by the unnatural, so is the sense of taste and the experience of hunger. References to the smells of food also demonstrate the perverse connection—or disconnection—between sensory stimuli and their objects. The odor of nail polish, improbably, stimulates Offred's appetite. Recalling the sexual violation termed "date rape" in her former life, she remembers that the term sounded like "some kind of dessert. *Date Rapé*."

In fact, like sex in Gilead, food serves only functional, not emotional, appetites. In a parody of the Lord's Prayer, Offred makes the connection between bread and spiritual sustenance, observing, "I have enough daily bread. . . . The problem is getting it down without choking on it." The yeasty aroma of baking bread, one of the few pleasant smells in Gilead, also recalls comfortable kitchens and "mothers": both Offred's own mother and herself as a mother. Accordingly, it is a "treacherous smell" that she must resist in order not to be overwhelmed by loss. Later she provides another context for these ambiguous associations as she recalls her childhood confusion about the extermination of the Jews: "In ovens, my mother said; but there weren't any pictures of the ovens, so I got some confused notion that these deaths had taken place in kitchens. There is something especially terrifying to a child in that idea. Ovens mean cooking, and cooking comes before eating. I thought these people had been eaten. Which in a way I suppose they had been."

Late in the narrative, Offred extends this link between eating and sacrifice. She describes another "Salvaging," the public execution of handmaids accused of treason and sacrificed before breakfast; she and the other handmaids grip a rope that reeks of tar, the other end of which is used to hang the offending women. Offred's reaction to her compulsory complicity in the horrifying event discloses the extent of her emotional numbing and deprivation. The tar odor makes her feel sick; yet at the same time,

> Death makes me hungry. Maybe it's because I've been emptied;
> or maybe it's the body's way of seeing to it that I remain alive,
> continue to repeat its bedrock prayer: *I am, I am*. I am, still.

I want to go to bed, make love, right now.
I think of the word *relish*.
I could eat a horse.

Offred's hungers are both literal and symbolic. Earlier, she had been "ravenous for news." When her Commander, having sought her out for forbidden companionship, allows her the proscribed act of reading, she reads like a starving person finally given food—"voraciously, almost skimming, trying to get as much into my head as possible before the next long starvation. If it were eating it would be the gluttony of the famished, if it were sex it would be a swift furtive stand-up in an alley somewhere." The pieces in the Scrabble game she plays with her Commander remind her of candies: peppermint, lime, "delicious." In Gilead, the act of intellectual intercourse is the equivalent of sin; as Offred puns, "Quick, eat those words."

"Nature" is also invoked in Gilead as justification for male sexual dominance and female oppression. Offred's Commander advises her that the era of romantic courtship and marriages based on love—the older dispensation—was "an anomaly, historically speaking. . . . All we've done is return things to Nature's norm." This "norm," however, leaves something to be desired for men who still prefer sex in the old manner, as conquest rather than duty. Those with power have access to a nightclub–brothel called Jezebel's. Resembling a Playboy Bunny Club, it is stocked with women in provocative costumes (primarily females "unassimilated" into other Gileadean roles) and private rooms for sexual assignations. To Offred's assumption that such things are "strictly forbidden," the Commander rejoins, "'but everyone's human, after all. . . . [Y]ou can't cheat Nature. . . . Nature demands variety, for men. . . . [I]t's part of the procreational strategy. It's Nature's plan.'" Even at Jezebel's, the ubiquitous, cattleprod-wielding Aunts preside, supervising the women's "rest breaks" and reinforcing the sense of sexual slavery that prevails in Gilead. The "forbidden" is accommodated, but only to serve traditional assumptions about male, not female, sexuality.

Offred's dark story of female exploitation concludes with an ambiguous event. A van arrives for her and—like an experience described by one of Kafka's characters—she has no way of knowing whether she is approaching her own "salvaging" or her salvation: whether she is being delivered into the hands of spies or rescuers. Entering the vehicle, she faces either her "end or a new beginning. . . . I have given myself over into the hands of strangers, because it can't be helped." The ambiguity corroborates the earlier conflations of death and birth: "And so I step up, into the darkness within; or else the light."

In the narrative's ironic coda, "Historical Notes on The Handmaid's Tale," the reader discovers that Offred's story was originally spoken onto audio tapes, presumably after her escape from the Republic of Gilead. From the distant perspective of the year 2195, at the Twelfth Symposium on Gileadean Studies held in Nunavit ("None-of-it"—presumably somewhere in the Arctic reaches of Canada), anthropologists and historians meet to debate the chronology and authenticity of events detailed in Offred's story. (One imagines Atwood wryly anticipating her commentators at the annual rites of MLA!) In this pseudopedantic coda, the imagery of nature that is so consistently inverted in the handmaid's own narrative is briefly parodied. The conference facilitators bear names (presumably analogous to Canadian Inuit) with associations with nature: Professors Maryann Crescent Moon and Johnny Running Dog. Program participants can avail themselves of special activities, including a fishing expedition and a Nature Walk.

From the more "objective" perspective of scholarly research, Professor Pieixoto, an archivist whose remarks comprise most of the coda, focuses less on the details of Offred's life than on the *men* who shaped it. Yet, as he concludes, "the past is a great darkness, and filled with echoes. Voices may reach us from it; but what they say to us is imbued with the obscurity of the matrix out of which they come. . . ."

Along with the professor's concessions to the limits of interpretation, his choice of words is particularly resonant, given the narrative that precedes his remarks. The "matrix" of Offred's experiences—with its linguistic associations with mother and matter—is the matrix out of which Atwood has written her dystopian fantasy of female oppression. If "nature" and "nurture" are the matrices out of which we come, *The Handmaid's Tale*, by inverting both, demonstrates the "broad outlines of the moment in history" in which we live: the inhospitable environment in which female identity must discover itself. Appropriately, the narrative ends with the interrogative, "'Are there any questions?'"

MADONNE MINER

# "Trust Me": Reading the Romance Plot in *Margaret Atwood's* The Handmaid's Tale

Midway through Margaret Atwood's *Handmaid's Tale*, the Commander sends a message to his wife's handmaid, Offred, that she is to meet him that evening in his study. Imagining that the Commander may ask her to engage in some kind of forbidden sexual activity, Offred is surprised when he expresses his desire: "'I'd like you to play a game of Scrabble with me.'" As the Commander takes the Scrabble box from his desk drawer and dumps out the counters, Offred realizes that this game *is* forbidden sexual activity. Under the Commander's watchful eye, Offred, no longer allowed to read or write, takes up the wooden counters, delicious, "like candies, made of peppermint, cool like that," and shapes them into luxurious words: "*Larynx*, I spell. *Valance. Quince. Zygote.*"

On subsequent evenings, Offred and the Commander repeat their game. Initially, she moves slowly: "My tongue felt thick with the effort of spelling. It was like using a language I'd once known but had nearly forgotten, a language having to do with customs that had long before passed out of the world." During early meetings, Offred and the Commander obey the rules of the game, of the language. When Offred, for example, spells "Zilch" ("A convenient one-vowel word with an expensive *Z*") the Commander challenges her, and she suggests "'We could look it up. . . . It's archaic.'" But as time passes, these two Scrabble players begin to alter the game. After a few

From *Twentieth Century Literature* 37, no. 2 (Summer 1991). © 1991 by Hofstra University.

drinks, the Commander "becomes silly, and cheats at Scrabble. He encourages me to do it too, and we take extra letters and make words with them that don't exist, words like *smurt* and *crup*, giggling over them."

I suggest that in this sequence, and various others throughout *The Handmaid's Tale*, we readers receive instructions in the reading process, lessons in how to construct meaning out of disparate pieces. Like Offred, we obey a grammar, set of rules, as we put together episodes, make chains ("words") out of segments of *The Handmaid's Tale*. First, Offred's words must belong to that club of words adjudged legitimate by a dictionary; our readings are similarly legitimized by signs of their membership in acceptable schools/traditions of reading. Second, when composing words, Offred must restrict herself to letters she draws from those spread out on the desktop; similarly, we are to compose our readings of *The Handmaid's Tale* relying upon what is "in" the text. But finally, just as Offred and the Commander "bend the rules" to allow for more free-wheeling creativity, so too we may find that "taking up extra letters" and playing with seemingly bizarre connections actually may lead us to some new understandings of the text.

*The Handmaid's Tale* worries over the plight of women in a society governed by religious fundamentalists committed to bolstering a seriously low birthrate (the result of toxic wastes, acid rain, and other environmental disasters which lead to sterility). In this "Republic of Gilead," fertile women are trained to serve as handmaids to infertile ones; each month, upon ovulation, the handmaid copulates with her mistress's husband (a Commander) and prays "let there be fruit." If conception occurs, the handmaid receives assistance in her labor and delivery from other handmaids, and then surrenders the child to her mistress. Having given birth successfully, the handmaid can rest assured that she will not be sent to the Colonies, where "unwomen" clean up toxic dumps and radiation spills.

Most readings of *The Handmaid's Tale* approach the text, quite rightly, as a dystopic novel, a cautionary vision of what might happen if certain attitudes are carried to extremes. Reactions to the *Tale* focus on its horrific presentation of "theocratic ambitions of the religious right," on its understanding of the sinister implications of an exaggerated cultural feminism (Ehrenreich), and on its critique of our own gender arrangements (Gileadean "solutions" highlight the problematic nature of sexual/social interactions in the 1980s). Many of these reactions also posit love as a force subverting Gilead's power. Coral Ann Howells, for example, argues that "heterosexual love is the excess term which the system can neither accommodate nor suppress. Its stubborn survival continually subverts the regime's claims to absolute authority, creating imaginative spaces within the system and finally the very means of Offred's escape from Gilead." In like fashion, Barbara Ehrenreich maintains that in *The Handmaid's Tale*, "as in *1984*, the only truly subversive force appears to be love." And Amin Malak suggests that as the novel "upholds and cherishes a man-woman axis," it enables its heroine to progress from "helpless victim" to "sly, subversive survivor." These reactions to the text make sense; but I argue that if we pay attention to the *Tale*'s own statements about signifying systems and the construction of meaning, we may put together other readings, readings that further complicate the political signification of love in the novel. In pages that follow, I "play Scrabble" with three "counters" from *The Handmaid's Tale*: Offred's relationship with Luke, with the Commander, and with Nick. Moving these counters, occasionally superimposing them, I suggest that the novel expresses real ambivalence about its characters' enactment of "the love story." As much as we readers may want to posit love as a revolutionary force, we must attend to the novel's statements about love's tendency to follow decidedly conservative narrative forms.

In *The Handmaid's Tale*'s first few sentences, Offred describes her situation at the Rachel and Leah Center:

> We slept in what had once been the gymnasium. The floor was of varnished wood, with stripes and circles painted on it, for the games that were formerly played there. . . . I thought I could smell, faintly like an afterimage, the pungent scent of sweat, shot through with the sweet taint of chewing gum and perfume from the watching girls. . . . Dances would have been held there; the music lingered, a palimpsest of unheard sound, style upon style.

This suggestive mixing of past and present typifies speculative fiction, which most often generates other worlds as comment upon our own. Such fiction raises questions not only about what might happen, but also about what is happening. Certainly, *The Handmaid's Tale* belongs to this genre; but to a greater extent than many other speculative novels, *The Handmaid's Tale* also asks questions about how we put together future, present, and past, how we construct meaningful connections across time and place. Offred's description above, for example, insinuates connections between past basketball games and the "games" to which Offred and her fellow handmaids are subjected, between past "dances" (sexual interactions) and those performed by the handmaids. As the novel proceeds, however, it insists upon probing the nature of these connections. In what ways are they arbitrary, and if arbitrary, how meaningful can they be? If such connections resemble those between layers of writing on a palimpsest, can we claim significance for readings moving both forward *and* backward between layers? What about those readings that move across a layer, picking up resemblances between discrete units (in the above quote, for example, between the smells of sweat, chewing gum, and perfume)? Attempting to "compose" herself and her world, Offred cannot escape these questions. Nor can we, who attempt to "compose" some kind of reading of *The Handmaid's Tale.*

Offred confronts such questions several times in the novel, but I want to look closely at just two such moments as introduction to my larger claims about how we might read the novel. The first moment occurs early on, as Offred describes a typical walk she takes with her "double," Ofglen. The two women do their shopping, then pause before "the wall" where bodies of traitors are hung on display, the heads covered with white bags. Blood stains one of these bags, blood that seeps from the dead man's mouth and takes the shape of "another mouth, a small red one, like the mouth painted with thick brushes by kindergarten children." Offred finds herself drawn to the red mark, and she meditates on its connection with other red marks:

> I look at the one red smile. The red of the smile is the same as the red of the tulips in Serena Joy's garden, towards the base of the flowers where they are beginning to head. The red is the same but there is no connection. The tulips are not tulips of blood, the red smiles are not flowers, neither thing makes a comment on the other. The tulip is not a reason for disbelief in the hanged man, or vice versa. Each thing is valid and really there. It is through a field of such valid objects that I must pick my way, every day and in every way. I put a lot of effort into making such distinctions. I need to make them. I need to be very clear, in my own mind.

Although we might accept Offred's assertion that "each thing is valid and really there," I think we must question her claim that "there is no connection" between the red of the blood and the red of Serena's tulips. Obviously, Offred herself sees a connection; she yokes the two together metaphorically: the red is the same. Thinking about the red of a smile and that of tulips, we might argue that at least superficially, both items suggest a type of sensual pleasure; both convey positive connotations. But we can sustain this positive reading only as long as we repress the source of the red; the smile of the hanged man is a smile of blood. This fact must then push us to ask about the source of the tulips' redness; metaphorically, it is the blood of other women that allows Serena the time to cultivate her colors. In other words, for some women to enjoy the freedom of playing with red flowers, other women must wear the red of handmaids.

Although Offred herself enjoys the flowers, they, like the bloody smile of the hanged man, signify her own dismal state; as beautiful as they may be, they finally are only "fruiting bod[ies]," subject to the breeding policy of their gardener. Later in the novel when Offred comes upon Serena, shears in hand, snipping at the seedpods of the tulips, Offred wonders: "Was it . . . some blitzkrieg, some kamikaze, committed on the swelling genitalia of the flowers? The fruiting body." This elaboration on the flowers as fruiting bodies points us once more to connections between the flowers and Offred.

Thus, once having suggested a connection between flowers and the bloody smile of a dead man, Offred cannot stop a flowering of associations unless, like Serena, she takes a kitchen shears and insists upon dissection—which is precisely what she does. Why does she retreat from relationships of similarity? As if anticipating such a question, Offred insists that she *needs* to make distinctions, needs to be very clear. But such insistence provides no real answer and so again we ask why, and ask what kind of clarity Offred achieves by cutting off these connections at the bud. If allowed to come to fruition, the connection cited above (between the red smile and the red tulips) pulls in Offred herself; in her red outfit, an outfit signifying both her fertility and her oppression, she is like a blood-red smile, like a flowering plant. She, and they, may provide a moment's pleasure, but at tremendous cost. Such metaphorical representations of her dismal situation can make Offred only more dismal. She represses them. Again, although I accept Offred's claim that distinctions are important, that objects exist separately, I read her denial of connection as reflecting a desire to protect herself from the hardest truths in her life.

A second moment of reflection on connection (and denial thereof) occurs somewhat later in the text, as Offred sits in a chair and prepares for breakfast: "I sit in the chair and think about the word *chair*. It can also mean the leader of a meeting. It can also mean a mode of execution. It is the first syllable in *charity*. It is the French word for flesh. None of these facts has any connection with the others." Once more, as Offred allows her mind to play with the signifier *chair*, she spins out a series of signifieds, connected only in sound. But the fact of this connection forces us to consider other connections: do these signs comment upon each other in some way? Does their juxtaposition force new meanings, new readings? Again, Offred says no. But her denial is suspect, especially in light of two subsequent narrative facts. First, in the sentence following those quoted above, Offred observes: "These are the kinds of litanies I use, to compose myself." That is, to keep from falling into emotional disarray, Offred chants ritual sequences of words. But to keep herself from the other extreme—a kind of emotional overload, a composition that has no boundaries—Offred denies connections between the words. The second fact that should prompt our suspicions with regard to Offred's denial is that in the "Historical Notes on *The Handmaid's Tale*" pompous Professor Pieixoto opens his commentary on the *Tale* by referring to the same string of signifiers Offred has played upon in the *Tale*: "I am sure we all enjoyed our charming Arctic Char last night at dinner, and now we are enjoying an equally charming Arctic Chair. I use the word 'enjoy' in two distinct senses, precluding, of course, the obsolete third." Here Pieixoto highlights the connection between "char" and "chair" which Offred does not want to acknowledge: in a sexist society, women and flesh are interchangeable. It is precisely this interchangeability that characterizes Gileadean culture, and that Offred would prefer to keep out of the "composition" which she calls herself.

These two moments—Offred contemplating a blood-red smile and tulips; Offred spinning out a chain of "chairs"—suggest that the signifying system cannot be arrested, cannot be contained. Containment attempts may tell us something about the desires and fears of a person who declares "there is no connection," but should not constrain us to some limited reading; repeatedly, the novel declares that there *is* a connection, numerous connections (hence, I would argue, Pieixoto's play on "chair" in "The Historical Note" is connected to Offred's earlier play on this same word; the later reference forces us to make comparisons, to look for similarities and differences in the two chains of signifiers).

Having laid out these operating premises, I now turn to the novel's representation of Offred's relationships with three men: Luke, Commander Fred, and Nick. Not surprisingly, Offred wants to imagine these men as unique: Luke as her "real love," husband, and father to her child; the Commander as her Gileadean "sugar-daddy"—powerful, distant, in control of her future; Nick as her illicit love, companion in crime. For example, before Offred begins her affair with Nick she gazes hungrily out at him from her window (just as she looks hungrily at the Scrabble counters). She tells herself: "They [Luke and Nick] cannot be exchanged, one for the other. They cannot replace each other. Nick for Luke or Luke for Nick. *Should* does not apply." And Offred most certainly would not imagine the Commander replacing either of them; as far as she is concerned, the Commander exists in a different realm altogether (a realm of duty, obligation; a realm in which love does not exist). But the text makes a very different argument. All three men merge, and this merging requires us to reassess supposed distinctions among husbands, lovers, and commanders. Other readers have noticed some of the similarities among these men: Mary McCarthy, for example, observes: "Characterization in general is weak in *The*

*Handmaid's Tale*. . . . I cannot tell Luke, the husband, from Nick, the chauffeur-lover who may be an Eye (government spy) and/or belong to the 'mayday' underground. Nor is the Commander strongly drawn." But no one has pursued implications of this blurring.

In looking first at Luke and the Commander, I attend to two categories of character definition: personal characteristics, and what we might call situational characteristics (relational dynamics). In the former category, I locate Luke's familiarity with various languages, his interest in "old things," and his insistence upon certain "old values." The latter includes his position of relative power in a culture that requires women to depend on men, his enactment of this power relationship within marriages or affairs, and his history of past involvements with women.

Several times throughout *The Handmaid's Tale*, Offred comments upon her husband Luke's knowledge of and interest in foreign languages. He frequently provides her with etymologies and translations. For example, when Ofglen remarks "'It's a beautiful May day,'" Offred finds herself thinking about the word "Mayday," a word whose derivation Luke explained to her in her pre-Gileadean life, "*Mayday, mayday*, for pilots whose planes had been hit, and ships—was it ships too?—at sea." He asks if she knows what the word comes from, and then tells her, "It's French, he said. From *m'aidez*." He is the "word authority" in this marriage, as we see in yet another example. Wishing she might sit and talk with the servant Rita, gossip and exchange secrets, Offred muses upon the word "fraternize":

> *Fraternize* means to behave like a brother. Luke told me that. He said there was no corresponding word that meant *to behave like a sister. Sororize*, it would have to be, he said. From the Latin. He liked knowing about such details. The derivations of words, curious usages. I used to tease him about being pedantic.

"From the Latin": Luke, obviously, has had a somewhat different education than the narrator. Like so many men of privilege throughout history, he knows the language of the classical curriculum and he uses this knowledge in a subtle reaffirmation of classical gender roles and inequalities (men can be brothers, one to the other; women cannot).

Two other male characters employ their knowledge of Latin in similar fashion: the Commander and Professor Pieixoto. Pieixoto is beyond my consideration here; I limit myself to consideration of fraternal language bonds between Luke and the Commander. Like Luke, the Commander both knows Latin and likes to play with "curious usages." We get some insight into the Commander's learning on the evening that Offred asks him to translate "*Nolite te bastardes carborundum*" for her (she has found this phrase carved into the floor of her closet). Unable to pronounce the phrase so as to make it intelligible, Offred writes it out on a pad; as soon as the Commander reads it he begins to laugh: "'That's not real Latin,' he says. 'That's just a joke.'" Offred does not want to believe that the phrase that means so much to her might be a joke (presumably the previous "Offred," the handmaid who occupied the room before our Offred, carved out the phrase for those who were to come later); and she gratefully accepts a dog-eared textbook that the Commander pulls down from the shelf:

> What I see first is a picture: The Venus de Milo, in a black-and-white photo, with a mustache and a black brassiere and armpit hair drawn clumsily on her. . . . 'It's sort of hard to explain why it's funny unless you know Latin,' he says. 'We used to write all kinds of things like that. I don't know where we got them, from older boys perhaps.' Forgetful of me and of himself, he's turning the pages. 'Look at this,' he says. The picture is called *The Sabine Women*, and in the margin is scrawled: *pim pis pit, pimus pistis pants*. 'There was another one,' he says. '*Cim, cis, cit* . . .' he stops, returning to the present, embarrassed.

The Commander stops, because the next word in the series is "cunt"; this little joke exemplifies typical schoolboy play, play that exploits the female body. Certainly, the Commander's Latin games are cruder and more childish than those of Luke, but both men wield their language prowess so as to keep women in the position of the unempowered.

Further reinforcing this positioning is the interest taken by both Luke and the Commander in "old things" and the ways of the past. When the Commander gives Offred a popular women's magazine from the 1970s and she asks why he has such forbidden material in his study, he responds, "Some of us . . . retain an appreciation for the old things." Other "old things" appreciated by the Commander are on display at Jezebel's, a Felliniesque whorehouse with women dressed in an amazing mélange of costumes from the past:

> Some of these have on outfits like mine, feathers and glister, cut high up the thighs, low over the breasts. Some are in olden-day lingerie, shortie nightgowns, baby-doll pajamas, the occasional see-through negligee. Some are in bathing suits, one piece or bikini; one, I see, is wearing a crocheted affair, with big scallop shells covering the tits.

As the Commander escorts Offred through this display of flesh, he observes, "'it's like walking into the past,'" and Offred senses that "his voice sounds pleased, delighted even." She tries to remember "if the past was exactly like this," and concludes that although it contained these things, "the mix is different." The "past" called up by the Commander, the past that brings delight into his voice, is one in which women are on display for men, and are dependent upon men.

Luke too enjoys "old things." When married to him, the narrator works translating books onto computer disks; occasionally she takes books home, pleased with "the feel of them, and the look." Luke tells her she has the "mind of an antiquarian." She comments, "He liked that, he liked old things himself." We might discuss the narrator's antiquarian pleasures, but more important here, I think, is the association of Luke with items from the past; he likes old books, and, as we learn more about Luke we realize that he likes old ideas as well. Perhaps one of his favorite old ideas involves differences between the sexes. Twice in the novel we hear about Luke's position with regard to difference. First, when the narrator and Luke are shopping, he attends to the meat purchases:

> He liked to choose what kind of meat we were going to eat during the week. He said men needed more meat than women did, and that it wasn't a superstition and he wasn't being a jerk, studies had been done. There are some differences, he said. He was fond of saying that, as if I was trying to prove there weren't.

Although we might accept Luke's comments as simple, good-humored teasing, there is more at stake here; Luke is the one who introduces the topic of difference, as if intent upon sustaining it (we have no evidence of the narrator denying difference).

Luke's comments on this topic become more exaggerated when he is in the company of the narrator's mother, who pushes on such questions much more seriously than does the narrator. Thus, we hear for a second time about Luke's chauvinism when the narrator tells us that in answer to her mother's claims that there is something missing in men, Luke teases her, "pretending to be macho, he'd tell her women were incapable of abstract thought." Again, we might dismiss Luke's comment as teasing and good fun, were it not for the fact that the specific charge he levels against women is repeated, in slightly more specific form, by the Commander, when he tells Offred that women cannot add: "For [women] one and one and one and one don't make four." In both cases, the men hang on to their belief that abstract thought is beyond women, who seemingly cannot put concepts together.

The personal characteristics of Luke and the Commander examined above contribute to an overall pattern of relational dynamics between these two men and women in the text. If, for example, women are incapable of abstract thought, then women will have to accept such thought from men; once this dynamic is established, others follow as a matter of course: women depend on men intellectually, economically, physically, emotionally. We see the evolution of this dependence in scenes depicting the narrator and Luke immediately after she learns that all women have lost their jobs and that their credit accounts have been transferred to their nearest male relatives. Devastated, terrified, the narrator turns to Luke for consolation:

> Did they say why? I said.
> He didn't answer that. We'll get through it, he said, hugging me.
> You don't know what it's like, I said. I feel as if somebody cut off my feet. I wasn't crying. Also, I couldn't put my arms around him.
> It's only a job, he said, trying to soothe me.

Notice that although Luke is sympathetic during this exchange, he does *not* respond to the narrator's question: "Did they say why?" Her question suggests that Luke may have access to an answer; his sidestepping implicates him in some way. But more damning is the text's juxtaposition of the narrator's thought, "I couldn't put my arms around him," with Luke's "soothing" statement: "It's only a job." Reading these lines one after another, reading them in light of what we know about women's jobs in Gilead, we cannot avoid the insinuation that even before Gilead, it was women's job to put their arms around men. Although reluctant to address such an insinuation (look what it does to one's belief in "love"!) the narrator does express certain doubts about what happens between her and Luke:

> He doesn't mind this, I thought. He doesn't mind it at all.
> Maybe he even likes it.
> We are not each other's, anymore. Instead, I am his.

Although she chastens herself for such thoughts ("unworthy, unjust, untrue") the narrator also notes that she never discusses her doubts with Luke: "I was afraid to. I couldn't afford to lose [him]." Newly subordinated, the narrator relies upon him and so must retain the good will of her superior. Honesty in such a relationship becomes impossible.

Similarly impossible is any kind of equal interaction (and therefore, any kind of honesty) between Offred and the Commander. Like Luke, the Commander has control over Offred's life; she knows as much, and knows she must remain in his good graces. When she receives the first call to his study, for example, she enters the room determined to engage in a good bargaining session; she envisions their interaction, quite rightly, as an exchange: "I'm not giving anything away: selling only." She goes yet further on later reflection, thinking about the Commander's desire as something that "could be important, it could be a passport." She might say the same about the importance of maintaining Luke's desire in the scene above; it may provide her with a way out.

And, as a matter of fact, an extremely significant moment in her relationship with Luke involves their use of passports. As the narrator tells the story of their attempt to cross the border into Canada, she suggests that Luke undertakes this journey out of love for her and their child, but the actual text of her account turns this suggestion on its head. She explains that the three of them drive the car to the border, where they hand their false passports to a border guard who takes the forms inside the immigration building:

> Then Luke got back into the car, too fast, and turned the key and reversed. He was picking up the phone, he said. And then he began to drive very quickly, and after that there was the dirt road and the woods and we jumped out of the car and began to run. A cottage, to hide in, a boat, I don't know what we thought. He said the passports were foolproof, and we had so little time to plan. Maybe he had a plan, a map of some kind in his head. As for me, I was only running: away, away. I don't want to be telling this story.

Failing to specify antecedents for the various "he's" above, the narrator incriminates Luke. Who said the passports were foolproof? Who had a plan? And what kind of plan? Encompassing whom? It may very well be that Luke's "plan" is larger than the narrator realizes. We can read her final comment, "I don't want to be telling this story" as suggesting that "the story" she does not want to tell (and does tell only through mistakes and gaps) is the story of Luke's betrayal of her.

If the term "betrayal" sounds too harsh, perhaps we need to think about Luke's treatment of his wife—that is, of his first wife. We do not meet this wife in the text; the narrator never has seen her, only has seen pictures and heard her "voice on the phone, late at night, when she was calling us, before the divorce." The narrator also has heard Moira express disapproval of the narrator's affair with a married man: "She said I was poaching, on another woman's ground. I said Luke wasn't a fish or a piece of dirt either, he was a human being and could make his own decisions." But the decision he makes is to betray his wife. We do not know whether he is tired of her, bored with her, angry with her; whatever the reason, Luke begins an affair, spending afternoons in hotels rooms with the narrator.

Quite appropriately, when Offred begins her "affair" with the Commander (another man married to another woman), he takes her to the very hotel in which she has spent time with Luke: "I know where I am. I've been here before: with Luke, in the afternoons, a long time ago." As if to underline the overlap between these two affairs, Offred comments on "sameness" when she enters the hotel room with the Commander:

> Everything is the same, the very same as it was, once upon a time.
> The drapes are the same, the heavy flowered ones that match the
> bedspread, orange poppies on royal blue, and the thin white ones
> to draw against the sun. . . . All is the same.

The setting is the same, because the interaction is the same: unmarried woman with married man.

Although the narrator protests against Moira's disapproval of her affair with Luke, she is not immune to the force of Moira's arguments. The narrator tells us, for example, about a dream in which she stands in the apartment she shares with Luke. The apartment is bare, empty, except for clothes hanging in the cupboard:

> they're my clothes, but they don't look like mine, I've never seen
> them before. Maybe they're clothes belonging to Luke's wife. . . .
> I pull out dresses, black, blue, purple, jackets, skirts; none of them
> will do, none of them even fits, they're too big or too small.
>     Luke is behind me, I turn to see him. He won't look at me,
> he looks down at the floor. . . .
>     *Luke*, I say. He doesn't answer.

The narrator has this dream after she and Luke are married; but notice that in her account she refers to Luke's ex-wife as his wife. Yet further suggestive of the narrator's difficulties as "the second woman" is the fact that the clothes do not fit; although they are hers, they also are not hers. And finally, in the dream Luke will not look at her or answer her. One imagines that his response to his first wife is precisely the same; that is, he undoubtedly looks away from her, refusing to answer her questions. We can easily make the argument that this dream expresses the narrator's otherwise unexpressed reservations about her relationship with Luke, and about Luke himself, a man who betrays women.

Offred's understanding of male betrayal is sharper with regard to the Commander. Because her own feelings are not entangled with his, she recognizes the banality of his statement that he seeks Offred's company because he and his wife "don't seem to have much in common, these days." Offred observes: "So there it was, out in the open: his wife didn't understand him. That's what I was there for, then. The same old thing." In other words, in this instance, Offred has read the story, knows the plot line, and she is not impressed. As a matter of fact, she feels some guilt with regard to Serena Joy, and expresses this guilt in terms similar to those used by Moira earlier:

> I felt I was an intruder, in a territory that ought to have been hers. . . . I was taking something away from her, although she didn't know it. I was filching. Never mind that it was something she apparently didn't want or had no use for, had rejected even, still, it was hers, and if I took it away, this mysterious 'it' I couldn't quite define . . . what would be left for her?

While Offred may be awakening to the costs of extramarital affairs (costs borne most heavily by the wife who is betrayed), the men with whom she enacts these betrayals give no signs of a similar awakening. Luke expresses no repentance for his affair, and the Commander, rather than repent, multiplies his sins (Offred is not the first woman to spend time with him in his study and at Jezebel's, the handmaid preceeding Offred did so, and ended up hanging herself).

What am I arguing here? Looking at both personal characteristics and relational dynamics, we see that *The Handmaid's Tale* provides us with two male characters who mirror one another; structurally, these two are twins. Offred does not draw attention to parallels between the two men, and might protest against such connections ("None of these facts has any connection with the other") but the text insists upon them. *The Handmaid's Tale* encourages us to read the future in light of the past, and the past in light of the future; doing so, we cannot exclude male figures from our consideration—no matter how disquieting the results of such consideration. Here, recognition of similarity between Luke and the Commander *is* disquieting; it casts doubt not only upon the narrator's story of Luke's love, but also upon love stories generally.

"But wait," the romantic reader may object, "there's a third male in this story, and he does credit to the love plot." Lucy M. Freibert, for example, argues that "Offred's real breakthrough to her courageous sexual self comes not with the Commander, who soon bores her, but with Nick. . . . Her joyous reaction to her desire embodies precisely the French *jouissance*." Certainly, we may argue that it is through Nick's intervention that Offred seemingly "comes to life," escapes from Gilead, tapes her account, and thereby provides us with the story of her past. Nick, unlike Luke and the Commander, does not exhibit any penchant for "old ways," any knowledge of patriarchal languages of power, or any inclination to implicate Offred in triangulated desire (there is apparently no wife in Nick's life). Also unlike Luke and the Commander, Nick risks his own life to save that of Offred; he instructs her to go with the two Eyes who have come to take her away: "'It's all right. It's Mayday. Go with them.'" Although we may suspect Nick, just as Offred does ("My suspicion hovers in the air above him, a dark angel warning me away"), the fact that we have a text at all suggests that Nick tells the truth, that he has arranged for Offred's escape. In other words, he functions as a fairy-tale prince, setting the princess free with a kiss. Early in the novel, Offred expresses her faith that Luke will perform as her fairy-tale savior—"sooner or later he will get me out, we will find her [their daughter], wherever they've put her. She'll remember us and we will be all three of us together"—but Luke never makes a showing. So Offred makes do with what is available, and falls in love with Nick.

In paragraphs above, I suggested that parallels between the Commander and Luke should prompt us to read the narrator's "love story" (that is, the story in which she and Luke are stars) with real skepticism. When the cast of this story changes, with Nick standing in for Luke, can we forgo the skepticism? Despite differences between the two men, the text pushes us to answer in the negative; it continues to represent the love plot as something potentially dangerous to women who entangle themselves therein. Let me pinpoint three narrative components that qualify the positive representation of Nick's and Offred's affair.

First is Offred's seemingly casual reference to mushroom-colored carpeting on the stairs to Nick's room: "I feel my way up, stair by stair: carpet here, I think of it as mushroom-colored." The only other mushroom-colored carpeting in this novel is that at Jezebel's, the whorehouse to which the Commander takes Offred earlier on that same evening she climbs Nick's stairs, the former-hotel whorehouse in which the narrator met Luke for afternoons of illicit sex. Although it is too dark for Offred actually to see the color of the staircase carpeting, she imagines it to be the same color as carpeting on which she trod in moving toward other bedrooms. Thus, Offred herself suggests connections between this affair and those, suggests similarities at work.

If the sole similarity between this affair and those were carpet dye, we might dismiss the suggestion of parallels, but two more features of the narrative militate against this dismissal: the effect on Offred of "being in love" and the grammar according to which she articulates being in love. When in love with Luke, the narrator tends to give in to him, to accept his direction of her toward passivity. For example, when a woman kidnaps Luke's and the narrator's child in a supermarket, Luke dismisses the incident as an individual woman's craziness, encouraging the narrator to see such kidnappings as isolated events rather than as structural phenomena demanding a response. Later, when the narrator considers joining marches to protest women's loss of their jobs, Luke again intervenes: "Luke said it would be futile and I had to think about them, my family, him and her." And finally, when several weeks pass without a word from the narrator's mother, the narrator searches her mother's apartment, and determines to call the police:

> Don't, said Luke.
> Why not? I said. I was glaring at him, I was angry now. He stood there in the wreck of the living room, just looking at me. He put his hands into his pockets, one of those aimless gestures people make when they don't know what else to do.
> Just don't is what he said.

And so the narrator doesn't.

Similarly, after Offred begins her affair with Nick, she loses all interest in Mayday and in the possibility of escape. She comments, "The fact is that I no longer want to leave, escape the border to freedom. I want to be here, with Nick, where I can get at him." She barely listens to Ofglen, who "whispers less, talks more about the weather." Whatever political commitment Offred might be capable of making vanishes in light of her commitment to romance. This evanescence is particularly frightening in light of Offred's childhood memory of a televised interview with the mistress of a man who supervised a death camp during World War II. This woman "said she didn't notice much that she found unusual. She denied knowing about the oven. . . . He was not a monster, she said." While the accommodation of this Nazi mistress may be extreme ("She was thinking about how not to think"), it is not different in nature from Offred's accommodation:

> I said, I have made a life for myself, here, of a sort. That must have been what the settlers' wives thought, and women who survived wars, if they had a man. Humanity is so adaptable, my mother would say. Truly amazing, what people can get used to, as long as there are a few compensations.

So, Offred "makes a life for herself," a life involving no community or political commitment, but only commitment to "having man."

Perhaps equally worrisome is Offred's reliance upon traditional grammars with which to structure her relationship with this man. For example, in Offred's first account of her visit to Nick's room, she relies heavily on the language of Harlequin romances. She and Nick do not talk:

> Outside, like punctuation, there's a flash of lightning; almost no pause and then the thunder. He's undoing my dress, a man made of darkness, I can't see his face, and I can hardly breathe, hardly stand, and I'm not standing. His mouth is on me, his hands, I can't wait and he's moving, already, love, it's been so long, I'm alive in my skin, again, arms around him, falling and water softly everywhere, never-ending.

"A man made of darkness"? "Falling and water softly, everywhere, never-ending"? Offred's account comes right out of mass-market bodice rippers (a dangerous source of role models for women who want to maintain any sense of integrity). As if aware of the silliness of this version of her encounter with Nick, Offred revises: "I made that up. It didn't happen that way. Here is what happened." And then we get a second version, in which the new lovers have trouble talking to one another, until they fall into the language of old movies. They toss "lines" at one another, "quoting from late movies, from the time before." This act of quotation is bizarre because, as Offred realizes, the movies themselves do not quote from "real life": "Not even my mother talked liked that, not when I knew her. Possibly nobody every talked like that in real life, it was all a fabrication from the beginning." These two lovers enact the fabrication, hoping to conjure forth something real with these magic words. Offred cannot sustain the illusion for very long. She senses the talk is "faded music, faded paper flowers, worn satin, an echo of an echo"; that is, she senses that the words actually keep the two of them apart, referring, as they do, to "echoes of echoes." After concluding this account, Offred again admits: "It didn't happen that way either. I'm not sure how it happened; not exactly. All I can hope for is a reconstruction."

Sadly, both of the reconstructions she offers us, as well as the fairly-tale construction she employs when she thinks about this affair, limit the range of activities and options available to male and female characters. Operating within this traditional grammar (men are princes or made of darkness; women are princesses or damsels in distress), Offred can individuate neither herself nor Nick; both fall into roles assigned to them by fairy tales and romances. Is the novel's reliance upon fairy tale/romance paradigms so destructive as to counteract its positive representation of Nick as "the prince"—the daring young man who saves the maiden? "Counteract" may be too strong a claim, but I argue that every representation of romance in *The Handmaid's Tale*, including that most positive representation, Nick with Offred, is highly qualified, highly ambivalent. The novel seems to want to believe in its own novelistic representations of love (and, by implication, in "real-life" love) at the same time it expresses extreme reservations about how we (authors, characters, readers, real-life lovers) typically realize this emotion. In one of the most perceptive reviews of Atwood's novel, Gayle Greene argues precisely this point. Greene observes that when Offred answers the Commander's question about Gilead's possible lacks—"What did we overlook?"—with the response, "Love, falling in love," it is tempting to hear Atwood's voice in Offred's. But, according to Greene, we also must hear her voice in the Commander's: "oh yes . . . I've read the magazines, that's what they were pushing, wasn't it?" That is, while there may be something importantly human about falling in love, narratives enact this emotion according to a limited number of scripts (those provided in magazines, romance novels, fairy tales) and we readers all too easily buy the line these scripts are pushing. Sadly, at the moment such scripts promise us individual love ("you, yes you, can love and be loved") they undermine the very possibility of individuality (and love) as they restrict experience to a small number of decidedly limited plot lines.

Thus, I must take exception to Barbara Ehrenreich's claim that in *The Handmaid's Tale*, "the only truly subversive force appears to be love" and to Victoria Glendinning's assertion that "what has been overlooked by the regime is the subversive force of love. On this the plot turns, as in all romantic narratives since the world began." I also must question Amin Malak's optimistic assessment that while *The Handmaid's Tale* condemns a "male misogynous mentality, [it] upholds and cherishes a man-woman axis." Instead, I argue that the novel subverts the subversive force of love, and that it raises serious questions about a man-woman axis, when this axis models itself upon patterns that restrict rather than liberate. In its representation of such patterns in relationships between Offred and Luke, Offred and the Commander, Offred and Nick, the novel insists upon love's limitations, rather than upon its latitudes.

I began this essay by suggesting that my way of reading *The Handmaid's Tale* parallels the way Offred and the Commander play Scrabble: like them, I draw letters from the text, rearrange them, and thereby compose new words, new text. I like that parallel, and enjoy the element of playfulness in both versions of Scrabble (Offred and the Commander take extra letters and make words that do not exist; I juxtapose characters and push on connections that, at least according to the narrator, do not exist). Here, at the end of this essay, I return to the Scrabble episode, again employing it as parallel—this time, not to the act of reading *The Handmaid's Tale*, but to the act of "falling in love" as represented in *The Handmaid's Tale*. Unlike my first analogy, however, this one leaves me feeling uneasy, uncomfortable, as it points to the closed nature of the games in question. Playing Scrabble, the Commander and Offred generally operate within certain rules; the two of them occasionally bend these rules, coming up with words like *smurt* and *crup*. In my first parallel, I suggest that such breaches are examples of creative play; here, in contrast, I argue that they actually are part of the game. That is, they do not change underlying grammars, do not question essential rules (note, for example, that the "made-up" words follow conventions within English with regard to consonant blends and the presence of vowels). Similarly, the romances enacted in *The Handmaid's Tale* operate within the rules, within the conventions of "falling in love." In case we have forgotten our fairy-tale education in this process, Offred reminds us of its elements in a lengthy meditation thereon:

> Falling in love. . . . Falling into it, we all did then, one way or another. . . . It was the central thing; it was the way you understood yourself. . . .
>
> *Falling in love*, we said; *I fell for him*. We were falling women. We believed in it, this downward motion: so lovely, like flying, and yet at the same time so dire, so extreme, so unlikely. . . .
>
> And sometimes it happened, for a time. That kind of love comes and goes and is hard to remember afterwards, like pain.

The narrator "falls" for Luke; later she "falls" for Nick. In both instances she becomes a "fallen woman"—a woman who surrenders herself to a plot already written, a story already told. Following the rules, the narrator enjoys love's loveliness and its pains—and never does she stop to ask if this game is the only way love can be played. Although some readers might see the narrator's premarital affair with Luke as stepping outside the game, I have to read this affair, finally, as akin to made-up words like "smurt" and "crup"; the affair, like the words, may not be accepted in polite company, but it, like them, is an integral part of the game. Similarly, Offred's affair with Nick (an apparent violation of her love-marriage to Luke) does nothing to challenge the general rules of romance; the affair simply provides readers with yet another example of "*J.H. loves B.P. 1954. O.R. loves L.T.*," "short stories" carved into the wooden desktops at the Rachel and Leah Center. Rather than engaging in a radical revision of such stories (which remind Offred of "inscriptions I used to read about, carved on the stone walls of caves, or drawn with a mixture of soot and animal fat," Offred accepts these archaic plot lines as model for her own.

But is *The Handmaid's Tale* structured according to "the story" or "the plot"? Although the novel does not provide an alternative vision of love's enactment, its portrait of love's typical realization is highly qualified. Yes, Offred's love for Nick leads to her escape from Gilead, but as that love is associated with her love for Luke (a love that colludes in the very foundation of Gilead) it must be interrogated. Such interrogation does not lead to a rejection of the importance of love, but it must lead to a critical assessment of how we have shaped love's plot, and how it has shaped us. The structural power of this plot is apparent in a seemingly casual description, from Offred, of the handmaids preparing for a Prayvaganza:

> We line up to get processed through the checkpoint, standing in our twos and twos and twos, like a private girls' school that went for a walk and stayed out too long. Years and years too long, so that everything has become overgrown, legs, bodies, dresses all together. As if enchanted. A fairy tale, I'd like to believe.

If this is a fairy tale, a prince will arrive and make life better with a kiss. Because Offred so much wants to believe in the fairy tale, she closes off other plot options: what would happen if she were to work with Ofglen, to spy on the Commander and communicate his secrets to Mayday? The novel does not give us these stories; but it does encourage us to break out of the old plots, to shape a future different from those offered us in the *Tale* and its *Historical Note*.

J. BROOKS BOUSON

# The Misogyny of Patriarchal Culture in
# The Handmaid's Tale

Like *Bodily Harm, The Handmaid's Tale* reflects on the antifeminist backlash of the 1980s. Observing that every "backlash movement has had its preferred scapegoat," Susan Faludi remarks that feminist women became "a prime enemy" for the New Right in the 1980s. Claiming that feminists were against the family, New Right spokesman Jerry Falwell, for example, warned that feminists had begun a "satanic attack on the home," and Howard Phillips charged that feminists were behind "the conscious policy of government to liberate the wife from the leadership of the husband." "Under the banner of 'family rights,'" observes Faludi, the leaders of the New Right lobbied for "every man's right to rule supreme at home—to exercise what Falwell called the husband's 'God-given responsibility to lead his family.'" Countering women's independence and autonomy, these so-called "pro-family" activists called for the restoration of women's traditional roles and for the return of women to the home.

"A lot of what writers do is they play with hypotheses . . . ," comments Atwood in a discussion of *The Handmaid's Tale*. "It's a kind of 'if this, then that' type of thing. The original hypothesis would be some of the statements that are being made by the 'Evangelical fundamentalist right.' If a woman's place is in the home, then what? If you actually decide to enforce that, what follows?" In *The Handmaid's Tale*, which reflects on the antifeminist messages

From *Brutal Choreographies: Oppositional Strategies and Narrative Design in the Novels of Margaret Atwood.* © 1993 by The University of Massachusetts Press.

given to women by the fundamentalist New Right in the 1980s, Atwood delineates in chilling detail just what might follow: the virtual enslavement of women, their reduction to mere functions, to mute, replaceable objects. Described as "bleak, unnerving" and as "disturbingly believable," *The Handmaid's Tale*, like *Bodily Harm*, exposes female anxieties about male domination and sexual exploitation that have always plagued women. "I didn't invent a lot" in *The Handmaid's Tale*, Atwood remarks. "I transposed to a different time and place, but the motifs are all historical motifs." Atwood describes her novel as "a study of power" and as "[s]peculative fiction," a "logical extension of where we are now." Although Atwood "avoided writing" *The Handmaid's Tale* for some four years because she thought it was "zany," when she did begin working on it she discovered it to be "a *compelling* story," one she "had to write."

A novel that many readers also have found strangely compelling, *The Handmaid's Tale*, as the critical conversation surrounding the text indicates, provokes both affective and cognitive responses from readers. *The Handmaid's Tale* is "disquieting and not nearly as futuristic nor fantasmatic as we might wish," writes one critic. "In a very real sense, the future presaged by 'The Handmaid's Tale' is already *our* history . . . ," comments another. "History repeats itself with minimal variations and the major source of fear for the reader is that nothing in this futurist society is new," observes yet another. And yet, if Atwood's talent is ignited by "fear," there is also a "hyperliterary quality" to her work. *The Handmaid's Tale* has been described as "intricately written" and as "an intense good read, almost a game or a puzzle." Atwood makes her readers "into detectives, trying to reconstruct the political history from which Offred's daily chronicle emerges." If Atwood draws readers into the persecutory world of her novel, she also prompts them to recognize and appreciate the literary puzzles and artistic complexities of her narrative.

Confining readers to Offred's subjectivity and then abruptly shifting to an objective academic discussion of Offred's tale in the "Historical Notes" which conclude the novel, *The Handmaid's Tale* uses a narrative strategy designed to call attention to the acts of reading and interpretation. In Offred's narrative, memories of her pre-Gilead and her Gilead past in the Red Center where she was indoctrinated are layered with descriptions of her present 'reality' as a Handmaid. Because Offred's memories are narrated in interrupted fragments, the reader is forced to assemble and construct her story. Moreover, the fact that Offred's narrative never reaches a definitive conclusion compels reader speculation about and participation in her story. Reader collaboration in the process of assembling the text is reinforced by the novel's inclusion, in direct addresses to an implied reader, of self-reflexive discussions about the difficulties inherent in the narrative reconstruction of events. Just as these devices serve to partially deflect attention away from the horrors being described, the "Historical Notes"—which are appended to Offred's narrative and which describe the Gileadean world from the perspective of twenty-second century historians—also diffuse or defuse some of the affective intensities of Offred's account. The epigraph taken from Swift's *A Modest Proposal* found at the beginning of the novel serves a similar purpose, and it also, as several critics have observed, points to the novel's use of satire. Like the historians who play the game of historical detective as they reconstruct Offred's story from some thirty tape recordings, critic/readers of Offred's narrative become involved in the process of reading clues and unraveling puzzles. Even though the "Historical Notes" section of the novel implicitly denounces what it dramatizes—the critical objectification of texts— *The Handmaid's Tale* nonetheless invites just such an interpretive process. But Atwood's novel is also designed to discomfort readers as it immerses them in a regressive—and voyeuristic—sadomasochistic fantasy. Indeed, while some readers find themselves "consumed" by the novel, others find themselves sinking, "not without intermittent spasms of resistance," into "the deepening masochism" of Offred's tale. If sadism demands a story, the story of *The Handmaid's Tale* demands sadism as it dramatizes the sexual oppression of women who, bound in a master-slave relationship, are forced to consent to femininity.

A feminist dystopia, but also part lurid Gothic fantasy and domestic romance plot, *The Handmaid's Tale* lays bare the inherent misogyny of patriarchal culture. In the Republic of Gilead, a theocracy established in the Untied States by New Right fundamentalists, the masculine code is carried to its absolute extreme in the regime's consignment of woman to various classes—the Wives, the Handmaids, the Marthas, the Econowives, the Aunts—according to the their functions. Through its imposition of a rigid system of hierarchical classification, the Gilead regime effectively robs women of their individual identities and transforms them into replaceable objects in the phallocentric economy. The thirty-three-year-old narrator of the tale is named Offred, her name identifying the Commander to whom she temporarily belongs. She is "Of Fred." Her name, as numerous commentators have pointed out, also suggests the words "afraid, "offered," and "off-read" (misread). In prompting the decoding of Offred's name for hidden meanings, the text encourages readers not only to repeat Offred's act of reading and interpretation as she attempts to unravel the mystery of the hidden message left by the previous Handmaid, but also to participate in the same word-association game Offred plays as she rehearses litanies of words to assuage her anxiety. If Offred is "misread" by her culture and also by the misogynist historians who later reconstruct and comment on her narrative, she is also "afraid" as she is forced to "offer" her sexual services to the state. Echoing the novel's wordplay and pointing to its political aim, one critic describes *The Handmaid's Tale* as "an impassioned sermon" that is "offered" by Atwood "as a warning to make her readers afraid." Moreover, the fact that Offred's real name is hidden in the narrative seems intended as a kind of "password into the text," observes another critic. Since careful readers of the novel can deduce Offred's name from the list of names provided at the outset—for all of the names, with the exception of "June," are assigned to other characters as the narrative unfolds—the fact that the historian who reconstructs and comments on Offred's tale does not know her real name is a "sign" of his "inability" to read Offred's story.

"Ordinary," the Handmaids are told, "is what you are used to. This may not seem ordinary to you now, but after a time it will." Repeatedly and with didactic intention, the narrative contrasts Offred's pre-Gilead past—her life in the United States in the 1970s and 1980s—with her Gilead present. A "refugee from the past," Offred recalls how women once felt as if they "were free to shape and reshape forever the ever-expanding perimeters" of their lives and how they were once depicted in the glossy women's magazines as "bold, striding, confident, their arms flung out as if to claim space, their legs apart, feet planted squarely on the earth." In Gilead, in contrast, the Handmaids are infantilized. Like the Surfacer who feels that words come out of her "like the mechanical words from a talking doll" when she speaks in an inauthentic, feminine voice, Offred responds mechanically when Serena Joy lays out the ground rules for their relationship. "They used to have dolls, for little girls, that would talk if you pulled a string at the back; I thought I was sounding like that, voice of a monotone, voice of a doll." Treated "like a child" in the Commander's household, she "must not be told" certain things; allowed to watch television news on the evening of the ceremony, she is like "a child being allowed up late with the grown-ups"; when she asks one of the Marthas for a match, she feels "like a small, begging child."

The Handmaids are forced to a life of utter passivity and submissiveness. They are "ladies in reduced circumstances. . . . The circumstances have been reduced; for those of us who still have circumstances." Because they are women with "viable ovaries" in a world of mass sterility, they are forcibly enlisted in the regime's project of reversing the precipitous decline in the Caucasian birthrate. Objectified by the culture and used solely for breeding purposes, the Handmaids, in Offred's description, are "containers," "two legged wombs . . . sacred vessels, ambulatory chalices." Those Handmaids who do not capitulate to the new regime are severely punished or executed. Making a conscious allusion to and an intertextual comment on the paradigmatically female story of *The Red Shoes* which, as we have observed, occurs in other Atwood novels, *The Handmaid's Tale* describes the brutal foot punishment suffered by disobedient Handmaids. "It was the feet they'd do, for first offense. They used steel cables, frayed at the ends." When Moira undergoes this punishment, her feet resemble "drowned feet, swollen and boneless, except for the color. They looked like lungs." Although Offred's shoes are red, they are "not for dancing." Observing the dangling feet of women who have been "salvaged"— that is, executed by hanging—Offred remarks that "[i]f it weren't for the ropes and the sacks it could be a kind of dance, a ballet, caught by flash-camera: midair." Offred does not want to be such "a dancer, my feet in the air, my head a faceless oblong of white cloth." "Women's Salvagings," as she observes, "are not frequent. There is less need for them. These days we are so well behaved." Offred is part of the "transitional" generation. "For the ones who come after you," she is told, "it will be easier. They will accept their duties with willing hearts"; they will freely submit, she recognizes, because "they will have no memories, of any other way."

Although Offred remembers the pre-Gilead era as a time of relative freedom and choice for women, she also describes another, partially censored, version of the past. Relentlessly exposing the misogyny underlying present-day culture, *The Handmaid's Tale* constructs a feminist reading position as it continues *Bodily Harm*'s critique of the sexual degradation and violence to which women are subjected. "Nothing changes instantaneously: in a gradually heating bathtub you'd be boiled to death before you knew it," Offred comments as she recalls the pre-Gilead world, the America of the 1970s and 1980s. "There were stories in the newspapers, of course, corpses in ditches or the woods, bludgeoned to death or mutilated, interfered with, as they used to say, but they were about other women, and the men who did such things were other men." Similarly, the pornographic films from the same historical period which Offred sees in the Red Center make manifest the hidden cultural script of male violence against women. The films show "[w]omen kneeling, sucking penises or guns, women tied up or chained or with dog collars around their necks, women hanging from trees, or upside-down, naked, with their legs held apart, woman being raped, beaten up, killed. Once we had to watch a woman being slowly cut into pieces, her fingers and breasts snipped off with garden shears, her stomach slit open and her intestines pulled out." Providing a graphic depiction of the sexual victimization of women, these images disclose the diseased underside of patriarchal culture. Subject to the killing male rage which mutilates, dismembers, and destroys, woman is a sexualized and dehumanized object in a sadomasochistic master-slave relationship.

"In the days of anarchy, it was freedom to. Now you are being given freedom from. Don't underrate it," the Handmaids are told. In Gilead the Handmaids have been promised "freedom from" the sexual degradation and violence—the pornography and rape—which existed in the pre-Gilead period. But the clichéd messages Offred gets from her culture repeat the masculine discourse from the past: "Men are sex machines"; it is up to the woman to "set the boundaries"; men do not want sex to be "too easy"; and "[n]ature demands variety, for men." "Think of yourselves as pearls," the Handmaids are told, while other women perceive them as sexually debased and contaminated. "She thinks I may be catching, like a disease or any form of bad luck," Offred thinks to herself when one of the Marthas shuns her. After the ritual insemination ceremony, Offred hears "loathing" in the voice of the Commander's wife, "as if the touch of my flesh sickens and contaminates her." And at the Prayvaganza, the Handmaids are segregated, presumably to protect the other women from "contamination."

The sexual object for male consumption and the marginalized woman who is shunned and despised by other women, the handmaid is the good/bad woman, the saintly prostitute. Her red, nunlike uniform symbolizes her imprisonment in the Handmaid's role. "Everything except the wings around my face is red: the color of blood, which defines us." A domestic and sexual captive—a "Sister, dipped in blood"—she is cast in the public gaze and yet remains invisible. The hostile male gaze that objectifies and obliterates what it sees becomes figured in the omnipresent Eyes—the Eyes of God—who are agents of surveillance and oppression. If to be seen, as Rennie recognizes in *Bodily Harm*, is to be violated, the enforced invisibility of the Handmaid serves as an even more insidious threat to the self. "Modesty is invisibility. . . . To be seen—to be *seen*—is to be . . . penetrated. What you must be, girls, is impenetrable," the Handmaids are taught. As the Handmaids walk in pairs, twinlike, they are iterable objects in the eyes of the body politic. Indeed, Offred imagines that she and Ofglen look "picturesque" from a distance, "like Dutch milkmaids on a wallpaper frieze . . . or anything that repeats itself with at least minimum grace and without variation." Returning to a concern voiced in other Atwood novels we have investigated, *The Handmaid's Tale* depicts women participating in men's desires and renouncing their own as they perform the feminine masquerade. When Offred catches sight of herself in a mirror, she appears "like a distorted shadow, a parody of something, some fairy-tale figure in a red cloak." Similarly, in the purple-sequined costume the Commander gives her to wear to Jezebel's, she is "a travesty, in bad make-up and someone else's clothes, used glitz."

"I'm doing my best. . . . I'm trying to give you the best chance you can have," Aunt Lydia tells the Handmaids. The Aunts, who ironically place a high value on "camaraderie among women," uphold the male supremist power structure of Gilead with its hierarchical arrangement of the sexes, and they play an active role in the state's sexual enslavement of the Handmaids. Anticipating *Cat's Eye*'s dramatization of the female-directed oppression of women which begins during the girlhood socialization process, *The Handmaid's Tale* describes the brutal reeducation of the Handmaids, who are coerced by the Aunts to forego the ideology of women's liberation and to revert to the "traditional" values of a male-dominant system. The "Historical Notes" describes the regime's use of women to control other women, explaining that in Gilead "there were many women willing to serve as Aunts, either because of a genuine belief in what they called 'traditional values' or for the benefits they might thereby acquire. When power is scarce, a little of it is tempting."

Repeating a pattern we have observed in other Atwood novels, *The Handmaid's Tale* is preoccupied with the bad mother, while the good mother is essentially absent from the text. Subject to the brutality of the Aunts—who are embodiments of the overcontrolling, fault-finding bad mother—Offred wants Serena Joy to be "a motherly figure, someone who would understand and protect" her. But she recognizes from the outset the Wife's hostility toward her. While the Wife is a menacing presence in Offred's life, her mother is both physically and emotionally absent. A "wiry, spunky" feminist, Offred's mother disappears soon after the Gileadean coup; branded an Unwoman, she is shipped to the colonies where she is forced to sweep up toxic wastes—a certain death sentence. "I thought she was dead," Offred tells Moira. "She might as well be. . . . You should wish it for her."

"Mother," Offred thinks to herself, "You wanted a women's culture. Well, now there is one. It isn't what you meant, but it exists." While "patriarchal in form," Gilead is also "occasionally matriarchal in content." Existing in an all-women's enclave, Offred is doomed to a "minimalist life" which consists of shopping, eating, taking a bath, listening to the gossip of the Marthas, whispering to other Handmaids, participating in the monthly insemination ceremony and the rare birthing rituals. Totally passive, Offred must endure long stretches of "blank time" with nothing to do but wait. "I wait, washed, brushed, fed, like a prize pig." Recalling nineteenth-century erotic art and its obsession with depictions of harems, she recognizes the true subject matter of these "[s]tudies of sedentary flesh." "They were paintings about suspended animation; about waiting, about objects not in use. They were paintings about boredom." For Offred, the "amount of unfilled time, the long parentheses of nothing," becomes oppressive. "Now there's a space to be filled, in the too-warm air of my room, and a time also; a space-time, between here and now and there and then, punctuated by dinner. The arrival of the tray, carried up the stairs as if for an invalid. An invalid, one who has been invalidated. No valid passport. No exit."

Treated as subordinate other—as body without mind—Offred is defined and confined by her reproductive role. "I used to think of my body as an instrument, of pleasure, or a means of transportation, or an implement for the accomplishment of my will. . . . There were limits, but my body was nevertheless lithe, single, solid, one with me. Now the flesh arranges itself differently. I'm a cloud, congealed around a central object, the shape of a pear, which is hard and more real than I am and glows red within its translucent wrapping." Submissively, Offred undergoes the monthly ceremony and attunes herself to her body's monthly cycle. "I become the earth I set my ear against, for rumors of the future. Each twinge, each murmur of slight pain, ripples of sloughed-off matter, swellings and diminishings of tissue, the droolings of the flesh, these are signs, these are the things I need to know about. Each month I watch for blood, fearfully, for when it comes it means failure. I have failed once again to fulfill the expectations of others, which have become my own."

But encoded in Offred's fervent—and orthodox—desire for pregnancy is the hidden fantasy that enforced pregnancy not only entails a loss of control but also poses a threat to the self. While the Handmaids are taught to intone "Blessed be the fruit," Offred sardonically likens herself, at one point, to "a queen ant with eggs." More significantly, Janine, the Handmaid who is depicted as utterly compliant and broken, is the only character in the novel who becomes pregnant and gives birth. At one point during the birthing process, Janine crouches "like a doll, an old one that's been pillaged and discarded, in some corner, akimbo." In a related description of childbearing, Offred recalls a film depicting childbirth in a pre-Gilead hospital: it shows a women "wired up to a machine, electrodes coming out of her every which way" so that she resembles "a broken robot." Convinced that it is her fault that she has given birth to an Unbaby—a "shredder"— Janine subsequently appears depleted, "as if the juice is being sucked out of her." And in the monstrous image of the Unbaby—"with a pinhead or a snout like a dog's, or two bodies, or a hole in its heart or no arms, or webbed hands and feet"—*The Handmaid's Tale*, like other Atwood novels we have examined, acknowledges female anxieties about pregnancy and motherhood.

"Maybe the life I think I'm living is a paranoid delusion," Offred says at one point, as she struggles to retain a sense of sanity in an insane world of sexual slavery. Examining the psychological origins of the sexual oppression of women, *The Handmaid's Tale* makes visible the pattern of desire laid down during female oedipal development by staging the female oedipal fantasy, in which the girl wishes to marry the father and take the place of the mother, who is viewed as a rival for the father's affection. "If female readers of a particular culture share certain fantasies, it is because particular child-raising patterns, shared across a culture, embed common fantasy structures in their daughters," remarks Jean Wyatt. Not only are family relations "the principal conduits between cultural ideology and the individual unconscious," but cultural ideology "is most subtle and insidious when it comes in the form of interpersonal relations in the family." In female oedipal development, the daughter's relationship to her father "trains her to idealize a distant and mysterious figure whose absences she can fill with glamorous projections." Some of the "behaviors that speak directly to the quirks of a female unconscious patterned by life in a patriarchal family are waiting, flirting, and the oedipal triangle," writes Wyatt. Because the "father's homecoming" is the "exciting event of a child's day," the waiting daughter comes to associate novelty and stimulation with the arrival of the father—a behavior that is repeated later in the romance scenario where "lover and waiting woman assume the active and passive roles first played out by father and daughter." The father enacts an important developmental role by "diverting his daughter's erotic impulses, first oriented toward her mother, into heterosexual channels"; he also engages in "sexual flirtation" with the daughter but does not follow through because of the incest taboo.

Providing a thinly disguised dramatization of the female oedipal situation in which the daughter views the mother as a rival and is drawn to the father, *The Handmaid's Tale* presents Serena Joy as a "malicious and vengeful woman" and the Commander as "not an unkind man." And the narrative also enacts the "waiting" and "flirting" behavior typical of the father-daughter relationship. When asked to meet secretly with the Commander in his study, Offred finds that these visits give her "something to do" and "to think about" and thus relieve the tedium of her life of passive waiting. But she also realizes that she is "only a whim" for the Commander, who likes it when she distinguishes herself, showing "precocity, like an attentive pet, prick-eared and eager to perform. . . . [H]e is positively daddyish. He likes to think I am being entertained; and I am, I am." But what is culturally repressed in this developmental scenario—because of the taboo against incest—is acted out in the novel's staging of the monthly insemination ceremony. If the narrative risks victimizing readers by positioning them as voyeurs and subjecting them to the obscene spectacle of the Ceremony, it also partially conceals what it reveals as it minimizes the horror of what is being depicted. For Offred protectively distances herself from what she is experiencing: she "detaches" herself, she "describes," she finds "something hilarious" about the impregnation ritual. Similarly, at least one critic claims to find a "humorous correspondence" between Atwood's description of the

Ceremony and its biblical source in the Rachel and Bilhah story, which is quoted in one of the epigraphs to the novel. For the barren Rachel's desire that Jacob impregnate her handmaid, Bilhah—"go in unto her; and she shall bear upon my knees, that I may also have children by her"—is dramatized in the novel not only in the birthing ritual but also in the impregnation ritual since in "both crucial moments, the Handmaid is between the Wife's knees." And another critic remarks that *The Handmaid's Tale* deliberately and with parodic intent deflates the Gothic suspense it has invoked in the description leading up to the Ceremony by depicting the impregnation ritual as "not so much dreadful as boring."

Although readers are encouraged to participate in the narrative's defenses by recognizing Atwood's parody of Gothic form in this scene or by locating the connections between the Gileadean Ceremony and its biblical counterpart, this pornographic and voyeuristic scene is, nevertheless, profoundly disturbing. As Offred lies between the legs of the Commander's wife, "my head on her stomach, her pubic bone under the base of my skull, her thighs on either side of me," the Commander services her. "What he is fucking is the lower part of my body. I do not say making love, because this is not what he's doing. Copulating too would be inaccurate, because it would imply two people and only one is involved. Nor does rape cover it. . . ." Despite the text's denial, this passage does dramatize a terrible kind of rape. Because the Handmaid takes on the role of the dutiful child-daughter in the father-commander's household, the Ceremony is presented as a thinly disguised incest drama. The actors in this degrading oedipal flesh triangle are the complicitous mother, the sexually violating father, and the sexually abused—and mute, silenced—daughter. In the displaced drama of Janine, the narrative explicitly refers to the forbidden theme of incest. "[S]o well behaved. . . . More like a daughter to you. . . . One of the family," Offred imagines the Wives saying when the pregnant Janine is "paraded" before them. "Little whores, all of them," is the remark made when Janine has left the room. And yet although the novel deliberately stages an incest drama, it also defends against it by focusing attention on Offred's involvement in an all "too banal" plot. In her relationship with the Commander, she has become the mistress of a man whose wife doesn't understand him.

"Is there no end to his disguises, of benevolence?" Offred asks at one point as she compares the Commander to a series of innocuous male figures: to a museum guard, a midwestern bank president, a man in a vodka ad, and the shoemaker character in a fairy tale. Yet another Atwoodian split male, the Commander is both the father-protector and the father-persecutor. For although he wants to make Offred's life more bearable and although he can be "positively daddyish" in his behavior, he also affirms the male supremist ideology which subordinates and sexually enslaves women. In Gilead, he claims, women are "protected" so that they "can fulfill their biological destinies in peace." The pre-Gilead years, in the Commander's view, "were just an anomaly, historically speaking. . . . All we've done is return things to Nature's norm." What lies behind the benevolent paternalism of the Commander and the culturally conservative ideal of protected womanhood, as *The Handmaid's Tale* makes apparent, is a rigid belief in the male use and control of female sexuality.

"Sexual objectification," remarks Catharine MacKinnon, "is the primary process of the subjection of women. . . . Man fucks woman; subject verb object." The fact that "consent rather than nonmutuality is the line between rape and intercourse . . . exposes the inequality in normal social expectations." Asking whether "consent is a meaningful concept" when sex is "ordinarily accepted as something men do *to* women," MacKinnon observes how "[r]ape in marriage expresses the male sense of entitlement to access to women they annex" and "incest extends it." As the experience of women "blurs the lines between deviance and normalcy, it obliterates the distinction between abuses *of* women and the social definition of what a women *is*."

Depicting the male objectification and sexual control of women, *The Handmaid's Tale* exposes the horror of woman's consent to femininity. But if the novel concerns itself with the troubling issues of incest and forced sex, it also incorporates an antagonistic, feminist-dialogic speech which serves to partially contain and master the female fears it dramatizes. Describing how this tactic works, Offred muses that "[t]here is something powerful in the whispering of obscenities, about those in power. . . . It's like a spell, of sorts. It deflates them, reduces them to the common denominator where they can be dealt with." "What'd you do wrong? Laugh at his dick?" Moira asks when Offred suddenly appears at Jezebel's with the Commander. When Offred explains that her Commander smuggled her in, Moira responds, "Who? . . . That shit you're with? I've had him, he's the pits." Indulging in a form of penis ridicule, Offred likens the Commander's penis to a stub, an extra thumb, a tentacle, a stalked slug's eye. When she attends a Gileadean group wedding, she imagines the impressive-looking Commander, who is officiating, in bed with his Wife and Handmaid. "[F]ertilizing away like mad" and "pretending to take no pleasure in it," he is "like a rutting salmon," in her view. "When the Lord said be fruitful and multiply, did he mean this man?" And she imagines sex among the Angels and their new brides as "momentous grunts and sweating, damp furry encounters; or, better, ignominious failures, cocks like three-week-old carrots, anguished fumblings upon flesh cold and unresponding as uncooked fish."

Externally compliant, Offred expresses her defiance through her "inner jeering" at the Commander and her "mean-minded bitter jokes" about Serena Joy. To Offred, the Wife's name is stupid-sounding, recalling the brand name of "something you'd put on your hair, in the other time, the time before, to straighten it." Serena Joy, who once made speeches about "the sanctity of the home, about how women should stay home," now stays in her home, but "it doesn't seem to agree with her. How furious she must be, now that she's been taken at her word." When Serena Joy wears one of her best dresses with flowers on it on the night of the Ceremony, Offred is scornful. "No use for you, I think at her, my face unmoving, you can't use them anymore, you're withered. They're the genital organs of plants. I read that somewhere, once."

Despite Offred's cynical inner voice, her anger remains largely censored. Although at one point in her narrative reconstruction of events she claims that she fantasizes stabbing the Commander when he firsts asks her to kiss him—"I think about the blood coming out of him, hot as soup, sexual, over my hands"—she subsequently denies this impulse. "In fact I don't think about anything of the kind. I put it in only afterwards. . . . As I said, this is a reconstruction." Whereas the film version of *The Handmaid's Tale* not only privileges this angry fantasy, it also enacts it, in the novel, Offred acts out her killing rage against her male oppressors only in the displaced drama of the state-sanctioned Particicution ceremony. When a man accused of rape is thrown at the mercy of a group of Handmaids, he is mobbed and brutally killed. "[T]here is a bloodlust; I want to tear, gouge, rend," as Offred describes it. On the fringes of her tale we find the partially expressed drama of female rage.

"Like physical abuse," writes Christine Froula, "literary violence against women works to privilege the cultural father's voice and story over those of women, the cultural daughters, and indeed to silence women's voices." Treating the Handmaid as an abused cultural daughter, the Gilead regime also attempts to silence her. "*Blessed are the silent,*" according to the revised Gileadean Bible. In Gilead, men have "the word" and women are rendered speechless. When Offred first meets her double Ofglen—the Handmaid she is assigned to go shopping with and to spy on—they exchange the "orthodox" platitudes sanctioned by the regime:

> "The war is going well, I hear," she says.
> "Praise be," I reply.
> "We've been sent good weather."
> "Which I receive with joy."

Later, after Ofglen informs Offred that she is a member of the anti-regime Mayday organization, their whispered conversations change but still their speech is, of necessity, "more like a telegram, a verbal semaphore. Amputated speech." Offred comes to feel that speech is "backing up inside" her. "Our big mistake," says one of the officials of the regime's original think tank, "was teaching them [women] to read. We won't do that again." In Gilead, women are forbidden by law to read books; after the third conviction, the offender's hand is cut off.

Ordered to make secret visits to the Commander's private, book-filled study, Offred does there what has become a perversity and crime in the new culture: she reads while he watches. His "watching is a curiously sexual act" and her "illicit reading . . . seems a kind of performance." And she and the Commander play Scrabble, a language game that is now banned and thus dangerous. As she uses "all the old tricks with consonants" she can recall, her tongue feels "thick with the effort of spelling," and her mind lurches and stumbles "among the sharp R's and T's, sliding over the ovoid vowels as if on pebbles." When the Commander, on one occasion, allows her to write with a pen, the pen seems "sensuous, alive almost" and she can "feel its power, the power of the words it contains." As Offred holds the pen, she remembers a Red Center saying—"Pen Is Envy"—which is meant to warn the Handmaids to avoid such forbidden objects. Since this Gileadean motto encodes yet another motto—"Penis envy"—it also may be a self-conscious allusion on Atwood's part to Sandra Gilbert and Susan Gubar's analysis of the "metaphor of literary paternity," the notion that the pen is a "metaphorical penis." In our phallocentric culture, as Gilbert and Gubar observe, "the text's author is a father, a progenitor, a procreator, an aesthetic patriarch whose pen is an instrument of generative power like his penis."

Because Offred recognizes the connection between the male control of language and male power, her dialogic resistance to the official, monologic discourse of Gilead is a conscious form of political disobedience. When, for example, Aunt Lydia tells the Handmaids to think of themselves as pearls, Offred resists this reeducation effort. "We, sitting in our rows, eyes down, we make her salivate morally. We are hers to define, we must suffer her adjectives. I think about pearls. Pearls are congealed oyster spit." Responding to another one of Aunt Lydia's sayings, "All flesh is weak," Offred mentally replies, "All flesh is grass. . . ." When greeting another Handmaid, Offred is compelled to use the orthodox speech of Gilead: "'Blessed be the fruit,' she says to me, the accepted greeting among us. 'May the Lord open,' I answer, the accepted response." But she also listens avidly to the "unofficial news"— the subversive discourse—exchanged among the Marthas. "*Stillborn, it was. Or, stabbed her with a knitting needle, right in the belly. Jealousy, it must have been, eating her up. Or, tantalizingly, It was toilet cleaner she used. Worked like a charm, though you'd think he'd of tasted it.*" Trapped in the male supremist world of

Gilead, Offred recalls her mother's oppositional discourse. What "use" are men, Offred's mother once commented, "except for ten seconds' worth of half babies. A man is just a woman's strategy for making other women." Gratified when she finds the "taboo message" left by the former Handmaid—"*Nolite te bastardes carborundorum*"—Offred feels that the written message is meant for her and is pleased that it has "made it through." If the mock-Latin phrase—"Don't let the bastards grind you down"—is alternately a prayer, a command, and a joke to Offred, it is also a whispered obscenity about those in power which is secretly passed from one Handmaid to another.

Through her dialogic wordplay and focus on words, Offred not only registers her resistance to the official speech and totalizing discourse of the state, she also signals her desperate desire to retain some sense of control. "I sit in the chair and think about the word *chair*. It can also mean the leader of a meeting. It can also mean a mode of execution. It is the first syllable in *charity*. It is the French word for flesh. None of these facts has any connection with the others. These are the kinds of litanies I use, to compose myself." Words, to Offred, are more than precious commodities. They are also signposts to the reality she is determined to hold on to. While the world can be read as if it were a text, it is not equivalent to a text. At one point Offred notices, on the white cloth bag covering the head of a hanged man, that blood has seeped through the bag, making a "smile of blood" on the white cloth. Associating the blood red smile of the executed man with red tulips, she thinks: "The red is the same but there is no connection. The tulips are not tulips of blood, the red smiles are not flowers, neither thing makes a comment on the other. The tulip is not a reason for disbelief in the hanged man, or vice versa. Each thing is valid and really there. It is through a field of such valid objects that I must pick my way, every day and in every way. I put a lot of effort into making such distinctions. I need to make them. I need to be very clear, in my own mind."

Realizing that a "danger" of her existence is "grayout," Offred also needs to make distinctions and be "very clear" in her "own mind" as she reconstructs her past and describes her present; for what she retains of her identity is bound up in her memories of what she was and is. "I wait. I compose myself," she says. "My self is a thing I must now compose, as one composes a speech." In the "Historical Notes" appended to Offred's tale, we learn that her narrative is really an oral diary, a transcription of some thirty cassette tapes. For Offred—who is "a blank . . . between parentheses. Between other people"—to compose her story, to speak herself into agency, is to attempt to recuperate herself.

To her imaginary audience, Offred admits that she wishes her story were "different" and "more civilized," that it had "more shape" and showed her "more active, less hesitant, less distracted by trivia." She would like to believe that the story she is telling is *only* a story because then she would have "control" over its ending. "I'm sorry there is so much pain in this story. I'm sorry it's in fragments, like a body caught in crossfire or pulled apart by force," she says. "But I keep on going with this sad and hungry and sordid, this limping and mutilated story, because after all I want you to hear it. . . . By telling you anything at all I'm at least believing in you, I believe you're there, I believe you into being. Because I'm telling you this story I will your existence. I tell, therefore you are." Although there are postmodernist appeals in the novel's repeated and self-conscious meditations on the act of narration, *The Handmaid's Tale*, as W. F. Garrett-Petts remarks, "invokes the conventions and themes of postmodernism . . . in order to reinsert them back into the narrative of daily experience." Despite its muted "postmodernist echoes," *The Handmaid's Tale* conforms to the purpose informing all of Atwood's novels: "her desire to teach her audience how to read the world." While Atwood's narrative thematizes the collaboration between writer and readers, it uses direct address to draw in readers, who assume the role of confidant and who "listen, sympathize, and learn from Offred's testimony." Moreover, Offred's open appeal to her imaginary audience—in particular to a female audience—is also designed to strengthen the reader's desires to make sense out of her fragmentary text and to see her rescued.

"I'm too tired to go on with this story. I'm too tired to think about where I am. Here is a different story, a better one. This is the story of what happened to Moira," Offred says at one point, interrupting her description of her life in Gilead to describe her "irreverent, resourceful" feminist friend from earlier times, who actively rebels against the Gilead system. Despite the horrible foot punishment Moira suffers after her first attempted escape from the Red Center, she remains undaunted. "I left that old hag Aunt Elizabeth tied up like a Christmas turkey behind the furnace. I wanted to kill her, I really felt like it . . . ," Moira later tells Offred, as she describes, in her characteristic feminist-dialogic speech, her second escape attempt. After her disappearance form the Red Center, Moira becomes a "fantasy" for the other Handmaids. Because of her rebellion, the Aunts are "less fearsome and more absurd," for their power is somehow flawed. And yet, the Handmaids also find something frightening in Moira's freedom. "Already we were losing the taste for freedom, already we were finding these walls secure. In the upper reaches of the atmosphere you'd come apart, you'd vaporize, there would be no pressure holding you together."

Ultimately cross-questioning the possibility of female heroism in such a regime, the narrative, while typecasting Moira as a feminist rebel, also dramatizes her defeat. Caught, tortured, and then forced into prostitution,

Moira ultimately loses her volition and becomes indifferent. "I don't want her [Moira] to be like me. Give in, go along, save her skin," says Offred. "I want gallantry from her, swashbuckling, heroism, single-handed combat. Something I lack." Although Moira's story does not "end with something daring and spectacular" as Offred and many readers wish it would, Offred's story does in the film version's rewriting of the novel: for in the film, which enacts a female revenge fantasy, Offred kills the Commander at the end and then is helped to escape Gilead by a Mayday rescue team.

If the text's rage is acted out in the film version of *The Handmaid's Tale*, the narrative, in contrast, intertwines its increasing anger about male oppression—which culminates in the displaced drama of the Particicution ceremony—with Offred's love affair with Nick and her at times lyrical, sensuous celebrations of the "minimalist life." Offred takes deep pleasure, for example, in observing the egg she is about to eat for breakfast. "The shell of the egg is smooth but also grained; small pebbles of calcium are defined by the sunlight, like craters on the moon. It's a barren landscape, yet perfect; it's the sort of desert the saints went into, so their minds would not be distracted by profusion. . . . The egg is glowing now, as if it had an energy of its own." She also takes delight in Serena Joy's garden: "A Tennyson garden, heavy with scent, languid; the return of the word *swoon*. . . . To walk through it in these days, of peonies, of pinks and carnations, makes my head swim." Having, from the beginning, hungered to "commit the act of touch," Offred finds it "good" to be touched by Nick, "to be felt so greedily, to feel so greedy." "Can I be blamed for wanting a real body, to put my arms around? Without it I too am disembodied."

"*Falling in love*, we said; *I fell for him*. We were falling women. We believed in it, this downward motion: so lovely, like flying, and yet at the same time so dire, so extreme, so unlikely," Offred thinks as she recalls the pre-Gilead ideology of romantic love. In the past, falling in love "was the central thing; it was the way you understood yourself." But in Gilead, this culture-specific notion of romantic fulfillment has been replaced with the arranged marriages that existed before the rise of romantic marriage in Western society. "Don't let me catch you at it," Aunt Lydia warns Offred (June) and the other Handmaids. "No mooning and June-ing around here, girls. . . . *Love* is not the point."

If Offred's situation "recalls that of a romantic heroine" who must choose between two men—the older, paternal Commander and the younger, dangerous and thus more sexually desirous, Nick—the "grim realities of Offred's actual existence resemble those of a concentration camp inmate, far more than those of a gothic heroine." That some readers may take comfort in the novel's love plot—which provides Offred temporary escape from the sexually repressive world of Gilead—is suggested in Lucy Freibert's remark that "Offred's real breakthrough to her courageous sexual self" occurs in her relationship with Nick, and that Offred's "joyous reaction to her desire embodies precisely the French *jouissance*." But despite the common claim that love is presented as a "subversive force" in *The Handmaid's Tale*, the narrative's representation of romantic love is, in fact, "highly qualified, highly ambivalent."

Although Offred's affair with Nick is presented as a form of female opposition to the State, the novel's invocation of the conventional romance plot may also appear to present a culturally conservative message: namely, that falling in love is the "central" thing, that a woman reaches self-fulfillment only in the love relationship. And yet if *The Handmaid's Tale* seems to recuperate the romance plot, it also interrupts it by having Offred tell two radically different versions of her initial sexual encounter with Nick. The first version is erotic. "His mouth is on me, his hands, I can't wait and he's moving, already, love, it's been so long, I'm alive in my skin, again, arms around him, falling and water softly everywhere, never-ending." Claiming that she invented this version of events, Offred then tells another story which actively undercuts and dialogizes the erotic discourse of the first description. In a telling role reversal, Nick becomes the sexual object and commodity. When he tells her that he could "just squirt it into a bottle" and she could "pour it in," she thinks that perhaps he wants something from her, "some emotion, some acknowledgment that he too is human, is more than just a seedpod." When they subsequently engage in "corny and falsely gay sexual banter" adopted from the late movies. "And what's a nice girl like me doing in a spot like this"; "Abstinence makes the heart grow fonder"—Offred realizes the purpose of such borrowed, stylized speech. "I can see now what it's for, what it was always for: to keep the core of yourself out of reach, enclosed, protected." That Offred subsequently admits that it "didn't happen that way either" points to the narrative's reluctance to commit itself to the romance plot. And if Offred's sexual relationship with Nick is presented as an important act of defiance against the Gilead regime, it is also entrapping; for when Nick becomes Offred's lover, she loses her desire to escape Gilead. Above all else, she wants to be near Nick; with him she feels she can make some kind of life for herself. "Humanity is so adaptable, my mother would say. Truly amazing, what people can get used to, as long as there are a few compensations."

"Thinking can hurt your chances, and I intend to last," Offred says at the outset of the novel, even as she contemplates the potential escape of suicide. "I know why there is no glass, in front of the watercolor picture of blue irises, and why the window opens only partly and why the glass in it is shatterproof. It isn't running away they're afraid of. We wouldn't get far. It's those other escapes, the ones you can open in yourself, given a cutting edge." "Oh God oh God. How can I keep on living?" Offred says on another occasion. "I could burn the house down. Such a fine thought, it makes me shiver. An escape, quick and narrow." Although the narrative repeatedly warns that Offred's story will end in the prescribed closure of suicide, it, instead, acts out the threatened ending of suicide in the displaced drama of Offred's predecessor, the Handmaid who defiantly leaves behind a written message. "I look up at the ceiling, the round circle of plaster flowers. . . . From the center was the chandelier, and from the chandelier a twisted strip of sheet was hanging down. That's where she was swinging, just lightly, like a pendulum; the way you could swing as a child, hanging by your hands from a tree branch. She was safe then. . . ." When Serena Joy discovers that Offred has been secretly seeing the Commander, she condemns Offred to the same fate. "Just like the other one. A slut. You'll end up the same." Although Offred thinks about setting fire to the house or killing the Wife, she finds herself unable to act. She is the victim of circumstances, not an active agent capable of directing the plot of her own life. In scenes that anticipate Atwood's next novel, *Cat's Eye*, Offred imagines herself freezing to death in the snow and she hears the former Handmaid—whose voice she has internalized just as Elaine internalizes the voice of Cordelia—telling her to kill herself. "Get it over, she says. I'm tired of this melodrama. I'm tired of keeping silent. There's no one you can protect, your life has value to no one. I want it finished."

Refusing the preestablished closure of suicide, *The Handmaid's Tale*, like *Bodily Harm*, intentionally leaves the reader in a state of suspense even as it invokes and promotes a rescue fantasy. As the Eyes help Offred into the black van, she is uncertain whether she is going to her "end or a new beginning," whether she is stepping up "into the darkness within; or else the light." Because Nick may be an Eye or a member of the Mayday organization—that is, a persecutor or a rescuer—readers do not know for certain whether Offred has been betrayed by Nick and ultimately sent to her death or rescued by the secret Mayday organization and the Underground Femaleroad. Although Offred's fate is left hanging in the balance at the end of her narrative, the "Historical Notes" section appended to her tale partially acts out the rescue fantasy generated by the narrative. Speculating on what probably happened to her, Professor Pieixoto, the twenty-second century historian who transcribes Offred's tapes, comments that while her "ultimate fate" is unknown, the weight of evidence suggests that Nick engineered her escape. And her narrative, he claims, has "a certain reflective quality. . . . It has a whiff of emotion recollected, if not in tranquillity, at least *post facto*."

Some critic/readers have similarly speculated about Offred's fate. In the view of Arnold Davidson, although "Offred's end is uncertain" in the main narrative, "the very existence of the tapes suggests that, aided by Nick, she did elude the rule of Gilead." In contrast, Leslie-Ann Hales argues that not only does Offred's narrative "not reach the security of conclusion," but readers never learn whether Offred "safely escapes Gilead, dies in the attempt, or is recaptured only to be hanged from a meathook on the Wall in Gilead. It is possible that only the tapes, not the maker of the tapes, survives Gilead." But for Coral Ann Howells, even though Offred's ultimate fate does remain uncertain, the fact that history proves that Gilead is "not invulnerable" builds "a shadowed optimism" into the novel. And Barbara Rigney feels that *The Handmaid's Tale* is "a novel about survival." Describing her intention in the closure, Atwood comments that *The Handmaid's Tale* "isn't totally bleak and pessimistic," for not only does Offred get out but also a future society exists which "is not the society of Gilead and is capable of reflecting about the society of Gilead in the same way that we reflect about the 17th century. Her little message in a bottle has gotten through to someone—which is about all we can hope, isn't it?" And yet despite the epilogue's reassurance that "there are nightmares from which one does eventually wake up," some critic/readers, like Arnold Davidson, find the professor's comments "in crucial ways . . . the most pessimistic part of the book."

Presented as a partial transcription of a scholarly meeting held in the far north of Canada in a nation ruled by native North Americans, the epilogue is set in 2195 at the Twelfth Symposium on Gileadean Studies at the University of Denay, Nunavit, a name that carries a hidden message to readers—namely, to "deny none of it." The setting, the names of the participants—Professor Maryann Crescent Moon who chairs the session and Professor Pieixoto—and the fact that Caucasian Anthropology is now a subject of academic study all serve to suggest a multicultural future in which the power of white patriarchy has been successfully challenged. But disturbing signs of the staying power of sexism soon emerge. Describing the joke behind the naming of Offred's story by a male colleague, Professor Pieixoto comments that "all puns were intentional, particularly that having to do with the archaic vulgar signification of the word *tail*; that being, to some extent, the bone, as it were, of contention, in that phase of Gileadean society of which our saga treats." This comment provokes laughter from the academicians, as does the professor's remark that "The Underground Femaleroad" has been "dubbed by some of our historical wags 'The Underground Frailroad.'" It is also telling that the professor seems to admire the "ingenuity" of the original members of the Sons of Jacob Think Tank while he belittles the intelligence of Offred who, in his words, "appears to have been an educated woman, insofar as a graduate of any North

American college of the time may be said to have been educated." As he
assumes an air of scholarly objectivity, Professor Pieixoto reveals his moral
obtuseness. "[A]llow me to say that in my opinion we must be cautious about
passing moral judgment upon the Gileadeans," he tells his academic audience.
"Surely we have learned by now that such judgments are of necessity culture-
specific." Because history's voices are "imbued with the obscurity of the matrix
out of which they come," we "cannot always decipher them precisely in the
clearer light of our own day," remarks Professor Pieixoto, who is blind to his
own interpretive biases as he reconstructs the history of Offred's society.

Atwood comments that one of her purposes in the "Historical Notes"
is to provide the reader with information about Offred's society which
Offred, given her limited circumstances, could not have known. But her
pedantic, misogynistic history professor, who is obsessed with facts but
ignores (or denies) the feelings generated by Offred's narrative, is also clearly
designed to provoke reader outrage. Again and again, critic/readers have
dialogically contested the authoritative speech of Atwood's fictional
professor. Leslie-Ann Hales finds the professor's "pompous attitude of moral
objectivity . . . appalling in the wake of the handmaid's own story." For Linda
Kauffman, the archivist not only "has little sensitivity to Offred's
predicament or her pain" but he and his cohorts "appropriate the female
voice for their own purposes—fame, fortune, power, self-aggrandizement,
and self-congratulation." According to Amin Malak, the epilogue reveals not
only the "absurdity and futility of certain academic writings that engage in
dull, clinically sceptic analysis of irrelevancies and inanities," it also shows
that the scholar who avoids taking a moral or political stand about issues such
as totalitarianism "will necessarily become an apologist for evil."

In providing a potent critique of the male appropriation and
objectification of the female voice, the "Historical Notes" expose the
ideological biases of literary interpretation. But if the epilogue "calls forth
strange emotions" and if the professor's witticisms "set the teeth on edge,"
the "Historical Notes" also function to disrupt and defuse the powerful
emotions generated by the novel and to focus attention, instead, on the act
of interpretation. Designed to make critic/readers aware of the author's
presence behind the text—indeed, Roberta Rubenstein imagines Atwood
"wryly anticipating her commentators at the annual rites of MLA"—the
epilogue also forces academic commentators to cross-question their own
critical activity. "Do we, as scholars, contribute to the dehumanizations of
society by our own critical work . . . ?" asks Arnold Davidson, who observes
how Professor Pieixoto objectifies just as the state objectified Offred. "Is this
what history is for? To round out the vitae of historians?" Lucy Freibert
thinks that "'serious' academics will turn bloody as they hear themselves

echoed" in the professor's "pedantic analysis." In the epilogue, "the small-mindedness of academe in dealing with reality cannot be missed." And for Michael Foley, the epilogue shows how "even in one of the temples of liberal democracy, namely the Western university, the deeply rooted sexual, racial or other biases of academics can anesthetize their critical faculties." Although "ostensibly a scene from the distant future," this is "actually the book's clearest depiction of a worrisome present."

Decrying the power politics of literary interpretation in the "Historical Notes," Atwood also asserts authorial power by urging commentators to reflect on their own critical practices and by suggesting that there are appropriate and inappropriate ways of responding to literary texts. In calling for a reading that, in the words of Harriet Bergmann, "combines emotional and intellectual perception," Atwood dramatizes her desire to save her novel from those readers who, like her fictional professor, treat the text as a verbal artifact to be coldly dissected and ultimately dismissed. And judging from the critical commentary *The Handmaid's Tale* has provoked, many readers find it difficult to dismiss Atwood's novel and its warning against the fundamentalist backlash against feminism. For David Cowart, readers who refuse "to concede any real prophetic plausibility" to *The Handmaid's Tale* miss "the contemporary actuality that fuels Atwood's speculation." Finding something "sickeningly familiar" in the novel's description of the pre-Gilead society, W. J. Keith feels that the "very suggestion" that Gilead represents a possible future for America is "a crushing indictment of our own times." "However we choose to look at it," writes Michele Lacombe, "Offred's world is not far removed from our own." While Atwood's fictional professor refuses to pass judgment, many readers do, as they are meant to. If Atwood wants to chill her readers, she is also determined to force them to pay attention. Indeed, as W. F. Garrett-Petts remarks, for Atwood the role of the reader "is one of considerable responsibility" and "reading is a matter of fierce interpretation."

"I would like to believe this is a story I'm telling. I need to believe it. I must believe it. Those who can believe that such stories are only stories have a better chance," Offred comments at one point. Although *The Handmaid's Tale* contains postmodernist echoes in passages that self-consciously reflect on the narrative process, it also insists on the existence of an historical reality that exists beyond the words of the text. Encouraging readers to speculate on the semifictive process of history-making and the ideological biases involved in any historical interpretation of the past, Atwood also enjoins her audience to recognize the terrifying reality—the material presence—of history. While history is an account we must attempt to decipher, it is also a lived experience. To reduce history to a mere story, as Offred recognizes, is to attempt to make it "less frightening." But history is more than a story we tell ourselves, Atwood reminds her "postfeminist" women readers, and it is a mistake to think that we can easily explain away its blood-stained smiles or use fiction to shield ourselves from the oppressive practices perpetuated by patriarchal ideology, with its hierarchical arrangement of the sexes—practices exemplified in the New Right's deliberate scapegoating of independent, autonomous women and its insistence on the restoration of women's traditional roles.

SHARON ROSE WILSON

# Off the Path to Grandma's House
## *in* The Handmaid's Tale

What do you think of when you see someone in red carrying a basket?"
asks Atwood. Although few critics have commented on the "Little Red Cap"
or "Red Riding Hood" intertext in *The Handmaid's Tale*, Red Cap again
meets the "wolf" in this text's sinister future. In addition, *The Handmaid's
Tale* draws on Triple Goddess myth and the biblical story of Jacob, Rachel,
Leah, and their handmaids, presenting not only a timeless vision of
oppression in any form, but exploring sexual politics in a feminist's hell.

Although Atwood says that *The Handmaid's Tale* is speculative rather than
science fiction, in the tradition of *1984*, in a broader sense *The Handmaid's Tale*
is an anti-narrative that both comments on and undercuts its varied intertexts,
especially the fairy tale. In this sense it is, in part, a metafairy tale: it is about
"Red Cap" and other fairy tales. In addition to subverting "true romance" and
utopian traditions, it self-consciously comments on, surrealistically distorts,
even reverses the Grimms' tale. *The Handmaid's Tale* is also metacriticism: like
*Bodily Harm*, it is about the reading process and literary criticism. The parodic
scholarly epilogue tells us that Offred's tale of doubtful authorship is oral,
supposedly tape-recorded, transcribed, reconstructed, arranged, and altered
over time like folktales and parts of the Bible. Flippant about the tale's title and
text and, like some discussions of *The Handmaid's Tale*, dangerously detached
about its horrifying events, these scholars undercut the value of their research

From *Margaret Atwood's Fairy-Tale Sexual Politics* by Sharon Rose Wilson. © 1993 by the
University Press of Mississippi.

and both the "truth" and fiction of the story we read. By linking the fairy tale with science fiction and satirizing those who would dismiss, redo, or overlook parts of fairy tales, myth, the Bible, and literature, Atwood projects past and present turbulence into the future, structuring a gender nightmare designed to move readers out of Rapunzel towers.

Implying a path through the nightmare, like most of Atwood's work *The Handmaid's Tale* is a distorting mirror: in order self-consciously to invert Little Red Cap's forest world and the biblical Eden, *The Handmaid's Tale* again incorporates the ancient myth of the Triple-Goddess. In addition to the usual Diana Maiden, Venus mother, and Hecate Crone, Atwood draws on early versions of the Persephone and "Red Cap" stories and on the Triple Marys of the Bible, all based in Goddess myth. All the females of the book figure in a paradic goddess trilogy. Interlacing the fairy-tale, mythic, and biblical intertexts, Atwood's novel presents Offred as already eaten Red Cap, raped Persephone maiden and Venus (Aphrodite), and biblical Bilhah; the Commander as wolf, Hades, Jacob, and biblical patriarch; and Serena Joy as witch-mother, Hecate, and Rachel. The goal of Red Cap's quest is reunion with Mother Earth or Persephone's return from "hell."

As previous chapters show, characters of myth often parallel those of fairy tales and the Bible; thus, Atwood's intertexts closely connect. All three intertexts share themes, images, motifs, settings, character types, similar character doubling and foiling, elements of plot, and narrative patterns that Atwood uses in *The Handmaid's Tale*. Like *The Handmaid's Tale*, the mythic, biblical, and fairy-tale intertexts all dramatize sexual politics: patriarchal power threatens or dominates the female and the submerged matriarchy behind her. In addition, the intertexts and novel all oppose green world (fertility) to the sterility of the underworld or civilization and are about familial conflict and mothers' separation from children. Most use red symbolism of the Triple Goddess or one of her aspects, feature journeys, and suggest literal or ritual dismemberment and cannibalism.

In the book's mythic intertext, the Demeter–Persephone (Kore) story, also embedded in Atwood's first published work, *Double Persephone* (1961), in *Surfacing* (1972), and in *Lady Oracle* (1976), not only portrays the Great Goddess but the kind of patriarchal displacement that occurred with the triple Marias and fairy tales. In the matriarchal version of the Demeter–Persephone myth, the goddess sacrifices herself to the earth. Demeter–Ceres is "reaped as the grain with her own moon-shaped sickle." Similarly, North American Natives' Corn Mother, whose limbs are severed, gives her blood to the earth so that her children, humanity, can cultivate corn.

In the best-known, patriarchal versions of the Demeter–Persephone story, however, Persephone leaves the earth, not of her free will, but because

Hades abducts and rapes her, symbolizing male usurpation of the female Mysteries. These versions are about a flower-picking daughter's rape, her abduction to the underworld, her separation from her mother (a second aspect of the fertility grain goddess), the sterility of the earth, the mother's efforts to recover her daughter, the daughter's taboo eating in the underworld, and her periodic return.

Similarly, at least in some versions, "Little Red Cap," like *The Handmaid's Tale*, is about a fertile daughter who delights in flowers, is separated from her mother (and in case of *HT*, also her daughter) in an off-limits area or underworld, participates in taboo eating or hunger, brings on her own rape by a wolf, and is eventually reborn. Whereas Demeter, the mother, is swallowed and disgorged by her father and tricked by her brother, the Grimms' Red Cap is swallowed and cut out of the wolf's stomach.

A "Modest Proposal" envisioning patriarchal theocracy, *The Handmaid's Tale* uses its mythical and other major intertexts as it uses Victorian and other literary or historical references: to suggest a distinctly feminist apocalyptic parody. According to Northrop Frye, Atwood's teacher at the University of Toronto, romantic, "realistic," and ironic literature suggest implicit mythical patterns. Undisplaced myth "takes the form of two contrasting worlds of total metaphorical identification, one desirable and the other undesirable. These worlds are often identified with the existential heavens and hells of the religions contemporary with such literature." Although apocalyptic and demonic archetypes are universal, pastoral myth, with its "nostalgia for a world of peace and protection, with a spontaneous response to the nature around it," is, as Frye suggests, particularly evident in Canadian literature. *The Handmaid's Tale* is no exception.

Rather than the heaven-on-earth or pre-fall world the fathers of Gilead say, and perhaps believe, they are building, *The Handmaid's Tale* ironically depicts Frye's "world of the nightmare and the scapegoat, of bondage and pain and confusion." As Jeremiah prophesized of its biblical namesake, it is "the desolation of the Promised Land." It is "the world also of perverted or wasted work, ruins and catacombs, instruments of torture and monuments of folly," replete with tree of death as well as tyrant-leader and sacrificed victim (pharmakos and sparagmos) in a parodic Eucharist. A Babylon rather than Jerusalem, it is an anti-apocalyptic world, with its euphemistic language, metaphoric wolf, sinister garden, urban waste land, temple prostitutes, and even technological Behemoths. More ironically, Gilead fulfills traditional scholarly definitions of "hell" primarily because of its treatment of "gender traitors," nonwhite races, religious minorities, and especially women.

*The Handmaid's Tale* also foregrounds the sexual politics of its main biblical intertext, Genesis, chapters 29 and 30. Literalizing and therefore parodying this passage, the book also implicitly satirizes aspects of Islam, Puritanism, Mormonism, and Christianity, particularly the contemporary fundamentalism represented by Pat Robertson. One Catholic sect even calls the wives of its coordinators "handmaidens." Atwood sets her narrative in what was once Cambridge, Massachusetts, and is now called Gilead. Named for a region in ancient Palestine, Gilead is the place where Jacob and Laban "made a deal" about Laban's daughters. Jacob's two wives, Leah and Rachel, are "played off against each other in the quest for status." Since an androcentric perspective values a woman for her ability to produce offspring and since the twelve sons of Jacob and his wives will represent the twelve tribes of Israel, Rachel and Leah are "having a baby contest to see who can have the most sons." "And when Rachel saw that she bare Jacob no children, Rachel envied her sister, and said unto Jacob, Give me children, or else I die. And Jacob's anger was kindled against Rachel; and he said, Am I in God's stead, who hath withheld from thee the fruit of the womb?" (Genesis 30:1–2) Atwood's retelling exposes and institutionalizes Rachel's envy and Jacob's power and anger. But it is Bilhah rather than Rachel who must produce children or die. Although Handmaids in Gilead could be punished with amputation of a hand for reading the Bible (or anything else), they are required to perform, literally, the "sacred" task that Bilhah fulfilled for Rachel in Genesis, 30.1–3: "she shall bear upon my knees, that I may also have children by her."

We know almost nothing about the powerless Bilhah except that her story is written for her by the collusion of her mistress with the patriarch; she is one of numberless biblical handmaids, including Hagar and Zelpha. "The custom of using the handmaid for progeny permeated Israelite history and custom," and legal documents pertaining to the practice date back to the fifteenth century B.C. But rarely has anyone looked at the passages about handmaids from handmaids' points of view. Whether or not Bilhah agreed to what a doctor recently called "genital rental" is unrecorded: Bilhah exists as a used object and, like Persephone and Red Cap, is violated. Ironically, like Offred and the Virgin Mary, she is designated to be a surrogate mother and bear a child with one of God's representatives. Resembling Offred and Demeter, she is separated from her child through patriarchal betrayal.

The sexual politics of the "Little Red Cap" intertext varies with the tale's different versions. Fairy and folk tales "have always symbolically depicted the nature of power relationships within a given society." Usual views of "Little Red Cap" focus on a girl who, taught to fear her sensuality, must be rescued by a "good father" devoid of sexuality. According to Zipes, however, the Grimms made substantial changes in oral folk tales. "It was the rise of authoritarian patriarchal societies that was responsible for (the) fear of sexuality and stringent sexual codes" evident in "Little Red Cap." "Whether the story is about initiation, warning, or both, one thing is clear: the folk tale celebrates the self-reliance of a young peasant girl." The original villain in oral folk tradition, "either an ogre, ogress, man-eater, wild person, werewolf, or wolf," attacked a child, characteristically "a good girl gone wrong," in the forest or at home. Charles Perrault, "who appears to have had a low opinion of women and of the superstitious customs of the peasantry," made the girl totally helpless in his "contaminated" literary version, "Le petit chaperon rouge," probably derived from French werewolf stories in which the girl escaped. The Grimm brothers, whose tale was originally based on the Perrault version, adapted it to "the *Biedermeier* or Victorian image of little girls and proper behavior" and provided a male savior, happy ending, and Christian moral.

Like Persephone (Diana), Demeter (Venus), early Christianity's Mary and Eve, and Snow White, Red Cap was part of a Virgin-Mother-Crone trinity; and she wore the same red garment the virgin Kali, British priestesses, and witches ("the flip side of the Maria cult") wore. According to Walker, the first werewolf was Moeris, spouse of the trinitarian Fate-Goddess (Moera or Moira or the Moirai, also associated with Mary); and the She-wolf was an aspect of the Triple Goddess. "Little Red Cap"'s wolf-clan traditions, emphasized in Angela Carter's twentieth-century retelling, "The Company of Wolves," are evident in "the red garment, the offering of food to a 'grandmother' in the deep woods—a grandmother who wore a wolf skin—and the cannibalistic motif of devouring and resurrection." As in many other werewolf stories, the original victim was the hunter (the Lord of the hunt), not Red Cap. Since the grandmother, traditionally seen as morally weak, even betraying, was, like Red Cap, identified with the displaced goddess, interpretations of the tale frequently reveal misogyny.

Sharing many feminists' disgust with "Red Cap" and apparently unaware of the tale's ties to matriarchal religion, Hélène Cixous ironically exposes the phallocentricism not only of popularized versions of the tale but also of its usual interpretations. According to Cixous, unlike "Sleeping Beauty," expressive of woman's place "[i]n bed and asleep—'laid (out),'" "Little Red Cap" is a story in which a woman "can be found standing up, but not for long." In Cixous's "little clitoris's" journey from one house to another (from mother to other), one "might imagine [the grandmother] as taking the place of the 'Great Mother,' because there are great men but not great women: there are Grand-Mothers instead." Although Cixous recognizes Red Riding Hood's detour "through her own forest," she feels the girl falls victim to her superego, the wolf. Unlike the disorder and laughter of a feminine "economy," this masculine "economy" generated by "the Law of the Father" silences and "decapitates" women through rigid inculcation. Continuing to read Red Cap as a brain-washed, passive victim, however, also silences and decapitates her.

Although Atwood gives no explicit indication of knowing either oral versions or goddess origins of "Red Cap," she refers to oral variations of another folktale in *Bluebeard's Egg* and in general uses the Grimms rather than Perrault because she prefers fairy tales with positive female images. As we have seen, Atwood frequently alludes to the Triple Goddess and even draws on Mary's early association with the goddess in *Cat's Eye. The Handmaid's Tale* not only evokes the goddess, but it revisions the best-known versions and interpretations of "Little Red Cap," finally restoring the Red Cap figure's inner resourcefulness and power. Among important features of the Grimms' tale that Atwood uses or parodies in her metafairy tale are the sexual politics, power politics, mothers' separation form children, familial conflict, quest, and initiation themes; the oppositions of house (culture) and green world (nature); the flower, fertility, sense, path, cannibalism, and dismemberment images; the red clothing, hood, and basket; the characterization (e.g., Red Cap's naiveté; the wolf's appetite, disguise, and use of deception); character doubling and foiling; aspects of the plot; and the narrative structure. By using a developing first-person, self-conscious narrator, initially with very limited vision, rather than the traditional reliable, privileged, third person, Atwood privileges Red Cap's point of view. By integrating the "Historical Notes'" commentary on the reading and writing process into *The Handmaid's Tale*, Atwood's metafairy tale also becomes metacriticism.

Initially, Offred is a grown up but naive Red Cap, whose conditioning endorses contentment in the wolf's embrace. Her ironic "innocence" or naiveté is, like the initial blindness of Atwood's other narrators, partially willed. In the world of the fairy tale, innocence or ignorance is equivalent to evil: failure to know what the wolf is brings the same disaster as choosing the wolf. Having gone with her society through the looking glass, Atwood's Red Cap is now trapped in a mirror, "a distorted shadow, a parody of something, some fairy-tale figure in a red cloak, descending towards a moment of carelessness that is the same as danger. A Sister, dipped in blood."

Reflecting the bizarre custom—not confined to Gilead—of giving a woman the name of the man who "commands" her, Offred's name also suggests "Off-red" as a secret rebel, the "Offered" in a blood sacrifice, and, especially, the "red" figure who goes "off" the path to immerse herself in nature. Like Red Cap, Offred is identified by her clothing. Offred, however, is owned by the wolf. Like her feared witch foremothers, including Atwood's relative Mary Webster (to whom the book is dedicated), she wears an official tatoo or cattle brand; the later evening rental tag also proves ownership. Unlike Red Cap but ironically resembling Jacob and other biblical characters renamed by God, a Handmaid is renamed when she changes households. Thus, in her ongoing encounter with the patriarch/wolf, she may be denied not only personal identity, but even gender identification: when she fails to produce a child after three fairy-tale chances, she becomes "Unwoman."

Like other women in Gilead, Offred is not only denied identity but symbolically dismembered. When Offred's Compucard is canceled because she is female, in a marriage no longer legally recognized, she feels as if her feet, symbolically the freest part of her, have been amputated. At the Red Center of indoctrination recalling *Jane Eyre's* Red Room, women's feet and hands, considered inessential for Handmaids, are sometimes disfigured. The name of Offred's friend and alter-ego, Moira, ironically suggests the virginal Aphrodite, another aspect of the goddess trinity; the death aspect of the Moira, Ilithyia (Birth), and Callone (Beauty) triad; the first werewolf's spouse; the Triple Fates; and Mary. This name also recalls Moira Shearer's filmed version of Andersen's "The Red Shoes," the fairy tale about a woman whose feet are cut off because she dances in red shoes. In the film that also functions as an intertext in *Lady Oracle*, a woman must choose between dancing or loving a man. In *The Handmaid's Tale*, choice no longer exists: Handmaids all wear red shoes and are forced to have sex with their Commanders. When Moira tries to assert herself against the system, like other "traitors" she receives a variety of torture practiced in Ayatollah Khomaini's Iran, in this case the bastinada: the soles of her feet are whipped with steel cables so that she is temporarily unable to walk.

Unable to speak out or even eat, Offred and the others steal packets of sugar for Moira, one of the few Gilead woman to still possess a mouth. In the patriarchy of Gilead, the Handmaid exists as a two-legged womb. If, for practical purposes, other parts of her remain, they are, as in Afghanistan or on Old Dutch Cleanser packages of Atwood's childhood, totally concealed. Adorned in her red "habit" with white angel wings "to keep [her] from seeing, but also from being seen," Offred is already a "seen" woman, controlled by the wolf even within the "home" that can never be hers.

Atwood's subversion of the "Little Red Riding Hood" story most readers know is evident in the book's distorted mirroring of the fairy-tale narrative. Near the beginning of the book, Offred, like Red Cap, leaves a privileged house of abundance on a journey both internal and external. Now equipped with a shatterproof window, however, this house is no longer either safe or home: this image of female initiation has already been violated, "chopped up," and consumed. Red Cap's movement is severely limited. Thus, her dusty pink path, ironically "like a carpet for royalty," now begins *inside* the house. As in Atwood's watercolor of the crowned Termite Queen in a red dress, the royalty of this "Mother Goddess," and of all the Handmaids and Wives imprisoned on a "pedestal," is a sinister variant of television's old "Queen for a Day." A Persephone cut off from the green world, Offred is a Red Cap who has been captured, violated, and debased. Despite her patriarchal society's ironic "worship" of the fertility symbolized in Red Cap, the matriarchal goddess, and the biblical Madonna, she is forced to be "the eternal fucking machine" rather than being honored as the bearer of life.

Significantly, the relationship of *The Handmaid's Tale* to "Little Red Cap" is even suggested by the convex pier glass Offred passes as she begins her journey. Anticipating the pier glass of *Cat's Eye*, the mirror seems to the blinkered Offred "like the eye of a fish, and myself in it like a distorted shadow . . . [of] some fairy tale figure." Red Cap's forest has become a polished hall, and all that is left of the enchanted vegetable world is Serena Joy's subversive "bleeding" garden and the Victorian banister (the remnant of trees and Great-Goddess Tree of life). Authority replaces magic, and daughters are separated from both natural mothers and Great Mother (die Grossmütter). This Red Cap, like her daughter, has been entrusted to futuristic versions of wicked stepmothers in collusion with the wolf. Thus, she is headed, not alone to Grandma's house, but to shops ironically named "Lilies of the Field," "Milk and Honey," and "All Flesh," accompanied by her double, another Handmaid vessel awaiting filling. Passing a grandfather clock that "doles out time," as the terrible fathers of Gilead measure pleasures and pains and segment women's bodies by color-coded functions, Offred next passes "The motherly front sitting room, with its fleshtones and hints. A sitting room in which I never sit, but stand or kneel only." Red Cap's "mother" is now represented by the black-gloved "Aunts" of the Red Centre, who hold electric cattle prods rather than "Cinderella" wands, and Serena Joy, who must participate with her in a ritualistic parody of sexual love. Thus, Red Cap is in a world of betrayed innocence. Ironically, it has been reached by a society's enforced travel *on* a narrow path, leading not to earthly heaven but to sexist "hell."

As Red Cap's stepmother in this demonic world, Serena Joy's role is as parodic as Offred's. Serena's name, reminding Offred of a feminine hair product, is, like Offred's, not her real one: it was selected for her former role as a television gospel singer. Undercutting the fate of all those who, Schlafly-style, are forced to practice what they preach, she is neither serene nor joyful once she is confined to "the sanctity of the home." As in the Grimms' version, it is her business to enforce the "rules" keeping Red Cap on the path, away from the flowers and any voluntary encounter with the wolf: Offred's predecessor hangs herself when Serena discovers her secret meetings with the

Commander. In the Grimms' tale it is also Red Cap's mother who warns Red Cap against "prying into every nook and corner." Gilead's bad-witch mothers bear partial responsibility for Offred's conditioned unseeing, which, along with patriarchal control and willed blindness, keeps her in the wolf's belly.

Serena is also both biblical Rachel and Crone Goddess in this fallen world. Consistent with the kinds of women portrayed in *1984* and the Bible, Serena, clad in Virgin-Mary blue, even plays Madonna to her opposite, Moira's Jezebel or Whore of Babylon, and to the intermediate figure dressed in red, Offred's Mary Magdalene. Although *The Handmaid's Tale* takes place in the United States and comments most directly on U.S. culture, it illustrates the tendency Atwood observes in other Canadian literature for the Crone or Hecate to predominate, characteristically incorporating Diana and Venus figures. Framing Offred on the marital bed during official sex for procreation, as Wives frame Handmaids during birth, Serena almost literally incorporates Venus. A Madonna unable to give birth to any savior, she—along with the Commander—symbolizes her world's sterility. Like Moira and Offred, Serena is trapped in her role, not only a bizarre parody of fairy-tale, Jacob/Rachel, and apocalyptic sexual union but another debasement of the Triple Goddess. She is forced to compete for the attention of her husband. Resembling the false mothers of "Hansel and Gretel" and "Little Snow White," Serena produces wool "children" and cultivates a Victorian garden, "something for them to order and maintain and care for" in the absence of either societal power or familial responsibility.

Serena's garden re-visions the sensuous fairy-tale flowers that tempt Red Cap to forget her mother's instructions, the apocalyptic rose identified with Christian communion, and, by association, the Tree of Life important in myth, religion, and fairy tales: "the garden . . . is large and tidy: a lawn in the middle, a willow, weeping catkins; around the edges, the flower borders, in which the daffodils are now fading and the tulips are opening their cups, spilling out colour. The tulips are red, a darker crimson toward the stem, as if they had been cut and are beginning to heal there." This garden is the domain of the Commander's Wife. Ruling over her depleted kingdom with "her knees on a cushion, a light blue veil thrown over her wide gardening hat, a basket at her side with shears in it and pieces of string in it for tying the flowers into place, . . . the Commander's Wife directs, pointing with her stick" while someone else does the digging.

Although the flowers forbidden Red Cap "are still allowed" in Gilead and even adorn the beds and sofas where Handmaids personally experience Giledean control, they must be cut and tied into an appropriate position; sometimes tulips (*two lips*, according to Lacombe) are also symbolically silenced and crucified. When Offred, carrying a basket of lambchops suggesting imminent slaughter, sees "Saint Serena" in early summer, Serena is again "on her knees, doing penance," in the garden. The tulips are "shedding their petals one by one, like teeth." This time, however, Serena is "aiming, positioning the blades of the shears, then cutting with a convulsive jerk of the hands. [Is] it arthritis, creeping up? Or some blitzkrieg, some kamikaze, committed on the swelling genitalia of the flowers? The fruiting body." Ironically, however, "to cut off the seed pods is supposed to make the bulbs store energy."

This divided Gileadean sensibility recalls not only "Little Red Cap" and the Bible but Tennyson's poetry, on which the gardens of *The Handmaid's Tale* are partly based, and the Victorian society behind it: in Gilead, as in Tennyson, we sense "a dialectic clash between the attraction of the deepest subjective levels and the resistance and restraint of other sectors of reality." In Tennyson's early poem, "Sense and Conscience," when Conscience is drugged by Sense and awakened by Memory and Pain, he futilely stabs "the pleasurable flowers" and ivy, which bleeds on his feet with blood resembling tears. Imprisoned like Offred in a role that has literally as well as symbolically crippled her ability to touch or express erotic feeling, Serena Joy is as passive as some consider the Catholic Mary after patriarchal persecution of Mariolatry. Serena Joy may share Offred's repressed desire to emasculate the "godhead" and the phallocentric society it represents. At the same time, she reinforces the Commander-wolf's power with submission and collusion.

If Serena's garden bleeds sacrificially, as a scapegoat, it is, nevertheless, storing energy for Persephone's return. One of the few remnants of life and fertility in the sexist wasteland resembling *Double Persephone's* "Formal Garden," flowers may be tied, dried, confined to straight borders, or captured in framed designs and stylized prints, as on the canopy bed used for "The Ceremony"; but they and the feelings they represent are not finally controlled by the Gileadean fathers. The power of Gilead, the power of patriarchy, is limited.

When the Grimms' Red Cap leaves the prescribed path to pick flowers, she is consumed by the world of the senses. Forgetting her infirm grandmother on her detour into the spontaneous and natural, she becomes vulnerable to the wolf, often considered an animalistic impulse, rapacious male, or "bad father" who hears, sees, touches, and then swallows her. Rescued by the "goodfather" huntsman, who carefully cuts open the wolf instead of impulsively shooting him, the reborn Red Cap learns how to deal with the next wolf, who can be fooled and trapped by his own senses.

Already consumed and inside the wolf's belly from the beginning of the book, Atwood's "reversed" Red Cap does, finally, go off the path to the flowers, this time associated with ancient female power. Unlike the Grimms'

Red Cap, Offred recovers amputated senses and is reborn in the sensory world. Seeming to radiate heat, breathe and breathe itself in, Serena's garden tempts Offred as well as Nick to journey off the patriarchal path to "distant pathways" of a paradoxically literal and archetypal past, goal of the future. Offred is drawn to no longer silenced flowers, to irises "like pastel water momentarily frozen in a splash" and to "the bleeding hearts, so female in shape it was a surprise they'd not long since been rooted out. There is something subversive about this garden of Serena's, a sense of buried things bursting upwards, wordlessly, into the light, as if to point, to say: Whatever is silenced will clamour to be heard, though silently." As Offred's dress "rustles against the flesh of [her] thighs and the grass grows underfoot," the willows whisper and she feels dizzy: "at the edges of [her] eyes there are movements, in the branches; feathers, flittings, grace notes, tree into bird, metamorphosis run wild." Significantly, not only is Demeter's dead world awakening, as if from a suspected spell of enchantment; but Offred's Red Centre conditioning, that has suppressed her appetite by "feeding" her scriptures for breakfast and lunch and attempted to blind, bind, gag, and obliterate a symbolically amputated body, is wearing off. Offred is no longer, like Tennyon's Conscience, repressing feeling. "Goddesses are possible now, and the air suffuses with desire." Even the mineral world, "softening, becoming tactile," begins to melt like the irises, and Offred is, like "a melon on a stem, . . . liquid ripeness."

In the Grimms' fairy tale, Red Cap remarks on the wolf's large ears, eyes, hands, and mouth, and the wolf does hear, see, touch, and then eat her. In *The Handmaid's Tale* it is Red Cap's "enlarged" sensory organs that save her: when Offred recovers her ability to hear, smell, taste, and, most significantly, touch, see, and speak, she begins to recover her self, her real name, and a position in time. In addition, by going off Gilead's theocratic path and experiencing the natural world, Atwood's transformed Red Cap begins to recover the Great Mother, displaced by phallocentric culture and its sanitized folklore in favor of the familiar figure of weakness or betrayal.

Offred expresses her recovered senses in her relationship with Nick, the huntsman figure who is in a sense also St. Nicholas, bestower of gifts and miracles, and Old Nick, or a parodic devil. The Grimms' Red Cap would presumably stay eaten without the assistance of the huntsman, the wolf's alter ego. In early oral versions of the tale, however, the girl never dies and saves herself without external help, sometimes by cutting her way out of the wolf's belly and in one later instance by shooting him with an automatic pistol. Again unnecessary to Red Cap's rebirth, Nick still assists Offred on her journey. Now an underground opponent to the patriarchy rather than a rational father or Disney prince, he doubles Offred both in becoming another patriarchal sex object, a "seedpod" to father the child the Commander can't, and a rebel of Gilead's monovalent "god." Although Serena selects Nick and even bribes Offred to cooperate, Offred goes back to Nick again and again. "I did not do it for him, but for myself entirely . . . , thankful, each time he would let me in. He didn't have to." Paradoxically, in a situation without freedom, Offred and Nick freely choose one another, creating a real relationship that foils the Commander's with either Wife or Handmaid. Loving touch is again a means of disenchantment, restoration, and personal magic. Although Atwood's huntsman helps "Red Cap" leave the wolf's belly as St. Nicholas sometimes saves girls from slavery, in *The Handmaid's Tale* only the narrator, who names herself again both to Nick and after the Particicution, is responsible for her rebirth.

Like her increased efforts to face painful memories of her lost mother, her daughter, Luke, and Moira, Offred's sisterhood with Moira, Ofglen, and her "ancestress" double are all evidence of her straying from the Gileadean path. Her visit to the Commander's forbidden room, however, not only dramatizes her metamorphosis but parodies "Little Red Cap" and the biblical intertext. The Commander is also Jacob, the father of Israel, the false god, the anti-Christ, Hades, a fairy-tale shoemaker, Bluebeard, and, significantly, the dispenser of the patriarchal "word." Comically, when Offred enters the door to be alone with this wolf, he wants her to play Scrabble, a word game, with him. In Gilead, as in the world of *1984*, the word is all, making the cruder disguise as a kindly grandmother unnecessary. Although he and his government have already swallowed Red Cap, this wolf not only hopes to make her stay more comfortable but wants her to kiss him with meaning and feel the "true love" of the now forbidden women's magazines. Like the Bluebeard figures of *Lady Oracle* and "Bluebeard's Egg," the powerful Commander is revealed as lonely and pathetic: not only does he have a belly, but he seems to shrink, "like something being dried." Resembling the wolf of "Little Red Cap," his attempt to fill his emptiness is unsuccessful: like the wolf filled with stones, he and his regime are sterile.

As in *Surfacing*, Offred's ability to laugh signals her opening and rebirth. Feeling she will burst, splashing red all over the cupboard, she rhymes "mirth" and "birth," listens to the sound of her own heart, and even breathes as in exercises "for giving birth." No longer thinking of herself as a chalice and abolishing the authority of the wolf (the hobbling forceps and other "fancy claims" Broumas's Red Riding Hood evades), Offred explodes like the blood-red tulips with the anarchistic "laugh of the Medusa." Turning herself "inside out" in a metamorphosis reminiscent of *Bodily Harm*'s Rennie as well as of numerous folk characters, Offred "blow[s] up the law," exploding her conditioning and defying Gilead's repressions.

Offred's regained ability to smell, taste, hear, touch, see, and speak accompany her desire to know. No longer afraid, like Atwood's camera-eye narrators, of seeing, she faces both dimpled and winged eyes and asks for knowledge when the Commander offers presents. Now keeping her eyes open, not only with Nick and the Commander but at the Salvaging and the Particicution, Offred records Gilead's attempt to displace and purge female rage. Witnessing the perversion of matriarchal ritual to Bacchic punishment of the regime's political enemies, she begins to understand phallocentric power. Nevertheless, her regained appetite at the Particicution is again symbolic: "Maybe it's because I've been emptied; or maybe it's the body's way of seeing to it that I remain alive, continue to repeat its bedrock prayer: **I am, I am**. I am still." Having traced the flowers' changes through the cycle of seasons from spring to fall, Offred, who is probably pregnant, prepares for a perennial return recalling the subterranean journeys of Persephone and the narrators of *Surfacing, The Journals of Susanna Moodie*, and *Bodily Harm*. She is still afraid of the red shoes and of the Bluebeard/wolf's power to turn her into a dancing doll or, like her double, a wingless angel. Nevertheless, the Handmaid's narration ends with Mayday and, like that of *Surfacing's* unnamed narrator, an act of trust: she steps into "a darkness within; or else the light."

Both Mayday (May Day) and light symbolism signify "a new beginning." In addition to being the international radiotelephonic signal for help, a labor holiday, and a feminist tatoo protesting artificial birth methods, May Day symbolizes the natural, anarchistic fertility that counters the "procreation by fiat" of Gilead and Ceaucescu's Romania. May Day was originally a goddess festival for Maya (Maj, Mary, Kale, Freya, Flora), the Virgin Goddess or Virgin Mother of Spring. Later Walpurgisnacht, the witches' festival, May Day is celebrated in a communal dance around the May tree (the god's phallus planted in the earth's womb) and by picking flowers and bringing them home, "the symbolic act of bringing home the May, i.e. bringing new life, the spring, into the village. . . . Carrying the May tree and garlands from door to door is the symbolic bestowing and sharing of this new creative power that is stirring in the world." Sometimes mock battles between summer and winter, with summer always winning, occur; the May Bride sings about nature's bounty and may even "wake" the bridegroom with a kiss. Contrasting to Red Cap's wolf filled only with stones, Offred resembles the May Queen in bringing the earth new life, symbolized by the body's magic—her probable pregnancy—and the zest for life she earlier envied in her mother and Moira. Thus, by making the fertility Gilead tried to control symbolize Offred's freedom, *The Handmaid's Tale* is profoundly ironic.

Similarly, an archetypal light in the darkness is not only paradoxical but hopeful. Elsewhere it is associated with the possibilities of the resistance, inner resources, prayer, and the post-Gileadean world of the future. In the Grimms' "Little Red Cap," the girl leaves the darkness within the wolf when an opening for her escape (rebirth) appears. We know from the existence of Offred's taped narrative that the dark van does finally take her off Gilead's theocratic path to a new life where she has a voice. Ironically, Offred "fall[s] from innocence to knowledge" and to "disgrace, which is the opposite of grace," suggesting the light symbolism of Lucifer and Luke's names as well as Saul's mystical transformation into Saint Paul, the much-quoted Apostle of Gilead as well as the Bible. Along with that of Nick, her fellow "devil" to Gilead's "god," Offred's fall not only parodies the biblical fall but also structures her path out of the sexist wasteland. Out of the books' fifteen regular chapters, seven of them—the fairy-tale, magic, and formulaic lucky number marking the end of a spell or period (e.g., week of creation) or the beginning of a transformation—are named "Night"; consciously or not, readers are prepared for light and change. Offred presumably takes the "Underground Femaleroad," a free and "true way" to counter the wolf's prescribed "demonic labyrinth of lost direction." Offred may reach at last the "safe house" of her sisters, a place where she can consume the sacramental cake and wine of healing once brought to the grandmother.

Thus, changing the direction of Little Red Cap's journey and going "underground," into uncolonized earth, Offred becomes an artist: she not only signals Persephone's cyclical return and reunion with Demeter but invents a time in our imaginations for Bilhah to recover her own lost child. Like the Robber Bride of the Grimms' "The Robber Bridegroom," she tells her story, in a sense "singing" as both artist and May bride. Resembling *Surfacing*, however, the book endorses respect for humanity and nature rather than worship of either Father or Mother God. Offred's tape recordings do more than speak against Gilead's atrocities: even inventing us as readers, her female narrative substitutes personal dialogue—within Offred, with people she misses, with various readers—for The Word.

The fate of Offred's descendants, represented by Professors Crescent Moon and Pieixoto at the University of Denay, Nunavit, may be, like our own, questionable, particularly if they, like we, continue to function in "Deny Mostofit." Still, the "Historical Notes" further develop and dramatize dialogue: this section functions intertextually to question not only how well we read folklore, myth, the Bible, history, newspapers, and our own lives but how well we are reading Offred, this book, and the book's intertexts. Parodying scholars and scholarly conferences and the novel's own double endings, neither of which is "the end," the "Historical Notes" decry the dangerous blindness of treating horrors of history, including witch burning and other sexism, fascism, homophobia, racism, and religious persecution, "objectively." Both formally establishing and undercutting Offred's story and its commentary as cultural artifacts, the "Notes" include readers in the communal group trying to decode the text.

Despite their unreliability, Moon and Pieixoto's narratives provide not only necessary information but postcolonial perspective. Atwood compares her "Historical Notes" to *1984*'s Appendix on "The Principles of Newspeak" since both futuristic postscripts prove the end of the dystopian society: the voice of the repressed woman we know only as Offred survives longer than the regime that tries to silence it. But the name and location of the University of Denay, Nunavit, where the Twelfth Symposium on Gileadean Studies occurs, is partly ironic. "Denay" recalls what Canada's historically repressed northern natives, the Dene, call themselves; and "Nunavit" refers to what Dene and Inuit would call their country if they had one, both words suggesting the fulfillment of thwarted dreams. Similarly, the chairship of Professor Maryann Crescent Moon, of the Department of Caucasian Anthropology, again dramatizes the end of the racist, patriarchal Gilead: the Caucasian race is now marginalized, an interesting subject for academic study. Maryann's name could also seem to suggest a futuristic return to matriarchal values associated with Diana, the new moon Goddess of virginity and childbirth, the three Marys, and the Triple Goddess Mari-Anna-Ishtar. Although the society of Crescent Moon, Pieixoto, Gopal Chatterjee, and Johnny Running Dog certainly appears richer in ethnic diversity and less patriarchal than Gilead, however, it, too, is characteristically undercut.

Too clearly in this book in which everything has happened or is happening somewhere around the world, the future once again fails to learn from the past, including the old stories that form intertexts in *The Handmaid's Tale*. Instead of replacing the Western ways of their oppressors, Denay, Nunavit, only reverses the usual hierarchies. Moon may introduce the main speaker, ironically from the "other" Cambridge, relatively untouched by Gilead; but Pieixoto's racist and sexist comments about their all "enjoying" their "Arctic Char" and "Arctic Chair" marginalizes her, mirroring not only women's treatment in Gilead but patriarchal confiscation and suppression of matriarchal myth and of the female voices in folklore and Biblical stories. Professor James Darcy Pieixoto, whose name links him to a macho character in an obscure Portuguese novel and to Darcy in *Pride and Prejudice*, cautions his audience to avoid passing moral judgment upon the

Gileadeans. Like male members of the Research Association, Moon finds Gilead important because it redraws the map of the world. Like some of us, Atwood's parodic traditional scholars too easily separate themselves from "the object" of their studies, ironically muting female text and voice and stories about both with all too familiar pedantic commentary. As Davidson argues, "the Biblical fundamentalism of Gilead poses crucial questions about the interpretative use of literary texts." Pieixoto's pre-Foucault, pre-de Beauvoir form of historical criticism, rampantly encoded with patriarchal imperatives, trivializes and finally disregards not only the text he proposes to discuss and the woman who created it but also our culture's major intertexts, including especially folklore, mythology, and the Bible. As Larson notes, Atwood's two "testaments," of Offred and the "Historical Notes," foreground the patriarchal sexual politics of the Bible and theology that have silenced scriptural women. If we take off our own blinkers to read and reread, however, *The Handmaid's Tale* restores the voices of Red Cap, Persephone, and Bilhah.

Although the final words of *The Handmaid's Tale*, "Are there any questions?" constitute a humorously pat question, they formally establish textual space for our questions and speculations. Mirroring the self-consciousness of Offred's narrative, these words return us to Offred's voice and "the matrix" from which it comes. As textual commentary, the "Historical Notes" deconstruct or unwind the text we have just read—which we cannot have read since it is a "tape recording" from our future—and then itself and its authority, from yet a further point in our future. Like Holland's "Little Red Readinghood," *The Handmaid's Tale* parodies both our theories and practices of reading, deconstructing the patriarchal myths of our cultural and literary texts. It also dissolves easy dichotomies such as the one some would draw between a contemporary Big Bad Wolf and a Canadian Little Red Riding Hood. Despite the mythic, fairy-tale, and biblical resonances, Offred is not a goddess, the book is an anti-fairy tale, and it utters words rather than The Word. But Atwood's postcolonial text does not simply catch us, like Holland's Grandma, in "a web of intertextuality." Unlike Handmaids, we are not forbidden to read; thus, rather than simplistic messages or icons, *The Handmaid's Tale* leaves us with questions and challenges.

By embedding a "reversed" fairy tale in *The Handmaid's Tale*, much as she has reversed myths in *Surfacing* and Gothic romance traditions in *Lady Oracle*, Margaret Atwood presents a timeless vision of sexual politics in a fallen world. Re-visioning Tennyson's poetry, history, scholarship, and current events as well as the Grimms' "Red Riding Hood," the Bible, and myth, *The Handmaid's Tale* again takes us *Through the Looking Glass* (1871) to a new *1984* (1949): through its intertexts it challenges us to stop reflecting nightmare visions of both past and present societies around the world, to stop being in the patriarchal mirror. Rather than being seen, silenced, and consumed, Atwood's Red Cap sees and speaks. If we cultivate our Mother's garden, the book implies possibility of rebirth: not a return to Eden or matriarchy, but harmony among animal, mineral, and vegetable worlds and peace within the human one.

SANDRA TOMC

# "The Missionary Position": Feminism and Nationalism in Margaret Atwood's The Handmaid's Tale

When Margaret Atwood's *The Handmaid's Tale* was published in 1985 it was to an almost unanimous adulation. The novel won Atwood her second Canadian Governor-General's Award, and won her equally distinguished, and laudatory, reviews by some of North America's foremost feminist scholars. Published at a moment when the American Religious Right had become a particular focus for American feminists, Atwood's prophecy of gender fascism was accepted pretty much unconditionally as an admirable banner of liberal feminist insurgency. Since the mid-1980's, however, presumably as a result of certain gains in historical perspective, many readers of Atwood's novel have, I think justly, questioned its character as a feminist critique. Why, for instance, does Atwood choose to resolve her drama of women's oppression by implementing a paradigm of female romance, such that the telos of the heroine's journey becomes her introduction to Mr. Right? How are we to read the heroine's barely ironized longings for hand lotion and old copies of *Vogue* when the novel provides these as symbols of women's former freedom? More important, and more troubling, what are we to make of Atwood's seeming refusal of a politics of emancipation? How do we interpret her apparently uncritical endorsement of the self-protective passivity of her heroine? For the critics who ask these questions *The*

From *Canadian Literature* 138/139 (Fall/Winter 1993). © 1993 by the University of British Columbia, Vancouver.

*Handmaid's Tale* is less a critique of andocentric political structures than a consolatory instruction on ways of "making do."

I want to begin my own reading of *The Handmaid's Tale* by stating that, in essence, I agree with this position. For a novel so overtly offered as a piece of feminist doctrine, *The Handmaid's Tale* delivers a curiously, and, for Atwood, an unwontedly, conservative interpretation of women's exemplary social actions, advocating what looks more like traditional femininity than an insurgent feminism. But I also want to propose that this conservatism is, in fact, politically motivated, not by Atwood's feminism in this case but by her nationalism. Although *The Handmaid's Tale* is not generally regarded as part of Atwood's nationalist canon, its understanding of female independence is nevertheless determined by Atwood's sexually coded understanding of the relation between Canada and America. In this, Atwood's only full-scale parody of American society, what concerns her is not a feminist politics of emancipation, but the nationalist politics of self-protective autonomy, an autonomy which, as I will argue, eventually translates into an advocacy of traditional femininity.

In Atwood's career-long promotion of Canada's cultural autonomy from the United States, national and gender issues have had for her a commensurate and almost interchangeable status. Her 1972 novel *Surfacing* overtly identified the "rape" of the Canadian wilderness by American investors and tourists with the abuse of the female narrator's body by men. *Survival: A Thematic Guide to Canadian Literature*, published in the same year, indirectly elaborated this identification of Canada and victimized womanhood into an explication of the essential Canadian identity as that of "the exploited victim." Although *Survival* did not venture expressly to characterize Canada's victimhood as feminine, Atwood's commentary since suggests the extent to which this notion of victimhood was for her a feminine construct. In a 1987 essay that strongly opposed the Canada—U.S. Free Trade Agreement, an agreement regarded by many Canadians as the beginning of the end of Canada's cultural autonomy, Atwood told her readers: "Canada as a separate but dominated country has done about as well under the U.S. as women, worldwide, have done under men; about the only position they've ever adopted towards us, country to country, has been the missionary position, and we were not on top."

While *The Handmaid's Tale* was a departure for Atwood in that it took up feminist issues to the exclusion of themes focusing on Canadian culture, her collapse of national and gender categories would, under any circumstances, make a consideration of her nationalism relevant to her feminist readings of contemporary culture. However, more than this, *The Handmaid's Tale* is not simply a non-Canadian novel, it is, as Catherine

Stimpson emphasizes, Atwood's first foray into an extended representation of America. Its story of gender oppression is situated within the object of Atwood's nationalist antipathy and the roles given both to America and to the novel's heroine are familiar: America is posed here, once again, as the male aggressor, its masculinist qualities literalized in the Gileadean patriarchy (which has, incidentally, mandated the missionary position); the heroine, to borrow a term from *Survival*, is the "exploited victim." If the geographical partition in *Surfacing*, the dotted membrane separating Canada from America, is not a central issue in *The Handmaid's Tale*, it nevertheless survives as a psychic and bodily construct, a membrane preserving the "victim" from total capitulation to the "victor." And accordingly, what Atwood defines as the optimum political response of her subjugated heroine is not a politics of liberation, if we understand such a politics to entail an active resistance to oppressive power, but a form of border patrol, a strategy of protectionism not unlike what she advocates for the survival of Canada's cultural autonomy: "good fences," as she puts it, "make good neighbours."

When Atwood's heroine Offred contemplates the power of the Patriarchal Republic of Gilead she understands it as a form of domination that wants to abolish borders, that has no limits:

> "This is the heart of Gilead, where the war cannot intrude except on television. Where the edges are we aren't sure, they vary, according to the attacks and counterattacks; but this is the centre, where nothing moves. The Republic of Gilead, said Aunt Lydia, knows no bounds. Gilead is within you."

Moving borders from continental to internal spaces and replacing colonization with indoctrination, Atwood goes on to define her heroine's response as a necessary preoccupation with the protection of her personal integrity—what Atwood in *Survival* terms "spiritual survival, . . . life as anything more than a minimally human being." Stating at the start of the novel that she "intends to last," Offred proposes to live outside of Gilead's amorphous discursive borders in a space of the self which its doctrines have yet to chart. She looks back to the days when "We lived in the blank white spaces at the edges of print. It gave us more freedom. / We lived in the gaps between the stories." Throughout the novel these empty, unwritten spaces are posed as sites of escape. There is first of all the blank space, surrounded by a plaster wreath, "a frozen halo, a zero," in the ceiling of Offred's bedroom where the chandelier has been removed, which offers the ultimate escape of self-annihilation: "Draw a circle, step into it, it will protect you." There is the hole in the washroom wall at the Centre where Offred touches Moira's fingers and hears of her plans to escape the Aunts. "The Canadian experience," Atwood once said, is "a circumference with no centre, the American one a centre which [is] mistaken for the whole thing." What counts as survival in the face of this appropriating wholeness is the integrity of the unscripted voids, one of which is Offred's real name:

> My name isn't Offred, I have another name, which nobody uses now because it's forbidden. I tell myself it doesn't matter, your name is like your telephone number, useful only to others; but what I tell myself is wrong, it does matter. I keep the knowledge of this name like something hidden, some treasure I'll come back to dig up, one day. I think of this name as buried. This name has an aura around it, like an amulet, some charm that's survived from an unimaginably distant past.

Unmentioned and surrounded by its aura, another border, Offred's identity is protected from appropriation. That the evasion of naming is paradoxically a form of self-affirmation is made clear in what Offred says about rhetorical strategies of evasion generally: their purpose is "to keep the core of yourself out of reach, enclosed, protected."

The degree of Atwood's investment in such strategies of self-protection is suggested by the fact that moments of crisis and horror in this novel are organized around threats to the internal and bodily membranes surrounding the uncharted space of the self. Of course, within Gilead's gendered economy of power, sexual penetration is the most obvious manifestation of threat, and appropriately, the Commander's penis, to which Offred must open herself once a month, is described not only as an invasive instrument but as a "delicate stalked slug's eye," "avid for vision," attempting to read a "darkness"—that blank of personal plenitude. When Offred and her husband Luke drive north in a desperate last-minute attempt to get over the borders of Gilead, Atwood describes Offred's fear of discovery as a fear of being penetrated, and of being read: "I feel transparent," she says. "Surely they will be able to see through me." It is appropriate, given Atwood's investment in blankness as a site of identity, that when Offred finally does move into a territory potentially free of Gileadean penetration, her narrative stops, thus literalizing the association of emptiness, of what might in other Atwood works be called wilderness, with spiritual survival.

Atwood's representation of her heroine as a special space or territory to be protected is perfectly consonant with her long-standing identification of the missionary position with America's missionary tradition of cultural and economic infiltration. Yet whether this use of nationalist models is entirely commensurate with the liberal feminist assumptions she calls upon to provoke her reader's outrage is another question. The problems critics have with *The Handmaid's Tale* focus precisely on the discrepancy between its overt invocation of feminist outrage and the heroine's self-protective avoidance of any form of political interaction with her circumstances. Glenn Deer, for example, remarks that Atwood "seems to privilege the female existential will, the realm of private consciousness, as an adequate recompense for . . . enslavement." And Barbara Ehrenreich points out: "Offred cries a lot and lives in fear of finding her erstwhile husband hanging from a hook on the wall, but when she is finally contacted by the resistance, she is curiously uninterested. She has sunk too far into the incestuous little household she serves—just as the reader, not without intermittent spasms of resistance, sinks into the deepening masochism of her tale." Ehrenreich, in fact, pinpoints a crucial problem. Atwood's internalization of a nationalist political paradigm produces a heroine whose sole resistance goes on inside her head, a resistance at once indistinguishable from passivity and masochism and uncomfortably synonymous with traditional stereotypes of feminine behaviour. It would be fairly easy to conclude that this incongruousness is simply an accident produced in the collapse of incompatible paradigms—that feminism, which historically has been based on a politics of liberation, is simply not synonymous with Atwood's notions of cultural autonomy and that, in assuming their interchangeability, she comes up with what her readers regard as a dubious response to "enslavement." Yet Atwood's politics of autonomy are more complicated than this suggests. It Offred's self-protectiveness is produced by Atwood's nationalist idea of the relationship between victim and victor, it also duplicates and fortifies this novel's generic idiosyncrasies, anchoring Atwood's formal choices in the heroine's efforts to maintain her integrity and suggesting that Atwood places herself as a colonial writer in the same victim category that she places her heroine. And here we have the second big problem critics have with this novel. What Atwood chooses as a colonial writer, what she lights upon to signify her own integrity, is not the political and anthropological density of feminist dystopian fiction but the highly formulaic fluff of popular female romance, the genre whose paradigms finally ground Atwood's formulation of colonial autonomy.

It is important to underline, first of all, Atwood's sheer reliance on the contrivances of women's junk fiction to structure the plot of *The Handmaid's Tale*. Like her prototypes in bodice-rippers and costume gothics, Offred is the innocent heroine who finds herself imprisoned in a menacing world over which she has no power, and indeed seeks to gain none for fear of compromising her womanly integrity. She falls in love with a man—in this case Nick the chauffeur—who is an attractive, ambiguous figure, stereotypically characterized by his roguish cynicism, his silence and his ability to melt the heroine with his ways in bed. Although like all of his strong and silent brethren, Nick initially seems to be part of the atmosphere of evil—he may, for instance, be a spy for Gilead—the heroine nonetheless trusts to feminine instinct and surrenders herself to him completely. For this leap of faith she is, of course, amply rewarded. The ambiguous lover turns out to be her saviour, the knight who rescues her from the menace—who, in this case, smuggles her out of the heart of Gilead into a space of relative freedom where she is at least able to articulate her story.

*The Handmaid's Tale* recapitulates the plot of a romance; but more than this, Atwood thematizes romance conventions themselves as agents of women's resistance and autonomy. Given that the "blank" space of the victim's autonomous self is framed as an essentially discursive territory, one whose scrawl the imperial order is incapable of deciphering, Atwood's particular thematization of romance conventions suggests that these form the cryptic writing on the victim's unreadable void. For Offred romance conventions provide the scripture that allows her to counter Gilead with a defense of hope. It is her belief in the fairytale narrative of the damsel rescued by her prince that both encourages Offred's self-protectiveness and saves her from capitulation. She says of her husband Luke: "I must have patience: sooner or later he will get me out . . . Meanwhile I must endure, keep myself safe for later." Likewise, what Offred wants from the renegade Moira, another source of hope, is "gallantry . . . swashbuckling, heroism, singlehanded combat." The very trappings of costume gothic, namely its costumes, its feminine trinkets and adornments, are posed as subversive alternatives to Gilead's institution of plainness and uniformity, so that Offred, catching sight of a group of Japanese tourists, notes the women's clothes, their short skirts and thin stockings and high heels, and says to herself: "I used to dress like that. That was freedom." In some of Atwood's other novels, in *Lady Oracle*, for instance, in which the narrator is actually writing a costume gothic, romance conventions function as the objects of parody and critique. They are things to be escaped, both by the heroine and by Atwood herself as a writer. But in *The Handmaid's Tale* romance conventions are presented as the *instruments* of escape, as much for Atwood as for the heroine. Indeed, the degree of Atwood's investment in romance paradigms as emancipatory structures is underlined by the fact that she does not—whether for her characters, her reader or herself—offer a way out of Gilead except through them. Moira, who engages in a tangible campaign of subversion and struggle, ends her days still imprisoned. Offred, who sits in her ersatz tower at the top of the Commander's house looking constantly out her window, is rescued by her hero.

Not unexpectedly, Atwood's critics view her reliance on popular female romance as an abysmal political lapse, one that is at least as glaring as the heroine's passive acceptance of enslavement. Chinmoy Banerjee argues that Atwood's invocation of costume gothic is there to dissolve feminist critique and to facilitate for the reader a soft commercialist consumption and enjoyment. Similarly, reading through what he regards as Atwood's obfuscations of history, Jamie Dopp concludes: "The Handmaid's desire for a man seems a part of the unchanging order of things, another emblem for the determination of political relations by sexual instincts and for the hopelessness of women's struggle." But if, as my own argument suggests, Atwood's endorsement of the romance is motivated by the same strategies of "survival" that determine her heroine's passivity—if Atwood, in other words, is cloaking a critique of Canada's victimization within the folds of the apparently complicitous costume romance, perhaps we should take a closer look at precisely what costume that romance is sporting.

Although the Republic of Gilead is generally accepted as an incarnation of the burgeoning American fundamentalism of the early 1980s, Atwood herself made a point of stressing that Gilead was in fact inspired by her studies in American literature and history. When asked by one interviewer whether *The Handmaid's Tale* takes place in "some amorphous Boston," Atwood responded:

> Not amorphous. It's enormously concrete. The Wall is the wall around Harvard yard. All those little shops and stores mentioned are probably there at this very minute. I lived in Boston for four years. It's also the land of my ancestors. They were people who left new England in 1775–1783, during the revolution and went to Nova Scotia. They were Puritans of the 1630–1635 immigration. They are all still in the Salem genealogical library. They are those people in the dour, black, strait-laced pictures that appear in *The Handmaid's Tale*. The book is dedicated to Perry Miller who was one of my teachers at Harvard who wrote American Puritans [sic]. . . . And the other dedication is to Mary Webster, who is one of my ancestors who was hanged as a witch. She's the witch who didn't die. They hadn't invented the drop then, so your neck didn't get broken. . . . She must have had a very sinewy neck and didn't die. Under the law of double jeopardy they couldn't execute her again. So there she was living away.

Several readers of this novel, including Cathy Davidson and Alden Turner, have commented on Atwood's invocation of the American Puritan tradition in her representation of Gilead. But what Atwood is invoking more specifically—in her reference to Miller, in her reference to Harvard, in her emphasis on a Puritan fear of women's sexuality, and even in Gilead's branding of the Handmaids in *scarlet*, though the actual letter is missing—is not just the persistence of a puritan strain in modern American culture but a tradition of American studies that celebrates Puritan intransigence as quintessentially representative of the American spirit. When Atwood was Miller's pupil at Harvard in the early 1960s, Americanists such as Richard Chase, Harry Levin, and Leslie Fiedler were busy transforming Miller's studies of the Puritans into *the* measure of authenticity in American writing. If Atwood was not herself a student of American literature, the efforts of these critics to define a national literary character were influential enough to inspire her to undertake a similar project for Canada and write *Survival*.

Atwood's exposure to 1950s and 1960s Puritan Studies provides her with the means to parody American culture. Aiming her attack at Americanist academics, Atwood holds up for condemnation their own most cherished national ideals: their approving construction of an uncompromising American spirit with its "tragic vision," its deep affection for allegory, for Manichean conflict and moral absolutism, and, above all perhaps, its iconoclastic reinventions of the social order. At the same time, Atwood's exposure to Puritan Studies arms her with a very neat, very precise definition of what constitutes the un-American mind. For the coterie of all-male critics writing during the 1950s and concerned to invest their national culture with a certain "toughness" and manly rigour, the one unequivocal un-American territory, the swamp which none of them could bring themselves to claim or settle under the national flag, was the morass of women's popular fiction—what Ann Douglas, another student of Perry Miller, would eventually term "the sentimental heresy." As later feminist critics were quick to point out, Puritan Studies scholars, having defined the American spirit as one distinguished by "an absolute refusal to give the feminine principle its due," went on to erase women's fiction from the "genuinely" American literary history which they themselves were engaged in constructing. And this, I would suggest, accounts for Atwood's commitment to the trashy feminine world of love and romance. Identifying autonomy as a discursive space, an illegible void within the victim's self, Atwood locates the site of resistance and the means of struggle—for her heroine, for herself and for her country—in a language America had not equipped itself to read.

It is thus no surprise to find in the concluding "Historical Notes" to *The Handmaid's Tale* that at centre stage is a male academic, a historian like Miller, who finds himself unable to read the essential content of Offred's story. Professor Pieixoto's appearance at the end of the novel as an expert on the now long-extinct Republic of Gilead fixes Gilead itself as an academically-inspired construct, flanked by Miller at the beginning of the book and Professor Pieixoto's at the end. As Arnold Davidson notes, Atwood's epilogue "loops back through the text that precedes it to suggest that the ways in which scholars (present as well as future) assemble the text of the past confirms the present and thereby helps to predict the future." And presumably, just as the text of the Puritan past read by Perry Miller foreshadows and inspires an American Gilead, so Pieixoto's reading of the text of the Gileadean past predicts the possibility of another gender tyranny, a future actualization of the forms of chauvinism he exhibits during his talk.

However, if part of Atwood's aim in the "Historical Notes" is to expose the complicity of academia in the formation of authoritarian institutions, another part is to offer strategies for slipping through what W.F. Garrett-Petts calls "the official discourse of History." The pairing of Professor Pieixoto and Offred at the end of *The Handmaid's Tale* mirrors the pairing of Perry Miller and Atwood's ancestor, the Puritan Mary Webster, at the beginning; and the issue in both cases is the failure of the female object of study to fit the patterns of inquiry set out by her male scrutinizer. Confronted with the Handmaid's refusal of politics for romantic introspection and history for passive self-absorption, Pieixoto cries, "What would we not give, now, for even twenty pages or so of printout from Waterford's [the Commander's] private computer!" Hailing from yet another Cambridge (England instead of New England), Pieixoto is implicitly as ill-equipped as his Puritan studies prototypes to read the hieroglyphs of feminine culture. Atwood's critics have, as I've said, condemned her endorsement of popular romance both for its gender conservatism and for its commercialism. And yet the "Historical Notes" indicate that a tribute to the "low brow," to forms of culture inadmissible to scholarly exchange, is part of her project. It is no accident that Offred's tapes are discovered among other tokens of popular passion and bad taste—Elvis Presley tunes, folk songs, Mantovani instrumentals, and the screams of Twisted Sister—nor that all of these are laughed at and dismissed by Professor Pieixoto. If the projected end of Pieixoto's academic efforts is only another tyranny, these tacky unreadable texts, like the romance itself, slip through his "official discourse" to signify the potential of resistance and hope.

Offred's failure to write the history that Pieixoto would be able to read is presumably mirrored by Mary Webster's failure to live the life that Puritan studies scholars could utilize in their constructions of the American spirit. Mary Webster's comic salvation by a weak rope contradicts the academically sanctioned "tragic vision" of a novel like *The Scarlet Letter*, which refutes the possibility of miracles precisely by redelivering its heroine to the scene of her tribulations. That Atwood duplicates Webster's miraculous escape in her own text, allowing Offred to escape Gilead through the implausible circumstance of falling in love, suggests this novel's challenge to the brutal teleology that produces a Hester Prynne, that celebrates and determines the female victim's capitulation to a "tragic" place in the history of persecution. The same might be said of Atwood's own choices for her novel. As her presentation of Pieixoto implies, imperial domination is for her as much an act of interpretation, a projection of cultural consciousness onto an uncharted self, as it is an economic or geographical domination. Finally, and much like her heroine, Atwood escapes interpretation along an "Underground Female Road," the illicit textual trail that leads over the border dividing American Tragedy from Harlequin Romance.

What fate does Atwood finally envision for Canada itself? In the nightmare future she imagines, women have succumbed to a totalizing patriarchy. Appropriately, given Atwood's conflation of feminism and nationalism, Canada, in some analogous gesture, has succumbed to its totalizing southern neighbour. Among the historical facts revealed in the "Historical Notes" is Canada's complicity in the Gileadean enterprise, its refusal to harbour female refugees escaping north for fear of "antagonizing its powerful neighbour," and, even more insidiously, its contribution of the design of the handmaid's costumes, which are modeled on the uniforms of German prisoners of war in Canadian P.O.W. camps of the Second World War. The logic behind such dour predictions seems to have its basis in 1980s history. Written at a moment when Canadians had just elected an unabashedly American-friendly Prime Minister, *The Handmaid's Tale* predicts a future in which the iconic move of crossing the border into Canada will no longer represent the escape from American persecution which it had, variously, in the eighteenth century to the United Empire Loyalists, in the nineteenth century to Southern American slaves, and in the twentieth century to refugees of the draft. In order to escape Gilead, Pieixoto tells us, Offred would not just have had to go north, as Atwood's ancestors did; she would have had to leave the North American continent altogether.

And yet if the epilogue predicts and, indeed, comments upon Canada's complicity in American aims, it also preserves the terms of Atwood's nationalist project, presenting in Professor Pieixoto the emissary of yet another of Canada's imperial rulers, this time Great Britain. In accord with the geographical trajectory of Atwood's nationalism, which equates northern wilderness with a final refuge, the scene of embattled autonomy has been pushed up almost into the Arctic itself. This scene is perhaps no longer identifiably Canadian. By Professor Pieixoto's era, Canada has disappeared as a geo-political entity. The academic conference at which Pieixoto speaks takes place at the "University of Denay, Nunavit," "Denay" apparently being a version of "Dene," one of the First Nations tribes, "Nunavit" being that portion of land in the Northwest Territories which the Canadian government has designated for the Innuit peoples and which, in Atwood's version of the future, has achieved its promised sovereign status. But if Canada itself has disappeared, the position of the feminized "exploited victim" has not. Maryann Crescent Moon, as the representative of native culture, itself an object of Caucasian imperialism, is also the object of Pieixoto's sexist remarks. The "Historical Notes" section, in other words, recapitulates the relations between female/colony and male/empire that Atwood's nationalism inscribes throughout this novel. In some sense, indeed, the prediction of Canada's dissolution, as well as Atwood's reference to Canada's unsavory participation in Gileadean fascism, only reinforce her call for national autonomy, precisely by painting so bleak a picture of the price of Canada's compliance.

There is no question that Atwood's attempt to warn against the dissolution of borders, whether national or personal, prompts her to propose models of autonomy for women that many feminists would consider too dangerously androcentric and heterosexist to be of much value. But by reading this novel outside the liberal/left feminist framework which its critics invariably bring to it, we can perhaps better understand its feminism not as part of a prescribed or consistent itinerary, but as protest contingent upon the idiosyncrasies of its contexts. Both the position of Canada with respect to Reagan's America in the mid-1980s and the self-designations of the Americanist scholars with whom Atwood was familiar determine her combined advocacy of self-protective autonomy and the unsanctioned tests of women's popular culture. But I would also suggest that such a reading might go further to question whether our standards for legitimacy in feminism don't sidestep the possible alterations required of it when gender is fused with seemingly unrelated political issues. Atwood draws on a conceptually skewed conflation of feminism and nationalism, but the very fact that she does so suggests the extent to which national selfhood is already a libidinally invested construct, one which enmeshes the discourses of citizenry and sexuality and which therefore potentially confuses the traditional coordinates of feminist response. The fantasies of drugstore romance may not seem like adequate weapons in the struggle for women's equality and recognition. But then, maybe lying in the missionary position under Uncle Sam, you need a little fantasy.

GLENN DEER

# The Handmaid's Tale:
## *Dystopia and the Paradoxes of Power*

Margaret Atwood has consistently written about women who are both powerful and vulnerable, strong enough to endure and retain a sense of self yet unable to elude the grimmer aspects of entrapment. Often Atwood's protagonists are writers or artists themselves and therefore have particular creative resources to help or even hinder them—Joan Delacourt in *Lady Oracle* (1976) is a writer of costume Gothics; Rennie Wilford in *Bodily Harm* (1981) is a lifestyle journalist; Elaine Risley in *Cat's Eye* (1988) is a painter. What will be considered here in greater detail is the voice of the most obviously entrapped artist-writer in Atwood's novels: Offred in *The Handmaid's Tale*.

This novel has received a great deal of critical and popular attention since it was published in 1985. Perhaps the popularity of *The Handmaid's Tale*, adapted into a film directed by Volker Schlondorff in 1989, can be attributed partly to the convenient opportunities it provides for teachers in the Canadian critical parlour to explain its generic inheritance from dystopian fiction (Orwell, Kafka, Zamyatin, Huxley) and to the postmodern design of the novel. Critics have been especially attracted to its metafictional elements and narrative frame. Among eight articles on *The Handmaid's Tale* published since 1987, four give prominence to the effect of the "Historical Notes" section on our reading. Out of these four, Amin Malak, Arnold

From *Postmodern Canadian Fiction and the Rhetoric of Authority*, by Glenn Deer. ©1994 by McGill-Queen's University Press.

Davidson, and Harriet Bergmann emphasize that the "Historical Notes" are
an ironic treatment of the failure of male academic readings of the oral
record left by Offred; the future historians fail to treat Offred's experience
with compassion or emotional sympathy. As Davidson suggests, the Notes
section is perhaps the most depressing part of the novel since it shows how
little has been changed by Offred's discourse: the male oppression of women
has persisted in a different form beyond the post-Gilead period, even into
the aboriginal Republic of Denay. W.F. Garrett-Petts goes further and
argues that the Notes section actually marginalizes and reduces the character
of Offred to a mere shadow: he tries to show that her character is
significantly deflated by the time we reach the end of the Notes. Constance
Rooke, by contrast, asserts that Offred's character retains integrity and
cannot be divorced from the politics of resistance.

Other tasks undertaken by various critics include the explanation of
generic sources (Malak, Lacombe), the identification of motifs of nature and
womanhood (Rooke, Rubenstein, Friebert), and the attempt to infer that
Offred's metaphorically significant real name is "June" (Rooke, Rubenstein,
Friebert).

Very little of the above criticism deals with the voice, ethos, or style of
the narrator in *The Handmaid's Tale*. Only Lucy Friebert comments that the
voice of Offred is the same "low-keyed" one that "B.W. Powe derides as
'virtually interchangeable' in all the previous novels." Friebert defends this
monotonous voice by arguing that this "voice, approximating the limited
scope of Offred's life symbolized by the blinkers on her veil, is precisely what
makes *The Handmaid's Tale* credible.

Amin Malak says that although Atwood is writing in an Orwellian
tradition, the novel "sustains an ironic texture" and is not filled with as many
"frightening images" as Orwell's *Nineteen Eighty-Four*: "the few graphic
horror scenes are crisply and snappily presented, sparing us a blood-curdling
impact. Some may criticize this restraint as undermining the novel's integrity
and emotional validity." I agree that Atwood's narrator does not present as
many overtly "frightening images"; nevertheless, the narrator does
consistently evoke a violent atmosphere that accords with the evil totalitarian
regime. In fact Atwood's narrator is a powerful user of language, a poet and
rhetorician who presents in a strategic way the true horrors perpetrated by
the Gileadean state. Although in the "Historical Notes" we learn that the
overall narrative arrangement is not Offred's, that her taped oral utterances
have been transcribed and arranged by Pieixoto and Wade, the power of her
rhetorical stance is distinctive and unusual.

Harriet Bergmann has recently written that "Offred was not, we can
tell, a person who cared particularly about the written word before the

establishment of Gilead." Actually, we don't know many details about the reading and writing habits of Offred before Gilead: we do know that she was university educated, that she loved books, and that she worked transferring books to computer disks. We should keep in mind that we are meant to read Offred's story as one composed retrospectively—and an extraordinary retrospective it is. Offred demonstrates immense skill in constructing her rhetoric; this "unskilled" storyteller pays expert attention to narrative point of view, to physical detail, and to remembered conversations. Indeed, Offred's discourse reflects a practised devotion to *written* rhetoric. And of course, one of the great compositional problems of the novel is that the *oral* qualities of Offred's taped discourse are always *imaginary* oral qualities: as we read the printed discourse, we attend to a complex syntactical and rhetorical play that is the product of the economy of writing, not speech. What we need now is an analysis of the paradoxical ways in which the language of the narrator scripts special footings of intimacy and authority with the reader.

In *The Handmaid's Tale* Atwood is caught in the dilemma faced by many creators of satiric dystopias: the author needs both to condemn particular social injustices and to portray the mechanisms of oppression as credible enough, as sufficiently powerful and seductive, to represent a believable evil, not an irrelevant or far-fetched one. While attempting to balance ethical interests with plausibility, the ambitious author risks falling into either transparent didacticism or a contradictory fascination with the rhetorical machinery of dystopic horror. Atwood's discourse in marked by stylistic and rhetorical features—habits of syntactic and lexical arrangement and strategies of managing point of view and addresser-addressee relations—that show she has succumbed to the latter: scenes of violence and horror meant to illuminate sites of oppression are also strategically designed to manipulate and horrify. Atwood's narrator is an authoritative and authoritarian storyteller, one who manipulates the reader as she tells her story but one who is also caught in the web of Gileadan power politics. Offred's powerful narrative skill conflicts with the powerlessness, the innocence, and the descriptive phenomenological cast of mind that also characterize her. It is as if Atwood's skill as storyteller continually intrudes, possessing her narrative creation. Narrative self-consciousness, in fact, does explicitly and strategically emerge.

To see *The Handmaid's Tale* as ideologically and rhetorically problematic is not a "politically correct" view, at least if one considers the majority of the above critical opinions, which aim at solidifying the conventionality of the text by inscribing it in an already readable canonical genre (dystopia, political satire, postmodern subversion), by deciphering allusions, or by weighing the effects of framing devices like the concluding

"Historical Notes" section. Only Frank Davey and Chinmoy Banerjee have recognized how the novel "participates not only in various literary conventions and bourgeois assumptions about the self but in various commercial formulas for capitalist book production" or how "Atwood is concerned with the aesthetic enjoyment of a particular kind of victimization, and not with a critical examination of its determinant relations." Atwood's politics in her earlier fiction have been cogently analysed by Larry Macdonald as bring fraught with contradiction (as are also, Macdonald points out, the fictions of MacLennan and Davies) because of the reduction of collective problems to "the psychic wounds of individual characters" and the tendency to undercut the possibilities of positive political change: "these novelists end by urging individual adaptation to a status quo which their fiction simultaneously urges upon us as intolerable."

The Handmaid's Tale is similarly caught in contradictory discursive impulses: it shows a world that is "intolerable," but it cannot avoid complicity in using the mechanisms or rhetoric of that very intolerable world. Hence, a trope that might characterize the rhetorical gestalt of the novel is *paralepsis*, the figure of verbal dissimulation and duplicity that asserts its lack of rhetoric while using rhetoric, that on the one hand critiques authority and on the other is complicitous with that authority, that feigns powerlessness in order to wield power, that disavows deliberate arrangement while arranging words with great care: "I'm sorry there is so much pain in this story," Offred apologizes, then proceeds to make us wince with her sharp, "fragments, like a body caught in crossfire or pulled apart by force." By examining these and other instances of such discursive contradictions and paradoxes, I will provide a close reading of the novel and subject key sections to lexical, syntactic, and rhetorical analysis; I will try to get a grip on the authority and style of Atwood's storyteller while remaining close to the play of addresser-addressee relations, those social relations that metonymically reflect the implied storyteller's attitude to power.


### The Authoritative Voice of the Victim


In The Handmaid's Tale the reader is addressed by a narrator whose authority is sanctioned by the implied author: she possesses an analytical intelligence that demonstrates her clear superiority over others. She is a reader of the social "signs" in her environment and in everyday objects. Offred is assigned the authority of an implied author; there is, in fact, no gap between implied author and narrator, no attempt to distinguish the voices. There is, however, a tension between Offred's narrative skill and the characterization of her as a

Handmaid. This narrator wants the discourse freedoms and powers normally granted only to men; yet she is in the position of Handmaid:

> The pen between my fingers is sensuous, alive almost, I can feel its power, the power of the words it contains. Pen is envy, Aunt Lydia would say, quoting another Centre motto, warning us away from such objects. And they were more right, it is envy. Just holding it is envy. I envy the Commander his pen. It's one more thing I would like to steal.

The intelligence and wit of the narrator is but one of various rhetorical tactics that Atwood uses to induce our acceptance of the didactic authenticity of her satire. Its social and intellectual validity as argument is enforced by a narrator who shifts between readerly footings of intimacy and equality to footings of authority, superior insight, and impersonal detachment. In the opening first chapter of the novel we are guided through the world of Gilead by a narrator who surveys her surroundings with a highly developed analytic sense, who possesses a writerly skill in evoking shapes, odours, and images:

> We slept in what had once been the gymnasium. The floor was of varnished wood, with stripes and circles painted on it, for the games that were formerly played there; the hoops for the basketball nets were still in place, though the nets were gone. A balcony ran around the room, for the spectators, and I thought I could smell, faintly like an afterimage, the pungent scent of sweat, shot through with the sweet taint of chewing gum and perfume from the watching girls, felt-skirted as I knew from pictures, later in mini-skirts, then pants, then in one-earring, spiky green-streaked hair. Dances would have been held there; the music lingered, a palimpsest of unheard sound, style upon style, an undercurrent of drums, a forlorn wail, garlands made of tissue-paper flowers, cardboard devils, a revolving ball of mirrors, powdering the dancers with a snow of light.
>
> There was old sex in the room and loneliness, and expectation, of something without a shape or name . . .
>
> We yearned for the future. How did we learn it, that talent for insatiability? It was in the air; and it was still in the air, an afterthought, as we tried to sleep, in the army cots that had been set up in rows, with spaces between so we could not talk. We had flannelette sheets, like children's, and army-issue blankets, old ones that still said U.S. We folded our clothes neatly and laid

them on the stools at the ends of the beds. The lights were turned down but not out. Aunt Sara and Aunt Elizabeth patrolled; they had electric cattle prods slung on thongs from their leather belts.

The first chapter contains an odd mixture of clarity and obscurity, hard detail and shadowy impressionism. The plural subject of the first sentence—"We"—and the institutional gymnasium setting signal a makeshift group cohesion, the unity of refugees, the homeless, prisoners, or recruits in some military training camp. By the end of the third paragraph we understand that they are somehow all three. The second paragraph, drawing on a particular cultural stereotype marking women as the receivers of male sexual agency, hints that they are women; when they are named at the close of the chapter, we know their sex.

The narrator's language indicates that she has detached herself emotionally from any memories associated with the gymnasium. (The past tense, "slept," indicates that this is a memory.) The language that she uses to describe the gymnasium in the second sentence is unusual because it is a more elaborate or expanded description of the commonplace than we are used to: she isolates in separate "snap-shots" features of the floor—the "varnished wood," the "stripes and circles," the "hoops for the basketball nets"—in the language of a person who is culturally distant from the place and the events that the gym was designed to host.

The emotional detachment in the tone of the narrator, an emotional emptiness, matches her surroundings: the gym, a place formerly meant for players, activity, and spectators, is empty; the hoops are stripped of their nets (netting has a delicate, membrane-like sensual quality, a quality absent from the gym). The rather long third and fourth sentences that complete this first paragraph sustain a ghostlike atmosphere in which human activity has ceased and all that remains are inanimate forms like the balcony, which "ran around the room," and vague odours that set off memories of tastes, images, and sounds in the narrator's mind. However, we are not expected to read the tastes, images, and sounds in these sentences as mere mental projections: the narrator's tactic is to present these as if they are present in the very room, ghostly presences that can be excavated by a consciousness sensitive enough to do so. The faint smell is "like an afterimage," hovering in the gym air, and the adjective clause "as I knew from pictures" is subtly inserted after the image of the "watching girls, felt-skirted" in order not to disturb the immediate impact of it as a raw perception of a tangible presence. Of course, this presence is but a shadow of the original; its faded and intangible quality, however, is what Atwood's narrator could be trying to get us to apprehend.

In the third sentence the narrator remembers the former fashions and changes in dating styles that the gym once was host to—basketball games give way to high-school romance; men and women playing competitively turn into different types of players. In the fourth sentence the sense that the gym is literally *haunted* by the past is even more forceful conveyed: the past-perfect verb cluster ("would have been held"), which suggests an already expired action, is followed in the second clause by an ongoing sound: "the music lingered, a palimpsest of unheard sound, style upon style, an undercurrent of drums."

As Atwood's narrator asyndetically tacks on modifying adjectival phrases, the language suggests both increasing action and increasing danger: the neutral "style upon style" shifts to the menacing "undercurrent of drums," then the surprising "forlorn wail," and finally the tragicomic carnival atmosphere of the death-dance suggested by the "flowers," "cardboard devils," "mirrors," and shadowy dancers powdered with "a snow of light."

Throughout this excerpt from the brief first chapter Atwood attempts to present the narrator as an innocent, a mere observer, a describer of her surroundings; this is a procedure that is retained in subsequent chapters. Chapter 2 begins "A chair, a table, a lamp." (The opening of chapter 2 and other meditations on physical objects and perception uncannily echo sections of Zamyatin's *We*, the obvious prototype for *The Handmaid's Tale:* "Are you familiar with this strange condition? You wake at night, open your eyes to blackness, and suddenly you feel you've lost your way—and quickly, quickly you grope around you, seeking something familiar, solid—a wall, a lamp, a chair").

Offred just happens to "notice" things. But her innocent eye always manages to present us with ideologically significant comparisons, observations, and details; this may hardly be surprising if one grants that ideology is partly an extension of material circumstances. But there is an incompatibility between Offred's narration and the position of subjugation she occupies as a Handmaid. One might wonder why and how such a narrative intelligence could be subjugated in this way. Of course one could argue that Atwood is suggesting that if Offred can be enslaved, anyone can be. Atwood needs to convince us that this Handmaid was subjugated, that the oppression she experienced was evil: the rhetorical intelligence of the narrator is meant to emphasize the power of the regime and the changes wrought upon society. When we finally read the Historical Notes, we also learn that the tale is meant to be read as an experience remembered, as a story recollected in a rather different setting from that of Gilead. However, even before we acquire this contextualizing information, we apprehend that the first chapter contains the polish of arrangement and aesthetic management of a narrative originating from a position of literary sophistication.

What I am trying to suggest is that Atwood's narrator in this novel does not speak entirely in the voice of the victim, the writer who pleads "Mayday"; rather, she speaks in the skilled voice of the rhetorician and the fabulator who is purposefully telling a story. Atwood has the narrator move through her thoughts in a plain style, joining modifying phrases to the main clause on the right side of the sentence, as if to suggest syntactically the artlessness of the narrator. The co-ordinate structures and right-branching sentences, however, are filled with an abstract lexis, a lexis of contemplativeness that emphasizes the narrator's wisdom, her philosophical and emotional superiority over those around her: "We yearned for the future. How did we learn it, that talent for insatiability? I was in the air; and it was still in the air, an afterthought, as we tried to sleep, in the army cots that had been set up in rows, with spaces between so we could not talk." (The rhetorical question here is another indicator of the author's artfullness.) Here we encounter a paradox: the voluble narrator speaks confidently and precisely about the silence she endured. To increase the sense of the macabre sinisterness of the setting, Atwood's narrator plays on the tension between the domestic softness and military harshness, between the cozy flannelette sheets and "Aunts" and the rough "army-issue" blankets and menacing "electric cattle prods slung on thongs."

## Orchestrations of Horror

The implied author's sanctioning of the narrator Offred suggests that the social world—its architecture, commodities, semiology—is open to systematic rational analysis: historical and political meanings are embedded everywhere; ideology is ubiquitously inscribed. Yet Offred is depicted as fascinated with the paradoxes of power. Offred's ethical assumptions would suggest that she is opposed to irrational modes of argument and persuasion; she is opposed to the tyranny of propaganda. Yet this ethical consciousness demonstrates its attraction to the rhetorical efficacy of violence, power, and the grotesque: Offred has, in her discursive practice, started to play the game of power politics like a true Gileadan.

Time after time Atwood's narrator demonstrates her ability to seize upon seemingly banal objects—a braided rug, the walls of a room, a pat of butter, a chair—and turn them into receptacles or symbols that have resonant metaphysical and political implications. Partly this is meant to illustrate the state of mind of an individual living in an ascetic and puritanically monotonous world: she is hungry for sensuous experience. Not only does this tactic supplement our sense of the repression and boredom in the

Handmaid's life, but it also leads to an epiphanic moment—one of those moments that expose how Offred always knows much more than she says, that she possesses powers of apprehension that are impressive. Atwood has endowed this narrator with conspicuous gems of compressed wisdom:

> I sit in the chair and think about the word *chair*. It can also mean the leader of a meeting. It can also mean a mode of execution. It is the first syllable in *charity*. It is the French word for flesh. None of these facts has any connection with the others.
>
> These are the kinds of litanies I use, to compose myself.
>
> In front of me is a tray, and on the tray with three slices of brown toast on it, a small dish containing honey, and another plate with an egg-cup on it, the kind that looks like a woman's torso, in a skirt. Under the skirt is the second egg, being kept warm. The egg-cup is white china with a blue stripe.
>
> The first egg is white. I move the egg-cup a little, so it's now in the watery sunlight that comes through the window and falls, brightening, waning, brightening again, on the tray . . .
>
> The sun goes and the egg fades.
>
> I pick the egg out of the cup and finger it for a moment. It's warm. Women used to carry such eggs between their breasts, to incubate them. That would have felt good.
>
> The minimalist life. Pleasure is an egg. Blessings that can be counted, on the fingers of one hand. But possibly this is how I am expected to react. If I have an egg, what more can I want? . . . I slice the top off the egg with the spoon, and eat the contents.

In the phenomenal world around her Atwood's narrator can find objects that remind her of her condition, that are models of the female life. It is important to note that the "litany" of chairs and eggs is in the "Birth Day" section, a chapter that presents the special birth ritual attended by the Handmaids: the pregnant Handmaid, Janine, literally gives birth—lays her egg—while seated in a special "birthing stool," a chair that allows the Commander's wife to sit behind and above the surrogate mother. The meaning of the word "chair" and the reflection on eggs takes on special significance in this context and contradicts the narrator's disclaimer that "none of these facts has any connection with the others," her need to retain an appearance of being artless, natural, spontaneous. The kinds of meanings that the narrator seizes on are connected to power and mortality—general concepts, to be sure, but concepts that are specifically linked to the exercise of power and the reminders of mortality that are dramatized when Janine gives birth. The birthing stool in retrospect is ambiguous. The mother can achieve prominence and power; or, if she fails to deliver a healthy child, a sentence of death.

The connection of birth to death, the fine line between power and failure, fertility and sterility, reflects the tendency of the narrator's mind to explore the ambiguities in her world, to delve under the affirmative and pull out the darker intimations of death. She utilizes this procedure when contemplating the egg: the two eggs, one on top of the other, are like a model of the Gileadean birth scene, with the Commander's wife seated up and behind the Handmaid. Offred begins with the neutral description "the egg is white"; she then moves into a figurative language that is resonant with female symbolism: the egg is compared to the moon; the moon becomes a desert; the desert, place of spiritual trial and of revelation. An alternating emphasis between fertility and sterility, energy and entropy, is played out—the egg literally seems to throb with temperature changes: "The sun goes and the egg fades. I pick the egg out of the cup and finger it for a moment. It's warm. Women used to carry such eggs between their breasts, to incubate them."

In this section the narrator's opening disclaimer would have us believe that her litany is artless, a stream of unconnected facts. Syntactically Atwood's narrator would have us perceive her thoughts as spontaneously stitched together: there are few logical connectors—however, moreover, therefore—that indicate argument. But there is a propositional cohesion here in the very juxtaposition of birth and death images. As I have already noted, one of the justifications for having the narrator produce these longish meditations—and displaying heightened sensitivity to the ordinary—is to portray the severe hunger for stimulation: Offred says, "In reduced circumstances the desire to live attaches itself to strange objects." At the same time, these meditations give us insight into the narrator's cast of mind: her values, fears, preoccupations. And what is highly significant in these preoccupations is that existing beside the analysis of the social condition of women is an attraction to pure power: "I slice the top off the egg with a spoon, and eat the contents" becomes an aggressive movement, a power signal.

There are times when Offred's discourses (or litanies, as she calls them) become redundant, a static piling up of grotesque descriptions. Unlike the previous examples, wherein the meditation upon the object yields a surprising turn, a transformation of meaning, a revelation of similarities, the presentation of the hanged men in chapter 6 involves the continuous reiteration of horror:

> We stop, together as if on signal, and stand and look at the bodies. It doesn't matter if we look. We're supposed to look: this

is what they are there for, hanging on the Wall. Sometimes they'll be there for days, until there's a new batch, so as many people as possible will have a chance to see them.

What they are hanging from is hooks. The hooks have been set into the brickwork of the Wall, for this purpose. Not all of them are occupied. The hooks look like appliances for the armless. Or steel question marks, upside-down and sideways.

It's the bags over the heads that are the worst, worse than the faces themselves would be. It makes the men look like dolls on which faces have not yet been painted; like scarecrows, which in a way is what they are, since they are meant to scare. Or as if their heads are sacks, stuffed with some undifferentiated material, like flour or dough. It's the obvious heaviness of the heads, their vacancy, the way gravity pulls them down and there's no life any more to hold them up. The heads are zeros.

Though if you look and look, as we are doing, you can see the outlines of the features under the white cloth, like grey shadows. The heads are the heads of snowmen, with the coal eyes and the carrot noses fallen out. The heads are melting.

But on one bag there's blood, which has seeped through the white cloth, where the mouth must have been. It makes another mouth, a small red one, like the mouths painted with thick brushes by kindergarten children. A child's idea of a smile. This smile of blood is what fixes the attention, finally. These are not snowmen after all.

The men wear white coats, like those worn by doctors or scientists . . . Each has a placard hung around his neck to show why he has been executed: a drawing of a human foetus. They were doctors, then, in the time before, when such things were legal . . .

What we are supposed to feel towards these bodies is hatred and scorn. This isn't what I feel. These bodies hanging on the Wall are time travelers, anachronisms. They've come here from the past.

What I feel towards them is blankness. What I feel is that I must not feel. What I feel is partly relief, because none of these men is Luke. Luke wasn't a doctor. Isn't.

The description of the executed men hanging on the wall exemplifies Atwood's narrator's penchant for the horrific. Presented as an innocent or guileless observer of her world, Offred in fact is an effective tale-teller; but while seeking to condemn the violence around her, her protracted gaze implicates herself, for she has made the vision and instruments of horror into objects of voyeurism rather than symptoms that point to more complex power problems.

This section is a skillfully orchestrated set-piece that begins tentatively and builds to higher levels of shock. Each paragraph takes us gradually and teasingly closer to the horror. Offred begins with a general declaration of the purpose of this display, "so as many people as possible will have a chance to see them." With the deft editorial camera eye of a Hitchcock, Offred avoids a direct description of the bodies and instead focuses on the unoccupied hooks set into the Wall. The pacing in this second paragraph is methodical and slow: sentences are cohesively joined with lexical repetition—anadiplosis and anaphora—as the narrator gradually moves from a plain description of the hooks, "set into the brickwork of the Wall," then shifts to shocking comparisons that carry an indirect hint on amputation and bodily injury: "The hooks look like appliances for the armless." And the final figurative comparison in this paragraph literally denotes the suspended questioning, the deliberately suspended interrogation: "Or steel question marks, upside-down and sideways."

The third paragraph serves up images that are more calculatedly grotesque: first the faceless "dolls," then the "scarecrows," and finally the "sacks, stuffed with undifferentiated material." Atwood's narrator skillfully intensifies the implied danger by keeping the face of violence just out of sight. It is the tension between the *absence* of life and the dead *weight* of the body that is effectively captured here; Offred's language is ponderous and weighty, but spiritless.

The fourth paragraph continues Offred's carefully paced revelation of the object of danger. The narrator begins to focus our gaze ever more closely on the covered faces of the hanged men, "the outlines of the features under the white cloth, like grey shadows." The metaphors in the last two sentences here reflect a typical tactic of Offred's for evoking the grotesque: an innocent, childhood image, a "snowman," metamorphoses into something more sinister, more tragic. The climax of this progression is finally reached in the fifth paragraph: "But on one bag there's blood, which has seeped through the white cloth, where the mouth must have been." But Offred continues to exploit the shock of the tension between childhood innocence and the bloody evidence of the execution. The blood on the face of the victim is "a child's idea of a smile. This smile of blood is what fixes the attention, finally. These are not snowmen after all."

After this detailed description, how do we read and react to the narrator's comment after she tells us that these victims were doctors who had performed abortions in the years before the present regime? "What I feel towards them is blankness. What I feel is that I must not feel. What I feel is partly relief, because none of these men is Luke. Luke wasn't a doctor. Isn't." The narrator asserts her "blankness," perhaps an emotionally protective measure to help her cope with the loss of Luke. But the presentation of her perceptions reveals much about her attitude to the reader and the scene she has witnessed: that she must orchestrate the feelings evoked by the scene in a deliberately shocking way, a rhetorically powerful way; that the impact of horror is as important as the reasons for it (and, after all, the Gilead authorities *are* setting the men up as human "scarecrows"); that a reader must experience the event's emotional impact before she or he can be introduced to its political or social background (i.e., the treatment of doctors as war criminals).

One might object that Offred is not meant to be seen as a character who is controlling the reader's perceptions, that the horror in her presentation is simply meant to illustrate how the authorities of Gilead have mastered the art of frightening people: Offred is simply testifying to the effectiveness of the rhetoric of the Gileadan police state. However, the type of discourse that Offred uses does not simply inform us that the executed prisoners are frightful deterrents: Offred carefully constructs a narrative that makes the reader look at the objects of horror in a prescribed and suspenseful way, a way designed to increase the shock effect. Again, the evidence suggests to me that Offred is intensely aware of the power structures around her, that she is not naïve. When she compares the "one red smile" on the hanged man's mask to the "red of the tulips in Serena Joy's garden," she advances a disclaimer that we can barely accept as valid: the obvious pun that relates the red mouth to the "tulips" is irresistible. As a reader, I am compelled to read the narrator as the originary force behind the pun, that she is well aware of the connections, but that she is simply withholding her comments:

> I look at the one red smile. The red of the smile is the same as the red of the tulips in Serena Joy's garden, towards the base of the flowers where they are beginning to heal. The red is the same but there is no connection. The tulips are not tulips of blood, the red smiles are not flowers, neither thing makes a comment on the other. The tulip is no reason for disbelief in the hanged man, or vice versa. Each thing is valid and really there. It is through a field of such valid objects that I must pick my way, every day and in every way. I put a lot of effort into making such distinctions. I need to make them. I need to be very clear, in my own mind.

"I put a lot of effort into making such distinctions," Offred says. But what distinctions are they? She gives us a glimpse of the philosophical and analytical interest in her mind, then abruptly stops. This seems to be an instance of Atwood's standing too close to her narrator, then shifting to limit the character's knowledge so that it does not merge with that of the omniscient author.

I have been trying to argue that Atwood's narrator is a deliberate storyteller, one who manipulates the reader as she tells her story, and that this shows how she has become caught in the web of Gileadan power politics. This sense of narrative skill conflicts with the powerlessness, the innocence, and the descriptive phenomenological cast of mind that characterize Offred. It is as if Atwood's skill as a storyteller keeps possessing her creation. The storyteller's self-conscious power, in fact, emerges at the end of chapter 7, a chapter that begins with a night-time series of fantasies of the past. Offred remembers her friend Moira, her mother, and her daughter:

> I would like to believe this is a story I'm telling. I need to believe it. I must believe it. Those who can believe that such stories are only stories have a better chance.
>
> If it's a story I'm telling, then I have control over the ending. Then there will be an ending, to the story, and real life will come after it. I can pick up where I left off.
>
> It isn't a story I'm telling.
>
> It's also a story I'm telling, in my head, as I go along.
>
> Tell, rather than write, because I have nothing to write with and writing is in any case forbidden. But if it's a story, even in my head, I must be telling it to someone. You don't tell a story only to yourself. There's always someone else.
>
> Even when there is no one.
>
> A story is like a letter. *Dear You*, I'll say. Just *you*, without a name. Attaching a name attaches *you* to the world of fact, which is riskier, more hazardous: who knows what the chances are out there, of survival, yours? I will say *you*, *you*, like an old love song. *You* can mean more than one.
>
> *You* can mean thousands.
>
> I'm not in any immediate danger, I'll say to you.
>
> I'll pretend you can hear me.
>
> But it's no good, because I know you can't.

There is no hint of this narrative self-consciousness in the opening chapter of *The Handmaid's Tale*, no indication that the story is meant *to be read as if originally spoken;* only in the "Historical Notes" do we learn that the text is meant to be a transcript of a tape recording. But as well there is no explicit signal in the introduction, such as the title-page to Richardson's *Pamela* ("In a Series of Familiar Letters from A Beautiful Young Damsel to Her Parents"), or the preface to Nabokov's *Lolita* ("The Confessions of a White Widowed Male"). Atwood's withholding of the contextualizing information creates a gap between our initial, heuristic reading of the book, a reading in which the narrator's authority is valorized through its writerly surface structure, and our retrospective reimaginings and rereadings that are informed by the "Historical Notes" (i.e., our retrospective reimaginings or our rereadings that postulate an oral consciousness rather than one originally cast in *writing*).

Offred's direct address to the reader emphasizes the artificial order that fiction imposes on reality: recognition of this artificiality is supposed to be consoling because "then I have control over the ending. Then there will be an ending, to the story, and real life will come after it." Yet Atwood's narrator wants her discourse to be *more* authentic than fiction, to have a privileged validity as a record of the *real*: "It isn't a story I'm telling." But if Offred's discourse is meant to be "like a letter," with a written sense of addressee, then why have the addressee markers been excluded from the earlier parts of the novel, especially in the introductory chapter?

I contend that Atwood's text compels us to see her narrator in two ways that are not entirely congruent: as innocent recorder and as a skilled self-conscious rhetorician and storyteller. Atwood needs to delay the revelation of this latter rhetorical self-consciousness because a self-dramatized narrator is immediately suspect, immediately prone to charges of unreliability and cunning artifice. And even when Atwood dramatizes the narrator in a self-conscious mood, as in the above, she inserts disclaimers, hoping to retain a sense of Offred's essential artlessness: the tale is a story she's telling "as I go along." Later, in the "Salvaging" section of the novel, Atwood has her narrator again profess that her discourse is artless and innocent: "I'm sorry there is so much pain in this story. I'm sorry it's in fragments, like a body caught in crossfire or pulled apart by force. But there is nothing I can do to change it." These apologies function to convey the ingenuousness of the narrator; but the stylistic evidence that we have gathered so far—her use of symbolic cultural objects, her deconstructions of them, her ingenious comparisons of images that connote power and mortality, her skillful rhetoric, which guides the reader to a special state of suspense and horror— these aspects of the narrator's discourse contradict her professions of artlessness.

The "Historical Notes" provide a significant shift in discourse. This is a peculiarly more comic section than the preceding narrative by Offred, and by being so is subject to ironic criticism. Ostensibly, these notes provide a gloss on the social, historical, and political origins of Gileadan society, as seen by a future society of scholars. The notes provide certain details that are not made explicit in the narrative (the escape of Offred to Canada, via Maine; the reasons for the extreme measures in the birthing process—disease, pollution, war, the President's Day Massacre). But more importantly, these "Historical Notes" are a further reinforcing of the *authority* of Offred's narrative: the academics are satirized as trivializers of history. They have turned Gilead into a matter of textual authentication and an occasion for levity and entertainment. The scholars are pompous cultural relativists; as Professor Pieixoto defends his objectivity, Atwood sets him up as hopelessly insensitive to Offred's story:

> Allow me to say that in my opinion we must be cautious about passing moral judgments upon the Gileadeans. Surely we have learned by now that such judgments are of necessity culture-specific. Also, Gileadean society was under a good deal of pressure, demographic and otherwise, and was subject to factors from which we ourselves are happily more free. Our job is not to censure but to understand. (*Applause*)

Pieixoto's attempts to "establish an identity for the narrator" are meant to be seen as demonstrative of his insensitivity to the text. Offred's story has not been understood by these scholars, who are rather poor readers of texts.

Since Offred's narrative is superior to that of the "Historical Notes," we should remind ourselves of how it operates, what kinds of discourses it contains, and whether these discourses are adequate to the task of exploring the power relations that she has targeted for criticism. I have tried to show how Atwood privileges the voice of her narrator in a paradoxical manner. The implied author attempts to suggest that Offred is ingenuous and artless. But she is unable to do this consistently because the intelligence and aesthetic knowledge of the writer, the storyteller, continually break through. Offred presents evil as both seductive and repulsive, an attitude that could be described as deriving from romanticism and the Gothic. Frank Davey, in *Margaret Atwood: A Feminist Poetics*, however, argues that "the Gothic element is a red herring" because it represents the distorted perspectives of Atwood's protagonists (specifically in *Lady Oracle*) who "lie and fantasize," "fictionalize on derivative models," and "exaggerate goodness and villainy, exaggerate the similarities between goodness and villainy" in order to escape from reality. We can remind ourselves, thus, that Gothic involves an element of parody and that an ironic poet like Byron or an ironic novelist like Jane Austen in *Northanger Abbey* deliberately undermines Gothic elements while using them. However, Davey also notes that there is a tension in Atwood's work between the objects of criticism and her own style, between the "rational, analytic, and male" mode of being and the "aphoristic, 'worldless,' and gestural" female mode: "Male order may constitute a travesty of female chaos and its gestural language, but only a wary appropriation of that order enables a speaking of either."

Satire is a form that cannot effectively manifest itself through "gestural" and cryptic language: the object of satire must be perspicuously framed (see Banerjee). However, in *The Handmaid's Tale* there is a peculiarly ambiguous attitude to male modes of power and authority. Atwood's narrator is made to observe much that is politically repugnant, but her discourse contains a powerful rhetoric that derives from the ethos of Gilead: Offred is preoccupied with power and authority. What kinds of lexical collocations with power and authority are found in Offred's language? She tends to emphasize tactics and techniques: one of the most significant collocates of power is "vision," or the dynamics of observation—the power of the observing subject and the observed object.

## Controlling the Observer

In *The Handmaid's Tale* the motifs of *vision* are an important part of the presentation of the politics of sexual control: these motifs connect masters to slaves, Commanders to Handmaids. The desires of both are controlled by state regulations: sex has been reduced to reproductive duty without contact and love, Commanders are forbidden to have contact with Handmaids in private. In Gilead even mere visual contact is severely regulated—Handmaids must not be looked at by men, nor may they look at men themselves. When Offred sees the Commander lurking near her room, she describes the act as a form of violation like "the signals animals give to one another: lowered blue eyelids, ears laid back, raised hackles. A flash of bare teeth, what in hell does he think he's doing?." Handmaids in Gilead have their vision obscured by the white winglike hats they must wear in public, making it "hard to look up, hard to get a full view, of the sky, of anything. But one can do it, a little at a time, a quick move of the head, up and down, to the side and back. We have learned to see the world in gasps." This presentation of the regulation of vision expresses the subjugation of the Handmaids (and their patient subversion, "in gasps"). No one is permitted to look at others freely, especially with desire; the exceptions are those agents of the state, Atwood's version of the thought police, the Eyes, who cruise the streets in the black vans "with the winged eye in white on the side. The windows of the vans are dark-tinted, and the men in the front seats wear dark glasses: a double obscurity."

In these visual motifs the power structure consists of the observer and a vulnerable object of vision. But this power structure is prone to reversal: the weakness of being observed is translated into the power of the controlling observer when Offred deliberately manipulates the Guardians:

> As we walk away I know they're watching, these two men who aren't yet permitted to touch women. They touch with their eyes instead and I move my hips a little, feeling the full red skirt sway around me. It's like thumbing your nose from behind a fence or teasing a dog with a bone held out of reach, and I'm ashamed of myself for doing it, because none of this is the fault of these men, they're too young.
>
> Then I find I'm not ashamed after all. I enjoy the power; power of a dog bone, passive but there. I hope they get hard at the sight of us and have to rub themselves against the painted barriers, surreptitiously. They will suffer, later, at night, in their regimented beds. They have no outlets now except themselves, and that's a sacrilege.

This use of the vision motif emphasizes the ambiguities of the power structure in Gilead and carries the implied author's belief that no matter how rigidly controlled master-slave or agent-object relations are, there will always be a point at which the observer is changed by that which he is trying to observe and control. Atwood thus questions the validity of the simple master-slave dichotomy: who really possesses power? The lover or the object of love? The desiring agent or the desired object? Can these agent-object relations be transcended?

Atwood presents Offred not simply as the object of subjugation but as possessing power herself: the power of the powerless, of the seductive prey. Atwood is continually tempted to endow Offred with the strength appropriate to a heroine, but instead she assigns the spectacular heroism to Moira, who mounts a daring escape from the Red Centre, an act of such dizzying audacity that it frightens Offred and the others, who "were losing the taste for freedom." Offred is not a Moira: when she is tempted to steal something from Serena Joy's living-room, or a "knife, from the kitchen," she admits that "I'm not ready for that." Offred, however, is assigned the kind of consciousness that both appropriates and transcends the power politics of Gilead. The implied author seems to privilege the female existential will, the realm of private consciousness, as an adequate recompense for her enslavement: "My name isn't Offred. I have another name, which nobody uses now because it's forbidden . . . I keep the knowledge of this name like something hidden, some treasure I'll come back to dig up, one day."

In a puritan society privacy is an important condition for retaining identity: the smallest bits of privacy can nurture the self's salvation and protect one's dignity. In Gilead private consciousness is all that is left; it cannot be regulated by the state. Offred may have lost most of the power to control others, to observe and control her world, but she still controls her private thoughts:

> I used to think of my body as an instrument, of pleasure, or a means of transportation, or an implement for the accomplishment of my will. I could use it to run, push buttons, of one sort or another, make things happen. There were limits but my body was nevertheless lithe, single, solid, one with me.
>
> Now the flesh arranges itself differently. I'm a cloud, congealed around a central object, the shape of a pear, which is hard and more real than I am and glows red within its translucent wrapping. Inside it is a space, huge as the sky at night and dark and curved like that, though black-red rather than black.

In this drama of power and powerlessness, Atwood clearly shows that certain types of oppression ensnare the oppressor along with the oppressed—power is always ambiguous. One of the explanations for the peculiarly ambiguous position of the implied author is her commitment to an essentially *romance* novel genre: she cannot help dramatizing horror and rhetoricizing violence, and she cannot help but make her "heroine" into a figure of compelling existential fortitude. This is not a negative judgment of the novel but simply an unveiling of its rhetoric's origins and intentions. Atwood has an ethical imperative, but she also has an rhetorical one—to create a convincing and suspenseful story. It is, of course, paradoxical that without imagining the dystopic situation, a conditional future of male tyranny, the implied author would not have a stage upon which to dramatize Offred's integrity.

I am suggesting that Atwood is experimenting with the deployment of compelling rhetorical form and with the rhetorical attraction of special conflicts. Take away the danger and repressiveness of Gilead—its Eyes, its Guardians, and its hangings—and you no longer have the persuasive climate that justifies Offred's quietly strident discourse:

> Maybe none of this is about control. Maybe it isn't really about who can own whom, who can do what to whom and get away with it, even as far as death. Maybe it isn't about who can sit and

who has to kneel or stand or lie down, legs spread open. Maybe
it's about who can do what to whom and be forgiven for it. Never
tell me it amounts to the same thing.

In *The Handmaid's Tale* we are guided by a cunning implied author, a
voice that feigns weakness in the guise of Offred, her narrative mask; but
this voice cannot help but advertise the control and strength of its origins:
Margaret Atwood. The implied author plays a narrator who subjects her
audience to a terrible nightmare in which she is the heroine. At one point
she asks our forgiveness: "I'm sorry there is so much pain in this story. I'm
sorry it's in fragments . . . Because I'm telling you this story I will your
existence. I tell, therefore you are." But even this request is followed by a
move that makes us conscious of the writer's power, for though this reader
has participated and intervened in the critical reconstruction of this story,
responsibility for its pain and power is shared with the rhetorical will of the
author.

HILDE STAELS

# Margaret Atwood's The Handmaid's Tale: Resistance through Narrating

In the futuristic novel *The Handmaid's Tale* the Canadian novelist Margaret Atwood presents a dystopian vision of a world in which the American neo-conservatives and the New Christian Right or New Puritans of the 1980s have seized power in a totalitarian theocratic republic named after the biblical land of Gilead. Like the New England Puritans of the seventeenth century, the rulers of Gilead establish a theocratic state in the area surrounding the city of Boston, Massachusetts, in the year 2000. The rulers of Gilead return to the Old Testament in a reaction against abortion, sterilization and what they consider to be dangerous kinds of freedom of the modern welfare state.

The ideal which Gilead's 'Sons Of Jacob Think Tank' devised is an imitation of the biblical land of Jacob and Laban, where Jacob restored hope and fertility with the help of a few Handmaids. Thus the regime uses Commanders who subject Handmaids to a monthly penetration in order to solve the problem of excessive and deliberate infertility in the past. The protagonist Offred, who is the Handmaid-slave of the Commander Fred and his infertile wife Serena Joy, is supposed to enact the biblical story of Rachel and Bilhah: 'Give me children, or else I die. Am I in God's stead, who hath withheld from thee the fruit of the womb? Behold my maid Bilhah. She shall bear upon my knees, that I may also have children by her' (*Genesis*, 30).

From *English Studies* 76, no. 5 (September 1995). © 1995 by Swets & Zeitlinger.

Margaret Atwood looks at the patriarchal biblical history from the perspective of its female 'victims.' All the women in Gilead are made to play subsidiary parts, the wives of Commanders included, as well as the elderly infertile women, the Aunts, who save their skins by collaborating and who train the Handmaids in self-suppression.

Gilead's victims can find refuge only in a secret Female Underground Road that leads from New England to Canada. Atwood here alludes to the escape route or the Underground Railroad by means of which the runaway slaves of the American South used to enter British-controlled Canada where slavery had been abolished in 1841. Historically, the underground is also a hiding place in the margin of society from which subversives attempt to disrupt the power of the regime above ground.

In my discussion of *The Handmaid's Tale*, I am particularly interested in recurring discursive forms, in the manner in which the first-person narrator delivers the story-material, and in the composition of the narrative text. For the investigation of the personal voice of the narrator, I use Roger Fowler's notion of 'mind-style.' Fowler was the first to introduce the concept into literary theory at the end of the 1970s. In *Linguistics and the Novel*, he defines mind-style as: 'the systems of beliefs, values and categories by reference to which a person comprehends the world.' In *Linguistic Criticism*, he gives the following definition:

> Cumulative ideational structuring depends on regular and consistent linguistic choices which build up a continuous, pervasive, representation of the world. This is the major source of point of view in fiction [. . .] Discussing this phenomenon in literary fictions, I have called it *mind-style*: the world view of an author, or a narrator, or a character, constituted by the ideational structure of the text. [. . .] I shall illustrate ideational structuring involving three different types of linguistic feature: *vocabulary*, *transitivity*, and certain *syntactic structures*.

Mind-style is a formal feature of the narrative text that serves the author's technique of indirect characterization. The study of mind-style combines stylistics and narratology, linguistics and literary theory. Mind-style analysis involves a scrutiny of consistent linguistic choices with which the narrator puts ideas or experience into words. I shall give special consideration to lexical forms and syntactic patterns, but also to the metaphors that convey the first-person narrator's conscious and unconscious mental operations.

I shall focus on two types of discourse used by the narrative voice, the discursive law of the theocracy and the narrator's personal, aesthetic discourse with which she counters the authoritarian speech of Gilead. For the description and interpretation of these types of discourse, I rely on some concepts used by the French semiotician Julia Kristeva. In her theory of literary discourse, Kristeva distinguishes between a codified or dominant discourse and another discourse that transgresses the boundaries of dominant sign systems: 'The poetic word, polyvalent and multi-determined, adheres to a logic exceeding that of codified discourse and fully comes into being only in the margins of recognized culture. Bakhtin was the first to study this logic, and he looked for its roots in carnival.' According to Kristeva, poetic discourse escapes the linguistic, psychic and social prohibitions of systematizing discourse. In poetic language, heterogeneity manifests itself, for instance, in non-calculable musical effects. Kristeva emphasizes that poetic discourse renovates language: it breaks through governing laws and ideologies and generates new meanings. It embodies a process between sense and non-sense, or that which does not yet signify, a rupturing of 'normal' communication rules or grammatical rules through rhythm. It is my contention that poetic language has a similar function in *The Handmaid's Tale*, as well as in Atwood's other novels.

The discussion of the narrator's mind-style is followed by an investigation of verbal forms used by the Cambridge dons in the epilogue to *The Handmaid's Tale*, entitled 'Historical Notes.' I am particularly interested in the historians' ironic repetition of Gileadean discourse. I would like to demonstrate that a critical evaluation of the scholarly discourse underlies the design of the text. The mind-style of the historians is judged or evaluated by the 'implied author.' Roger Fowler, among others, defines the implied author as follows: 'the design of a text situates the writer, and thus his reader, in a certain location relative to his represented content—the structure of the text contributes to the definition of its author.'

## 1.    Witnessing the Closed Morality of an Absolutist State

In *The Handmaid's Tale*, Offred retrospectively witnesses her personal victimization as a Handmaid in Gilead's theocracy. The totalitarian regime forces the inhabitants to submit to the power of one (moral) law, one true religion, one language code. Gilead's Newspeak makes all other modes of thought impossible. The new regime legitimizes its own meaning system and demands an unconditional allegiance to it. Where meaning is singular and final, ambiguity of meaning and variety of experience are excluded. People are indoctrinated into so-called traditional values that are expressed in terms of universal truths, maxims or slogans. In a society that functionalizes language to the extreme, the potential polysemy of discourse is replaced by absolutely homogeneous, univocal signs.

Though modernity is judged to have been a threatening force, the rulers highly esteem the values of logocentrism and materialism that typify the capitalist spirit. Everything is coded, measured and regulated to an economic value. All human qualities are instrumentalized, and reduced to quantitative values of exchange. In other words, the new rulers equate the value of something and someone solely with validity, usefulness, functionality, economic profit.

Everything and everyone is substantified. People's identity is supposed to coalesce with the coded concepts and the predicated state by which they are defined. Handmaids are supposed to merely think of themselves 'as seeds,' as objects with a procreative function that should save the world from the threat of sterility, as 'two-legged wombs, that's all: sacred vessels, ambulatory chalices.' The 'deadly' regime paradoxically aims at creating new life.

The governing discourse of the absolutist state is an artificial, so-called Biblical speech. In the theocracy, a metaphysics of truth reigns that conveys the full presence of meaning in what is said to be the Word of God. The rulers have the power over the use and abuse of language whereas lesser human beings are granted the freedom neither to see nor to speak personally, in their own name. Handmaids, who must neither see, nor be seen as individuals, are therefore freed from self-reflection and self-affirmation. Freedom from too much knowledge and from choice are said to be the privilege of the meek. Mirrors are practically absent, because freedom from self-reflection saves one from the traditional search for identity. The ideal is freedom from the constitution of an identity and from the struggle for self-definition. It is part of Gilead's double-think to disguise as privilege people's mindless, wordless condition.

Handmaids are allowed to see only the flat surfaces of the present, i.e. a wall of rules and regulations. The eyes of Handmaids are not allowed to move beyond the prescribed edges. Gilead excludes all agency functions of the colonized individuals: 'The active, is it a tense?' Offred wonders. Whereas Offred remembers the 1980s as the time when one could freely communicate and 'squander' words, Gilead excludes all exchange of personal speech. In a society where social interaction is excessively mechanized and people are reduced to passive recipients of the law, the constitution of subjectivity through interaction between human beings has become obsolete.

As there is no room for a shifting of boundaries, any aesthetic, creative use of language is necessarily outlawed. A bureaucratic rationality that is completely dehumanized censors all dangerous personal, irrational and emotional elements that escape calculation. The ideal is the absolutely unified individual, whose inner life is gradually stultified and in the end totally and finally conditioned by Gilead's law. Thus Offred is supposed to be a soulless object: 'My self is a thing [. . .] a made thing, not something born,' she says. She feels she is no-body in particular, a depersonalized 'it.' Gileadean logic mutes the flesh and numbs the blood. It mortifies the site of unconscious, 'irrational' feelings and desires; the site of heterogeneous elements. Offred says: 'That is how I feel: white, flat, thin. I feel transparent' or 'I too am disembodied.'

The indoctrination sessions supervised by Aunts aim at excluding nostalgia for the past or a yearning for the future. Memories of the past, together with personal desires, are supposed to fade away. Whatever unconscious irrational or emotional forces may remain, in the form of aggression and frustration against the regime, they are drained off, or are guided into collective ritual events. Rituals, ceremonies or clock time dominate in the theocracy to keep the oppressed away form social disruption.

In Gilead, hands and feet are pronounced non-essential tools: 'Remember, said Aunt Lydia. For our purposes your feet and your hands are not essential'; 'I feel as if somebody cut off my feet,' says Offred. With gloved, folded hands and encased feet, the Handmaid's body signals its dismembered condition. In the theocracy, the heart is supposed to be no more than a mechanical clock that counts time. The metaphor of cancelled hearts, hands and feet connotes uprootedness, or a soulless existence.

Ironically, the biblical land of 'healing balm,' appears in the new context as a waste land, a desolate area, whose inhabitants are spiritually and emotionally deadened. It is an 'unreal' place that resembles an infernal circle, a labyrinth without exit, the trails are dead-ends. Natural colours are 'a sickly yellow,' white, grey, dim or fading. With nature put to sleep, the womb of the earth is a tomb, or a place where absolute stillness reigns. The lifeless heart or centre of Gilead is a metaphor for the numbed hearts or souls of its inhabitants. The air communicates the reign of violent suppression, inertia, boredom, total stagnation, infertility. In this context, the instrumentalized wombs of Handmaids mainly produce stillbirths.

## 2.   A Tale of Silenced Voices

Offred's place of narration is an Underground Female Road that is associated with images of 'the dark realm within,' 'some other place,' a 'cellar,' an 'attic hiding place,' an 'obscure matrix.' Metaphorically, the underground is the space in the margin of law and order from which the creative artist ideally expresses her own voice. The dark subterranean realm from which Offred witnesses events of the past is penetrated by light. The image of light associates the tale with the imaginative activity of the mind. 'I step up, into the darkness within; or else the light,' says the retrospective narrator, who remembers the moment before she found a refuge in the 'Underground Female Road.'

By bringing into prominence a Handmaid's personal, aesthetic discourse spoken in the margin of a fundamentalist regime, the eye-witness account is both a report of and a challenge of the meaning system established by the rulers of the theocracy. Offred's tale is the personal expression of insights that move beyond the historical facts of Gilead, beyond the frontiers of Gilead's meaning system and, finally, beyond the identity of Handmaid-slave that the colonizing power imposed on her.

From the point of view of Gilead, personal discourse is disallowed, because it is considered too dangerous. However, among the colonized individuals, the total suppression of personal desire and personal speech causes an irrepressible yearning for gratification. In the margin of society, Offred articulates her muted insights and sacrificed feelings, and she evokes absent objects and meanings. Her individual speech produces a profusion of words and desires that are not allowed. Offred crosses the boundaries of accepted meaning by giving voice to an alternative perspective and an alternative discourse that continuously cut through the rigid logocentric texture of the superstructure.

By giving expression to her inner feelings and bodily sensations from her situation on the periphery of society, Offred breaks through the discursive Law of the theocracy. Gilead censors the threatening force of creative self-expression. Yet Offred defies the strict rules of authoritative discourse by giving life to a silenced discourse. She revives the capacity for individual spiritual and emotional life. In the margin, she speaks in her own name, the name that she was supposed to forget once and for all: 'I keep the knowledge of this name like something hidden, some treasure I'll come back to dig up, one day. I think of this name as buried.' In Gilead, Offred used to silently repeat her hidden name (June) to maintain her existence: 'I want to be more than valuable. I repeat my former name, remind myself of what I once could do, how others saw me.' By recalling her former name, June regenerates her creative energy. She is the grammatical subject and narrative agent of the tale, whereas Gilead reduced her position to that of (grammatical) object and patient.

In Gilead, where Offred is forced to lead a paralysed existence, she suffers from an almost uncontrollable physical desire to take in the smell of organic life—of earth, flowers and warm wet grass—that silently breaks through the hardened surface. She desires to feel alive and become united with the buried voice or life-cycle of the earth, in defiance of the power which the regime exercises over her. The narrator-witness reconstructs the will of the protagonist to survive, to liberate herself from the trap of 'here and now.'

The protagonist yearns spiritually and emotionally for a crossing of spatio-temporal boundaries. Offred wants to absorb the smell of objects that bring back to mind the context of the past. The connection with these memories, though it is a painful recollection, is necessary to her survival. She longs to move down, into and through the linear subdivisions on the surface of the petrified city. She desires to give expression to repressed corporeal and affective processes by opening up her hands and feel the blood flow again through the cancelled hands, feet and heart. She gives voice to a want, to a personal desire for touch and for being touched. Against the reign of economic exchange value between commercially valid objects, she posits a desire to create a contiguous, free-flowing relationship with the elements and with other human beings. Remembering what she felt while standing close to the Commander's servant Nick, she says: 'Whether it is or not we are touching, two shapes of leather. I feel my shoe soften, blood flows into it, it grows warm, it becomes a skin.'

The loving gestures contradict the reign of folded, gloved, coldly artificial hands. Offred wishes to regenerate subjectivity and undo frozen dichotomies in the object world. She wishes to resuscitate the life of the soul or the heart. She relates spatially and semantically polarized animate and inanimate objects in both/and relationships. From her own world of desire and in her own voice, everything becomes animated: 'Even the bricks of the house are softening, becoming tactile; if I leaned against them they'd be warm and yielding. It's amazing what denial can do.'

With her outstretched bare open hands, Offred communicates with the hidden organic, biological rhythm of nature that resurrects concealed corporeal and affective processes. She revives the exchange with ex-centric space in opposition to the sheer exchange between consumer objects in the centralized regime. Adverbials 'in,' 'into,' 'across,' 'out,' 'up' and 'through' point to the crossing of limits. The desire for warmth, fluidity, light and life ruptures the reign of cold, dead abstraction and violence.

The absolutist regime wants to abolish the past. Yet Offred re-enacts the past in the present. Her memory of the past brings back to life the excluded pole in Gilead, such as the existence of love and humanity, Offred's act of retracing the lost connection with her roots in the process of life is a desire to escape from the trap of paralysis and defeatism. It is an act of survival that saves her from despair and that resurrects the missing part of herself. 'I want to be with someone,' says Offred, who desires to be 'someone' who calls 'someone' into existence where subjectivity is pronounced obsolete. By activating her silenced inner body, she asserts her will to be visible.

The singularity of Offred's speech frees words from Gilead's communicative constraints of language, from denotative speech and from the sign as merely an element of commercial transaction. The narrator's poetic discourse resists the reduction of reality to coded concepts and of individuals to reified objects. In a society that censors aesthetic speech, Offred's poetic discourse reactivates the lost potential of language and the conditions for the production of meaning. She revitalizes an otherwise extinct language and inner life, deadened by the supremacy of codes. She resists Gilead's transparent, quantifiable products of meaning by creating heterogeneity.

Traces of unconscious processes are visible in the narrator's free flow of similes. She describes the posture of the Handmaid Ofglen as follows: 'Without a word she swivels, as if she's voice-activated, as if she's on little oiled wheels, as if she's on top of a music box. I resent this grace of hers. I resent her meek head, bowed as if into a heavy wind.' Consider also Offred's description of the dead bodies of 'subversives' that hang on the wall surrounding Gilead: 'The three bodies hang there, even with the white sacks over their heads looking curiously stretched, like chickens strung up by the necks in a meatshop window; like birds with their wings clipped, like flightless birds, wrecked angels.' Whereas the theocracy wants the gap between the word and its meaning to be filled, and the relationship paralysed, Offred compulsively opens up the gap by using an exuberant flow of similes.

Offred creates a contiguity between spatio-temporally and semantically discontinuous objects by an abundant use of metonymical speech and synaesthesia, as in: 'my hands; they fill with flowers of light'; 'Time as white sound'; 'a thin sound like the hum of an insect; then nearing, opening out, like a flower of sound opening, into a trumpet.' Compare also: 'Aunt Lydia pressed her hand over her mouth of a dead rodent' and '[Janine's] transparent voice, her voice of raw egg white.' The rhythmic features of her mind-style appear not only in semantic, but also in phonetic associations, as in: 'Sun comes through the fanlight, falling in colors across the floor: red and blue, purple, I step into it briefly, stretch out my hands; they fill with flowers of light.'

Offred sets against the impersonal, denotative scrabble game that she is made to play with the Commander, a personal connotative discourse that ideally unites the word and the flesh, that attempts to bridge the gap between language and feelings: 'I feel like the word *shatter*'; 'the [bullet] hole [. . .] the one flash, of darkness or pain, dull I hope, like the word *thud*, only the one and then silence.'

Offred connects the concrete and the abstract; remembered objects, impressions and sensations of the past (censored events) and events in the present; the visible (the 'true' and 'real') and the invisible (declared 'unreal' and 'irrational'); conscious and unconscious events. She awakens a sense of things that she has never experienced before. The narrator opens tunnels inside herself that lead towards the unrecorded. As a protagonist, the danger of silently creating relations that are based on fantasy fills her with both pleasure and pain: 'In a minute the wreath will start to color and I will begin seeing things [. . .] things at the sides of your eyes: purple animals, in the bushes beside the road, the vague outlines of men, which would disappear when you looked at them straight.'

Whereas Aunt Lydia warns the handmaids against the word *Love*: 'Don't let me catch you at it. No mooning and June-ing around here, girls,' June offers an alternative to the mechanized petrification by calling back to mind the power of ancient fertility (moon) goddesses. Offred remembers there once were primitive matriarchal societies that conceived of a goddess as the main element in the formation of the universe. The power of the Great Goddess, the Virgin-Mother who is renewed every month as moon-goddess, or once a year as earth-goddess, fills her with hope for renewal of life. The gift of creative life force which the Goddess offers counteracts the reduction of fertility to a functionalized procreative act. Thus Offred awakens an ancestral memory, a traditional world of culture and value. The Great Goddess is a recurring metaphor in Atwood's novels. She is the origin of life that can be reached only through death. The ancestral mother or Nature Goddess manifests herself in the novels as both a tomb and a womb. Through re-established contact with the Goddess, the protagonist retrieves the willpower to receive and to give new life.

Offred wants to make the 'unreal,' the 'irrational' and invisible happen, and make real fantasies of restored contact with the Great Goddess and creative energy. We read 'in the obscured sky a moon does float, newly, a wishing moon, a sliver of ancient rock, a goddess, a wink' and 'at the edges of my eyes there are movements, in the branches; feathers, flittings, grace notes, tree into bird, metamorphosis run wild. Goddesses are possible now and the air suffuses with desire.' Above ground, the air communicates a smell that emerges from the womb of the earth, from the dark matrix that hides the power of the (moon) Goddess of fecundity. Sensations of warmth and life force (water) fill the air, because they know no boundaries: 'It's started to rain, a drizzle, and the gravid smell of earth and grass fills the air.'

Offred, who creates an outpouring of words, the rhythm of which is a symptom of her oppressed inner life, notices how, in a similar vein, suppressed but inviolable natural space symptomatically disrupts the logocentric superstructure. From Offred's point of view, the garden of the Commander's wife Serena Joy communicates the invincible power of buried life energy. Offred says: 'There is something subversive about this garden of Serena's, a sense of buried things bursting upwards, wordlessly, into the light, as if to point, to say: What-ever is silenced will clamor to be heard, though silently.' She associates breaks in the social structure with symptoms of silent rebellion of the oppressed.

The narrator recurrently uses the image of an egg, an object that seems to be no more than white and granular on the outside. The egg is an image for the barren surface of Gilead and for the condition of the protagonist's outer body, which are 'defined by the sunlight' or by the logocentrism of the rulers. Yet the egg glows red from the inside. Underground, a red, hot pulsing process of life is hidden. Red is the colour of organic, free-flowing blood that reveals the existence of life energy: 'the life of the moon may not be on the surface, but inside,' Offred says.

Against the prescribed mono-tone voice, the narrator creates a personal, multivocal tale; 'this sad and hungry and sordid, this limping and mutilated story.' A range of feelings and responses calls into existence a vulnerable breathing subject. The voice shifts from hatred to resentment, despair, outrage, mockery, from nostalgia for the past to compassion for fellow-victims. Sometimes, Offred gives voice to hope and belief in new life: 'It's this message, which may never arrive, that keeps me alive. I believe in the message'; 'Out there or inside my head, it's an equal darkness. Or light.' Spiritual and emotional revival resides in hope for change and belief in love and vitality that will defeat the reign of stasis: 'hope is rising in me, like sap in a tree. Blood in a wound. We have made an opening.' Offred moves back through layers of history, opens the wounds and retraces the loss. Pain is still possible because of memory, and memory is what the narrator tries to keep alive. The destruction of memory, which Gilead aims at, involves a numbing of the site of personal desire and creative energy.

Offred's tale moves, emotionally, as well as rhythmically, in contrast with the deathly stillness that reigns above ground. In *The Handmaid's Tale*, the most striking traces of what Kristeva calls the 'semiotic' are rhythm and sound in poetic discourse. The rhythm of the text is symptomatic of traumatic events, and of excluded experiences. *The Handmaid's Tale* transforms or shifts the boundaries of the conventional dystopic genre. This defamiliarization of the traditional dystopia is an effect of the narrator's inner journey that results in the subject's creation of an alternative word and world to the everyday object world. Though the personal voice and perception (mind-style) of a female protagonist are at the centre of the tale, the language spoken from within the margin is not necessarily 'a woman's language,' but the discourse of a socially marginalized individual.

### 3.    The *Historical Notes*: Irony in Retrospect

On the twenty-fifth of June in the year 2195, academics organize a Symposium about the history of Gilead at the University of Denay, Nunavit. The names 'Denay' and 'Nunavit' allude to the first Canadians, the native Eskimos and Indians, victims of a politics of colonization. The Indians prefer to be called 'Dene' and the Eskimos 'Inuit.' Both words mean 'the people.' 'Nunavut,' the Northwest Territories (between Alaska and Greenland) is land claimed by the Eskimos in Canada. Yet Atwood alludes to the Canadian government which even today opposes the demands for autonomy. It also allows the territory of the Innu, who are a nomadic people, to be invaded by military exercises with airplanes that threaten animals and human beings by flying at low level (100 ft. only). The words 'Denay' and 'Nunavit' may also be Atwood's pun on 'deny none of it,' which both applies to the victimization of the native Eskimos and Indians and to the colonization of the inhabitants of Gilead.

At the Symposium, two Cambridge dons, Professor Wade and Professor Pieixoto, are proud of having discovered some thirty fragments of a tale which they have subsequently transcribed. They have entitled the anonymous narrative *The Handmaid's Tale*. Offred's tale turns out to be an oral account and taped narrative that was excavated after having remained buried for about a century.

A spoken text is transcribed, which implies that the tonal voice is deleted (a voice that adds meaning to discourse) and the discourse further hardened. The hardening further removes the meaning of the speaker from the meaning of her discourse. Even though in the taped text Offred insists that neither the truth nor the exact context of her experience can be retraced, let alone pinpointed, the historians attempt to reconstruct the reality about Gilead. Whereas the tale claims neither to be a factual document, nor simply a report and eye-witness account, the historians nevertheless try to figure out what really happened. The joint paper of the scientists, 'Problems of Authentication in Reference to The Handmaid's Tale,' indicates they are in search of closed interpretations. The narrator, however, repeatedly emphasizes that her tale is a reconstruction, an invention which necessarily involves the loss of the original story. At times, Offred explicitly states that she attempts to remember stories that went on inside her head while she was living above ground. The tale can never be an authentic account of lived experience or a mimetic representation of reality.

Offred asserts that the act of telling covers up the horror of reality, because lived experience is unnamable and irretrievable. Yet positivism pushes to the margins of experience what it cannot explain and control: the irrational and emotional elements that emerge from an 'obscure matrix.' The self-satisfied Pieixoto and Wade trivialize the expressions of pain to 'a whiff of emotion.' They exclude from their horizon of perception the act of telling as a re-articulation of reality, as an effort to give expression to inner sensations, or hope and faith in change. They aim at a reconstruction of the historical facts of a patriarchal history. They express more concern for the historical author of the tale and for the position assigned to her above ground, rather than for the unique narrating voice of 'someone' who speaks from within the periphery, and who draws strength from her marginalized position.

Proud of their own 'Enlightened days,' the academics announce the return to, or the continuation of, a supreme rationalism that typifies Gilead. The connection between the mind-style of the narrator and the context is utterly misunderstood by the academics in their own context. They fail to consider the narrator as generator of meaning in their search for 'objective' truth. By endowing the non-measurable aspects of the narrative with a sheer decorative value, the academics merely create another subjectivity in relation to the same history. By ignoring the narrator's attempt to witness to the unspeakable horror, the academics also negate the work of art as a moral instrument. June, who wants her own voice to be heard and her inner life to be visible, is muted once again. In her relationship to the future listeners, the story-teller has failed to be rehabilitated as 'someone' who speaks to 'someone,' for the male researchers turn a deaf ear to her personal voice. Offred fails to achieve her wished-for creative interaction between the 'I' who speaks and the 'you' who responds, as in: 'By telling you anything at all I'm at least believing in you, I believe you're there, I believe you into being. Because I'm telling you this story I will your existence. I tell, therefore you are.' In the academic world, 'June' means nothing more than the month during which the Symposium takes place.

The mind-style with which the academics approach Offred's narrative is characterized by sheer logical reasoning. The scholars attempt to track down clues, proof, evidence that should lead to definitive knowledge about the original identity of the narrator; of the Commander (Waterford?); the place of narration; the original meaning of the tale and the whole context of Gilead. They are interested in as many measurable facts as possible. They are concerned with deciphering the tale precisely 'in the clearer light of our own day.' This statement recalls the supremacy of 'the defining sunlight' or logocentricism in Gilead that fixes the position of everyone and everything. It is no accident then that the Commander Fred calls himself 'a sort of scientist.' The academics investigate the tale so as to establish its stable meaning and to pinpoint cause and effect relationships: 'Supposing, then, the tapes to be genuine [. . .] If we could establish an identity for the narrator [. . .] to identify the inhabitants [. . .] to trace and locate the descendants [. . .] this trail led nowhere [. . .] we pursued a second line of attack'; 'whatever the causes, the effects were noticeable [. . .] her original name [. . .] Offred gives no clue.'

'Many gaps remain,' says Pieixoto, who would love to see the gaps between the words and lived experience filled and the narrative ended. He would like to undo the ambiguities and indeterminacies and establish an original, transparent meaning instead. He ignores the narrator who emphasizes the necessity to maintain the gaps between the words and reality, and to be well aware of the existence of unrecorded experience.

The desire of the scholars for univocal, transparent meaning ironically mirrors the authoritative word of Gilead. The logocentric, categorizing mental structures or speech types are analogous to the logocentrism that underlies the tyranny of the Gilead regime. The desire for a metaphysics of truth is equivalent to Gilead's dogmatism and its illusions of stable, given meaning. The academic scientists similarly exclude polyvalence and ambiguity in favour of essential meaning.

In the manner of Gilead, the scientists push into the margin the subject's creative individual utterances, the connotative speech of the (female) subject. They (consciously) overlook the narrator's self-expression and self-affirmation, the rhythmic pulsations, intuitions, the creative power that underlies her poetic speech. Even though the researchers compare Offred to Eurydice, the Creation-death goddess whose voice emerges from a far distance, Eurydice escapes as soon as they try to 'grasp' her, that is, understand and control her by looking at her from their own rational perspective. Her voice remains enigmatic and returns to the womb of the earth, where it lies buried. The personal voice is lost to those who do not wish to acknowledge its existence, or who fear to listen. They simply neglect the tale as a work of art, namely Offred's restructuring of the order of language and her re-visioning of reality. As a result, the historical listener radically fails to coincide with the implied, ideal listener.

The scholars ignore Offred's conscious effort to call the lost, loved ones back into existence. They do not try to comprehend the articulation of her inner world as a deliberate attempt at survival. Instead, they approach the text in a utilitarian way. From their perspective, more historical data and exhaustive material facts about Gilead would have made the tale a commercially interesting exchange object. Because the document does not provide the complete picture of Gilead, and has too many 'obscure' passages, it fails as a commodity. The restitution of the whole context and of the meaning of the theocratic model would have been more valuable than the evanescent personal utterances, the woman's expression of hidden feelings and desires that is a wasted effort in economic terms: 'What would we not give, now, for twenty pages or so of printout from Waterford's private computer! However, we must be grateful for any crumbs the Goddess of History has deigned to vouchsafe us.'

The nightmare that underlies the Symposium has to do with the negation of Offred's tale as a timeless account, for the scholars trivialize the horror of which she speaks by simply regarding it as a moment in history, rather than comprehending it as a warning against the reification of a mental construct that may return at any time in history, in any form. Furthermore, the academics marginalize the narrator's personal mind-style, especially the pain, the hope and the belief in new life, the alternative world and word. Consequently, the novel affirms the survival of darkness, though the age is said to be enlightened. Darkness survives as well in the refusal of male intellectuals, of those who establish a literary canon, to acknowledge the value of a woman's perspective on patriarchal history.

I hope to have shown that mind-style analysis throws an interesting light on the complex psychological and ideological stance of Atwood's protagonists. In addition, readers of Atwood's novels need to pay careful attention to the ironic mirroring of discursive forms, as it is a typical formal feature of her novelistic practice. In her fiction, Atwood uses this technique to critically evaluate or judge a particular perception of reality. The evaluation underlies the compositional structure of the narrative text. It is up to the reader to disclose the design of the text as the hidden signifier.

Some readers apparently fail to do so. In her review of *The Handmaid's Tale*, the American author Mary McCarthy attacks Atwood for her failure to create a 'true' dystopia: 'the most conspicuous lack, in comparison with the classics of the fearsome-future genre, is the inability to imagine a language to match the changed face of common life. No newspeak. [. . .] This is a serious defect, unpardonable maybe for the genre: a future that has no language invented for it lacks a personality. That must be why, collectively, it is powerless to scare.'

I consider such criticism to be unjust, for the literal application of biblical texts, the anachronistic use of scriptural phrases, and other such devices that aim at making other modes of thought impossible, are functionally analogous to Orwell's Newspeak. Moreover, not only is it highly questionable that Newspeak is a necessary ingredient of the dystopic genre, but McCarthy's criticism of Atwood's novel also seems to stem from the reviewer's neglect of the context or ex-centric spatial position from which the tale is narrated. It is my contention that by 'designing' the text in such a manner, Atwood precisely aims at shifting the boundaries of the conventional dystopic genre.

KAREN STEIN

# Margaret Atwood's Modest Proposal: The Handmaid's Tale

Margaret Atwood begins her novel *The Handmaid's Tale* with two dedications and three epigraphs: a passage from *Genesis*, a passage from Jonathan Swift's "Modest Proposal," and a Sufi proverb. This abundance of preliminary matter establishes a frame through which we read the novel, just as a frame around a painting tells us to read the enclosed space in a certain way, as an art object, an object re-presented in a way that calls attention to its special relationship to surrounding objects. We look through—not at—the frame, but its presence has already categorized the object within and structured the way we will view it. Similarly, Atwood's interpolated texts set up a frame that asks us to read the rest of the book in a particular way.

To frame means, among other things, to utter or articulate, to fit or adjust to something, to enclose, to shape or fashion, to invent or imagine, to plan or contrive, to devise falsely (to frame up); all of these meanings resonate in *Tale*. In Gilead, women have been framed. Framed by their red robes and wide wimples, the handmaids are clearly visible, marked and delimited by their social status. For the wearer within the frame, the wimples serve as blinders; to look *through* them is to see only straight ahead, a narrowed view of the world. For us as readers, to look at the wimples is to read the authoritarian practice of Gilead which attempts to control women, and to permit only one view of reality. By decoding Atwood's framing texts,

From *Canadian Literature* 148 (Spring 1996): 57–71. © 1996 by the University of British Columbia, Vancouver.

we can read the frame itself as well as reading through it. Such a reading may in fact expand our view, for it adds layers of inference and possibility. Many critics have discussed one of the framing texts, the Historical Notes section at the end. Indeed, this topic is the focal point of articles by Arnold E. Davidson and Patrick D. Murphy. Davidson considers the political implications of the Notes, while Murphy examines this section of the novel as a structural device. For other analyses of the Historical Notes, see, for example, Deer, Lacombe, LeBihan, Rubenstein, Stein, Tomc. Thus, while this section has received substantial attention, few critics have spoken about the prefatory material. Lucy M. Freibert addresses the dedication and all of the epigraphs, although she speaks in detail only about the material from *Genesis*. She remarks that the epigraph from Swift prepares us for political satire. Nancy V. Workman analyzes the Sufi proverb and its meanings for the novel. She mentions the Swift epigraph in passing, notes that it is "readily understood" and relates Swift's exaggerated satire to Atwood's exaggerated satire of American Puritanism and the Moral Majority. Linda Wagner-Martin discusses the novel's dedications briefly. Sandra Tomc explores in greater depth some of the ironic implications of the dedications. I will consider all of the prefatory framing matter here, and focus in particular on the Swift epigraph. I shall argue that this epigraph serves larger thematic and stylistic purposes in Atwood's novel. By examining these initial framing devices, I hope to ask useful questions about the narrative voice and to extend our readings of the novel.

Before considering the preliminary framing matter which will be our central concern here, it will be useful to sketch out the workings of the book's "Historical Notes," the concluding frame. This chapter, a report of an academic conference about Gilead held at the University of Denay, Nunavit ("deny none of it"), serves many functions. For one, the academic discourse satirizes academic pretension. More seriously, through its sexism and moral relativism it establishes ideological parallels between the dystopias of Gilead and the post-Gileadean society. Rhetorically, the speaker at the conference, Professor James Darcy Pieixoto, continues the process of ironic layering of texts which the multiple epigraphs have initiated. Pieixoto has in fact assembled Offred's story, rearranging and transferring her audiotaped oral narrative into the written text that is the eponymous story. Thus, through his editorial acts, and now, in the novel's narrative present, through his conference presentation, Pieixoto provides another narrative voice, another layer of interpretation to frame the handmaid's narrative. His narrative includes information about Offred's escape from Gilead and her recording of the story which, puzzlingly, she does not provide. Moreover, in bracketing her tale, his text reiterates the tension between Offred's words and patriarchal control of her story which forms the crux of her tale. We shall have more to say later about the ways in which Pieixoto misreads Offred's tale.

Additionally, the "Historical Notes" section furthers the satirical purpose of the novel. In describing the function of this frame, Patrick Murphy explains it as a device to solve a problem facing writers of dystopian speculative fiction: if the dystopian world is too far removed from ours, our reading may lead to "cathartic reduction of anxiety" with no impulse to act in our own world. The reader who is too comfortable may read for escape or to "reinforce smug assumptions." To reduce this distance, and induce a "discomforting" reading, the author employs a framing device "intended to reduce the distance between tenor [relations in the empirical universe] and vehicle [relations in the fictional universe] and thereby further the fundamental purpose of this SF subgenre: to prompt readers to change the world." Murphy notes that while it has "historical precedents in the 'discovered manuscript' device used by Swift . . . and others, pseudo-documentary framing" is a more appropriate strategy for contemporary readers because it is closely related to "journalistic and academic writing conventions. . . [influenced by] 'new journalism' and the popularity of the 'non-fiction novel'." To Murphy's categorization of *Tale* as dystopian science fiction, I would append, as others have suggested, the label of satire (and also, the labels of journal, epistolary novel, romance, palimpsest). Satire, like dystopian science fiction, is a genre which addresses its exaggerated version of present evils to readers who have some power to act and, by this means, hopes to bring about social and political change. Offred's original text, recorded on audiotape, is presumably intended to inform a larger audience about Gilead and thus to serve the same purpose of bringing about action to extirpate the horrors of the dystopia.

This dystopian-science fiction-satirical-journal-epistolary-romance-palimpsest text then, this *Tale*, is the story of a rather ordinary, educated, middle-class woman who is framed by, but (presumably) escapes from, a dystopian misogynist society. How appropriate to frame (bracket) her story with a dedication to Atwood's ancestor, Mary Webster, who escaped hanging as a witch at the hands of the dystopian misogynistic Puritan Massachusetts. Because the rope broke and the law of double jeopardy saved her from being tried again, Webster escaped from death and subsequently moved to Nova Scotia, a more liberal society. Counterpoised to Webster, the novel's other dedicatee is Perry Miller, an American scholar of Puritanism (a teacher of Atwood's when she was at Harvard). Sandra Tomc demonstrates that the juxtaposed dedications posit the ironic relations between scholars and the texts they (mis)read, between the events of history and the historians who (mis)interpret them. In explicating and valorizing the texts they interpret, both Pieixoto and Miller ignore the deeply misogynist strain of Gileadean and Puritan cultures. Pieixoto urges the conference audience to suspend moral judgment in studying Gilead; Miller was in the vanguard of American scholarship that celebrated the Puritan vision as quintessentially American. Observing that the ironic pairing of Webster and Miller at the start parallels the pairing of the handmaid Offred and Professor Pieixoto at the end, Tomc notes "the issue in both cases is the failure of the female object of study to fit the patterns of inquiry set out by her male scrutinizer." Moreover, because they do not fit these "patterns of inquiry," Offred and Mary Webster are able to escape from the traditional plots scripted for (or rather against) women, and thereby to elude not only the scholars who study them, but also the rigidly punitive societies that seek to destroy them.

Like the dedications, the epigraphs chosen as framing texts are drawn from the domains of history, literary history and religion, thus pointing to a wide scope of issues, to a seriousness of purpose and, also, to the persistence over time of the problems the novel will raise. These preliminary interpolated texts signal the reader that several discourses will be juxtaposed; several layers of meaning and language will be superimposed upon each other, and played against each other to produce ironic effects.

Because irony is a chief feature of the novel, and one of the components of satire, a brief discussion of its purposes is in order. A useful place to begin our understanding of irony is Linda Hutcheon's discussion. Describing the complex, multifaceted uses of irony, Hutcheon notes that its tone extends along a range that begins with the mildly emphatic and continues through the playful, ambiguous, provisional, self-protective to the insulting, the subversive or the transgressive. She offers a definition of "irony as the interaction not only between ironist and interpreter but between different meanings, where both the said and the unsaid must play off against each other (and with some critical edge)." Moreover, irony may be a device which creates a community of knowing readers who are complicit in their exclusion of the targeted groups, those other readers who do not comprehend the point of the irony. With this in mind, let us resume our readings of the prefatory matter of *The Handmaid's Tale* to discover how the ironizing frame of the novel is constructed.

Just as the double dedication suggests ironic possibilities, the biblical, Swift and Sufi epigraphs open up spaces for further ironic readings. Because others have addressed the biblical and Sufi material, we shall consider them only briefly here, and then focus our attention on the Swift text which needs further critical explication. In her analysis of the Sufi proverb, Nancy V. Workman explains that punning, multiple meanings and paradox (discursive strategies central to *The Handmaid's Tale*) are central components of Sufi writings. She finds that the "inwardness and language play" important to the Sufi mystical tradition structure the novel and provide the narrator with "the power to shape reality." However, we must be aware that the reality Offred shapes is a private one; her world is a narrow cell-like room within which she is free to imagine and meditate as she chooses.

In contrast to Offred's constrained shaping of reality, the totalitarian government of Gilead appropriates biblical texts to institute and enforce harsh political control, to shape a political reality for its citizens. Lucy M. Freibert discusses the religious hypocrisy of Gilead and explores the comic implications of the biblical allusions and parallels, noting "humorous correspondence between the biblical account and Atwood's tale" and outright "high burlesque" in the prayer scene preceding the impregnation ritual. The epigraph biblical text *Genesis* 30: 1-3 suggests the importance of children to women and raises the issue of male control over women. Recontextualizing this passage, Gilead turns Rachel's anguished plea for children into the pretext for instituting a new domesticity based on the sexual triangle of a man and two women. In the guise of a re-population program, Gilead reads the biblical text literally and makes it the basis for the state-sanctioned rape, the impregnation ceremony the handmaids must undergo each month. In this recasting of the biblical passage, Gilead obliterates the emotional meaning of the story and, instead, turns a woman's desire into an instrument of male control.

Moreover, on a more figurative level, the choice of a biblical text for the epigraph suggests that spiritual as well as political significance is at issue in the novel. The state-controlled religion of Gilead, like the patriarchal Israelite society and the Puritan theocracy of Massachusetts, offers its adherents little spiritual sustenance. Its belief system is a harsh theology based on a judgmental father god rather than on a nurturing divinity. The state cynically selects the texts which it privileges to authorize its political control, and promulgates religious rituals (such as the Salvagings, Particicutions and Prayvaganzas) as "steam valve[s] for the female elements." Its written texts are subject to state control. Bibles are kept locked up, and only the men are legally allowed to read them. Computer-banks of prayer machinery print out prayer scrolls and intone them in metallic monotones, but no one reads or listens to the prayers: "you can't hear the voices from outside; only a murmur, a hum." Even worse, neither Offred nor her partner (and possibly no one else in Gilead) believes that the intended audience—God—"listens to these machines." Consequently, the computer prayers are voices which fall upon deaf ears, just as Offred's voice falls upon deaf ears, unheard or misheard. Since Pieixoto finds her audiotapes so many years later, hidden in a trunk in what was once the city of Bangor, Maine, we must assume they did not succeed in their purpose of conveying the story of Gilead to her contemporaries.

Another voice whose urgent, impassioned call to action was not heard by his contemporaries is the voice of Swift's Modest Proposer. Atwood's choice of an epigraph from "A Modest Proposal" invites us to explore thematic and stylistic parallels between her text and Swift's, and leads us to posit ironic readings of the narrative voices. The satire in each case depends upon an ironic narration, the "proposal" or "tale" of a supposedly artless observer who reports an appalling situation in a relatively flat style. The targets of satire are repressive governmental policies which produce worse harm than the problems they set out to solve. Swift, the brilliant Irish political satirist and clergyman, published his "Modest Proposal" in 1729 to expose the damaging consequences of British economic policy toward Ireland. Atwood, the brilliant Canadian novelist, published her *Handmaid's Tale* in 1985 to expose the damaging consequences of patriarchal misogyny in an imagined state, which Atwood alleges is not entirely fictional.

The passage which Atwood appends in her epigraph reads: "but as to myself, having been wearied out for many years with offering vain, idle, visionary thoughts, and at length utterly despairing of success, I fortunately fell upon this proposal." Whose is this voice? Is it the voice of Swift, the outraged public man who seeks to ameliorate the problems of a debt-ridden, colonialized Ireland? The Proposer, who frames—in a data-filled, matter-of-fact report—a most heinous solution to the problems of Ireland's poverty and overpopulation? Critics are still asking: How are we to read the connections between the voices of Swift and his Proposer? Swift chose the "Modest Proposal," a genre popular in his time, as his frame "to reduce the distance between tenor [relations in the empirical universe] and vehicle [relations in the fictional universe] and thereby further the fundamental purpose of this . . . subgenre: to prompt readers to change the world" (Murphy, bracketed text from Suvin). His satire is powerful in part because it is directed at its readers, both the educated business class of England and the oppressed Irish. English and Irish Protestant mercantile interests might speak in exasperated voices about the Irish poor, as does the Proposer. Or they might suggest policies as detrimental to Ireland as those of the Proposer, without realizing the tragic consequences of such legislation. On the other hand, many of the remedies the Proposer discounts as being ineffective or impossible to realize, such as the refusal to purchase foreign manufactured goods, are options available to the Irish themselves.

Whose voice(s) does the author of *Tale* mean to imply by the epigraph? Who are we to suppose is the equivalent of the Proposer? There are layers of authors: the imputed author, the handmaid Offred who narrates the tale, the archaeologist Pieixoto who pieces together the fragments of audiotaped oral narration to assemble the manuscript. Whose voices emerge from this layering, and with what degree(s) of innocence? And what are the targets of the novel's satire? What are we to make of the novel's use of romance story conventions? Should we conclude that because it uses the romance plot—the rescue of the helpless female victim by the mysteriously dark, silent lover—the tale is therefore retreating from politics and public life into romantic fantasy? Or is the tale satirizing those readers who do not see that the romance conventions are also a level of irony (Tomc)? Or is the tale satirizing all of the academics who attempt to pin down its voice and propound our own interpretations?

Swift's "Modest Proposal" and Atwood's *The Handmaid's Tale* share many stylistic and thematic features. Stylistically, both play with the range of possible irony. Both create characters (the Proposer, the Commander and the Professor) whose smug certainties are punctured by ironic narration. Thematically, both texts establish metaphorical links between women/animals/procreation/food. Both paint graphic pictures of the horrific consequences of misguided political policy. Swift's text demonstrates the tragic effects of English colonial policy which reduced Ireland to poverty and famine. Atwood's novel depicts the ravages of a fictional totalitarian regime (although Atwood insists, in an interview in *Quill & Quire*, that "there's nothing in the book that hasn't already happened"). In both cases, one social dilemma addressed is that of population. The "Modest Proposal" seeks to solve the problem of Irish overpopulation; the rulers of Gilead are obsessed with resolving their crisis of underpopulation, for industrial pollution and experiments in biological warfare have produced the sterility that led to underpopulation. In each case, the measures taken to rectify the population are draconian. Gilead resorts to the desperate remedy of enforced sexual servitude; the Proposer suggests another desperate remedy, cannibalism. The voice of the Proposer, like that of Gilead, is definitely hostile to women (note that the possibility that Swift was also a mysogynist is a matter of some critical debate). Both the Proposer and the government of Gilead seek to control and appropriate women's sexuality and to commodify their children

In both texts, there are deprecating references to women as animals, especially breeding animals. Ofglen is a "trained pig," the handmaids are like "caged rats." Offred sees herself as a "prize pig," and "an attentive pet." She refers to the handmaids as two-legged wombs. She thinks of a Commander as a "rutting salmon." In "Modest Proposal," a similarly reductive perspective prevails. Women are compared to brood mares, calving cows or sows in farrow. Charles Beaumont finds that in its thirty-three paragraphs of text "Proposal" uses the terms "breed" or "breeders" six times, and "dam" (in the sense of female progenitor) twice.

Body parts of men as well as women (often exaggerated or grotesquely depicted) figure prominently in each text. In *Tale*, Offred sees worms as "flexible and pink, like lips"; she describes the Commander's penis as a "tentacle," "blind," like a slug. The sexual politics of Gilead foregrounds sexuality as reproduction, and leads the narrator to view the world in terms of reproductive functions. Offred perceives flowers as "the genital organs of plants." As a result of this distorted vision, as Roberta Rubenstein notes, "distinctions between human and non-human are grotesquely inverted or reduced." The hanged bodies of Gilead's victims are suspended from the walls of the former Harvard Yard like slabs of meat on meathooks. With bags over their heads, they are anonymous, featureless. Offred contemplates this process of dehumanization: "This is what you have to do before you kill . . . You have to create an it, where none was before. You do that first, in your head, and then you make it real." The "Modest Proposal" employs a similar strategy of dehumanization; the Proposer describes infants as "useless mouths"; Beaumont counts five uses of the word "carcass," and four appearances of "flesh."

Just as women in Gilead have become property of the state as child-bearing machines, the children they produce are commodified. In *Tale*, bearing a child insures the handmaid's survival, while handmaids who fail to produce progeny after three postings are exiled to the toxic waste colonies. Because of their enhanced value, pregnant handmaids flaunt their status. But they lose all rights to the infants after parturition: the babies become the property of the Commander's wives. However, as a result of environmental pollution, many babies are born deformed and thus fail to actualize their commodity value: they are "Shredders" rather than "Keepers."

In "Modest Proposal," of course, the sole value of children is as marketable commodity. But market value here depends on weight and flavour. Children are described as "plump," "fat," or "fattest." Infants are reckoned up in terms of how many portions they will make: "a well-grown fat yearling child . . . roasted whole, will make a considerable figure at a Lord Mayor's feast, or any other public entertainment"; "a child will make two dishes at an entertainment for friends; and when the family dines alone, the fore or hind quarter will make a reasonable dish." Additionally, children are compared to venison or suckling pig, and recipes are offered.

The "Modest Proposal" continues to shock with its vitriolic satirical suggestion of cannibalism. But there are dark echoes of cannibalism in *Tale* as well, which it will be worth considering. Indeed, Atwood's first novel was *Edible Woman*, in which the narrator Marian MacAlpin perceives herself as a commodity that her fiancé Peter plans to consume. She thinks of herself as analogous to the rabbit he hunts and eviscerates; she runs away from the camera he seeks to "shoot" her with. In the conclusion, she bakes a cake in the shape of a woman and asks him to consume it instead of her. (For an exploration of the food imagery in *Edible Woman*, see MacLulich, who reads the novel as a version of the "Gingerbread Man" folktale.)

Atwood has clearly been fascinated with the idea of cannibalism. She has treated this subject playfully in at least one other context. In 1987 *The CanLit Foodbook: From Pen to Plate—a Collection of Tasty Literary Fare*, edited and illustrated by Margaret Atwood, was published. Written as a fund-raiser for Canada's Anglophone P.E.N., the book is a compilation of authors' favorite recipes, and selections from Canadian authors containing descriptions of food or meals. Atwood cautions her readers that this is not exactly a cookbook. Indeed, chapter nine is title: "Eating People is Wrong: Cannibalism Canadian Style." In her foreword, Atwood tells us:

> Chapter nine is devoted to cannibalism, metaphorical and actual, of which there's a surprising amount in Canadian literature. It appears to be one of those thrill-of-the-forbidden literary motifs, like the murders in murder mysteries, that we delight to contemplate, though we would probably not do it for fun, except in children's literature, where devouring and being devoured appears to be a matter of course.

In her selections for this chapter, Atwood includes the passage in which Marian MacAlpin bakes and decorates her woman-shaped cake. Atwood comments in the foreword that collecting recipes and "pestering writers" took a long time: possibly she had begun thinking about the *Foodbook* at the time she was writing *Tale*. Of course, the tone of the foodbook is much lighter than that of *Tale*. Alluding to cannibalism in connection with Hitler's policy of extermination establishes a much more serious context in *Tale* than in the tongue-in-cheek cookbook. Yet, this conflation of serious and comic is a recurring feature in Atwood's work. In fact, her playful *Foodbook* is a fund-raiser for the serious purpose of raising money on behalf of writers who are political prisoners.

Cannibalism, to the extent that it may ever have been actually practiced (apart from the desperate cases of stranded disaster survivors in extreme conditions), is an act of aggression against an other, a powerless, but somehow potentially dangerous and fearsome victim. We would apply the cannibal label only to alien others, whom we perceive to be savages beyond the pale of civilized humanity, for cannibalism is a powerful taboo, which has, as Atwood notes, the power to horrify and titillate readers. The cannibal theme is carried out in several ways in *Tale*. On some level, the foods the handmaids eat, symbolic representations of wombs and fertility (pears, eggs, chickens, bread described as baking in the oven), are analogues for their bodies. Additionally, one of Offred's flashback memories recounts her childhood fear of cannibalism. When her mother described the deaths of victims in Nazi concentration camps, she talked about people being killed in ovens. As a young child, not comprehending, Offred believed that these people had been baked and eaten. "There is something especially terrifying to a child in that idea. Ovens mean cooking, and cooking comes before eating. I thought these people had been eaten. Which in a way I suppose they had been." By means of this digression, Offred makes explicit the analogies between Gilead and Nazi Germany, and between her tale and "A Modest Proposal." In all cases, we have dystopian societies that are devouring their children.

Having explored some of the thematic parallels, let us now turn to the stylistic parallels between Atwood's and Swift's texts. These stylistic strategies hold the key to our readings of the texts, for through their styles the narrators establish their relationships to their texts and present themselves as subjects of the reader's interpretations.

Discussing the style of "A Modest Proposal," Charles Pullen writes that the Proposer "is quite capable of irony and anger: what he is incapable of seeing is how monstrous his marvelous solution is." Further, "The Proposer is . . . highly skilled, knowledgeable, imaginative . . . He is also a captive of his style which simply has no need or room for emotion, for morals, for human implication. Solving the problem is all: he possesses the rhetorical structure, the proper language and the necessary knowledge." This characterization of the Proposer's style applies equally to the first of the two male voices in *Tale*, the voice of the Commander (the state). The Commander, "highly skilled, knowledgeable, imaginative," is smugly certain that he has solved "the woman problem." But he is more sophisticated than the Proposer. Aware of the human implications, he is nevertheless pleased with his solution. In conversation with Offred, he lapses into cliché, thus signaling that his response is superficial, trivializing both the issue and the person he is answering. His response again relies on dehumanizing and cannibalizing the victims: "You can't make an omelet without breaking eggs." He also acknowledges that "better never means better for everyone. It always means worse, for some." Thus women become for him the eggs which are broken and consumed to create a better life for the patriarchal ruling class.

The Commander is evasive and trivializing about the human implications of his political revolution. On the other hand, we note that Professor James Darcy Pieixoto (the voice of the academy) who speaks in the Historical Notes section, is willing to remain oblivious to the "human implication" of Offred's tale, the story he has pieced together from fragments. His distanced, objective reading is at cross purposes with Offred's subversive political intent in recording her tale. Accordingly, his neutral stance highlights his links to the Commander, and serves to accentuate the satirical purpose of the novel. As Pullen notes in continuing his discussion of the Proposer's style: "Only a style of antiseptic distance could ignore the potential for horror in this." The last of the narrators of *Tale*, Professor Pieixoto prides himself on his "antiseptic distance," his fitting, proper, moral relativity. Ignoring the horror of Gilead, he warns his audience "we must be cautious about passing moral judgments upon the Gileadeans. Surely we have learned by now that such judgments are of necessity culture-specific. . . . Our job is not to censure but to understand." Thus, Pieixoto adheres to a reading practice that remains distanced from dystopian or satirical narratives, reading for escape or for comfort rather than as an impetus for action toward social change. It is this kind of distanced reading which perpetuates the dystopia of Gilead in its current avatar in Nunavit.

We now turn to the central narrative voice in *The Handmaid's Tale*. What are we to make of the voice of Offred, the handmaid whose oral narration has been transcribed by Pieixoto? Glenn Deer has analyzed the voice of the narrator, and finds her to be not as innocent as we might first suppose. Deer notes that Offred is a gifted storyteller; she does not remain an artless narrator. To some extent she is complicit in the story she tells, a story which foregrounds violence. "In *The Handmaid's Tale* we are guided by a cunning implied author, a voice that feigns weakness in the guise of Offred, her narrative mask; but this voice cannot help but advertise the control and strength of its origin: Margaret Atwood. . . [T]hough the reader has participated in the construction of this story, responsibility for its pain and power lies in the rhetorical will of the author." Deer argues that Atwood must create a skilled storyteller in order to achieve her rhetorical goals. I would like to push Deer's point somewhat further, to argue that the power of the novel comes precisely from the tension produced by just this layering of narrative voices. By reading the slippage between the voices of Offred and Pieixoto and the "rhetorical will of the author" we become aware of the layers of irony, "the interaction. . . between different meanings. . . with some critical edge" (Hutcheon). Similarly, it is in the slippage between the skillful speech of the Proposer and the "rhetorical will" of Swift that the irony of "A Modest Proposal" resides.

A key stylistic feature of *Tale* is its use of layers of textual material to establish frames that set up ironic oscillations of meaning. The epigraphs, historical notes and dedications are part of this process, but even within Offred's narrative the novel employs this ironic layering device. First, we note that Offred's text, the main portion of the novel, is Pieixoto's piecing together of recorded fragments. Second, within the tale puns, digressions, flashbacks, asides, rewordings, abound. Offred sometimes retells the same event in different ways, reminding us that this is a "reconstruction" or an "approximation." Thus, Offred's words continue the pattern of layered texts, overlapping voices within the novel. Jill LeBihan notes that this textual layering functions to problematize the Gileadean notion that there exists one truth, one officially sanctioned version of reality: "the novel constantly reiterates its uncertain, problematic relationship with the concept of a single reality, one identity, a truthful history." Further,

> the dystopian genre and temporal shifts are ways of drawing attention to the frame, the arrangers, and the white space and flat surfaces which make perception . . . possible. . . . *The Handmaid's Tale* is dystopian fiction, but also historiographic metafiction with a confessional journal-style first person narrator. The single identifiable generic frame is stretched to include as many different writing strategies as possible within its construction. But the story once in print . . . is not under the subject's control.

Thus, several narrative conventions exist in tension with each other, challenging the notion of a seamless reality and a unified narrative voice. Similar stylistic strategies are at work in "A Modest Proposal."

Returning to interrogate Swift's style, we find that its power stems from this very tension of layered voices. I quote at some length from Clive T. Probyn's discussion:

> [Swift] characteristically works from the margin inwards, leaving us with a false frame, or even several overlapping frames of discourse. . . . The background noise[s] (allusions, . . . genres, styles, . . . asides, . . . disconnections) are endless. There is no one voice for us to interrogate, and . . . [the] text . . . refuses to give us a definitive truth . . . [Swift situates] the crisis of interpretation within the narrative personality, *before* the text reaches the reader of print, when he or she recognizes that . . . to agree with Gulliver we must become horses, or that humanitarianism in Ireland depends on cannibalism . . . There is no solace or

privilege for the critic in all of this. Swift's narrators are always their own first critics, analytically adept, logical to a fault, keen students of the literary text . . . Swift's solution to warfare between overlapping texts is to rewrite, recycle, and permanently distort one text by [another]. . . version of it . . . . The subversion of a given text by an incursion from the margin which rewrites either in part or whole . . . [adds] a further and implosive level.

The overlapping frames of discourse, the background noises (puns, allusions, digressions, memories, retellings, multiplicity of genres, disconnections); these are among the devices which construct *The Handmaid's Tale*. There are many voices, starting with the dedication, moving through the epigraphs and the journal-entry novel to the Historical Notes. The "crisis of interpretation" is situated within Offred and Pieixoto. To agree with Offred, we must become complicit in the voyeurism of Gilead and its sexual and political violence; we must rectify the romance plot which engineers Offred's escape from Gilead. To agree with Pieixoto, we must acquiesce to moral relativism and patriarchal sexism. "There is no solace or privilege for the critic in all of this": we must interrogate our own readings; in the person of Pieixoto ("analytically adept, logical to a fault, [a] keen student of the literary text") we have already been subsumed into the text. Layers of overlapping texts "rewrite, recycle, and permanently distort one text by [another] . . . version of it." The incursions from the margins, the dedications and epigraphs which press in upon the text, the Historical Notes which rewrite the tale from a future time add "further and implosive level[s]." Atwood's scintillating satire appropriates and puts to powerful use the very strategies which built Swift's satire.

Let us now turn to the epigraph: "having been wearied out for many years with offering vain, idle, visionary thoughts; and at length utterly despairing of success, I fortunately fell upon this proposal." If we read this as the voice of the Modest Proposer, we see the man who considers himself a practical, decent person, exasperated by the folly and suffering of humanity, delighted to be able to offer a solution to the ills of Ireland.

Who is the equivalent of the Modest Proposer in *Tale*? Let us consider the options. Is it the Commanders of Gilead, who at last have fortunately come upon the solution to the political ills they addressed, and to the problem of women. In this context, we remember that the Commander tells Offred that men from the time before Gilead had lost the ability to feel, and believed "there was nothing for them to do with women." Or, is Atwood's Modest Proposer the voice of the somewhat obtuse, chauvinist historian

Pieixoto who at this point in his professional career (after what previous encounters with ideas, what manner of "thoughts"?) "fortunately fell upon" Offred's narrative, which may lead to conference papers and publications, and thus insure his professional "success"? Perhaps it is Offred, who was "wearied out for many years" thinking her "vain, idle, visionary thoughts" in her cell-like room in Gilead, and has now "fortunately [fallen] upon this proposal" to dictate her memoirs as a way to communicate the horrors of Gilead to a larger audience which possibly has the power to intervene in Gilead, or at least to commemorate its history. Or perhaps we have here the gently self-mocking, ironic voice of the imputed author (or of Atwood?). This author has "been wearied out for many years" speaking publicly, writing novels and essays "offering vain, idle, visionary thoughts" and has despaired because the political changes her texts propose have not yet come to pass. However, she has now "fortunately [fallen] upon this proposal" as the cautionary tale which will at last bring others to see the light and to mend their ways. Or perhaps, dear readers, it is we, the scholars who, like Professor Pieixoto, "fall upon" our texts and read into them our own obsessions. Perhaps, it is we who commodify the texts we read and evaluate according to our standards; we who offer up recipes for consuming the texts.

MARTA DVORAK

# What is Real/Reel? Margaret Atwood's "Rearrangement of Shapes on a Flat Surface," or Narrative as Collage

> On a map or in an aerial photograph the
> water pattern radiates like a spider, but in
> a boat you can see only a small part of it,
> the part you're in.
>
> (Atwood, *Surfacing*)

In Margaret Atwood's second novel *Surfacing* (1972), already a reflection on perception, the narrator discovered that "if you put your eye down close to the photograph [the figures] disintegrated into grey dots." The implicit need for distance, for perspective, in order to accede to a more faithful representation of reality, subtends Atwood's discursive and narrative strategies in later novels like *The Handmaid's Tale* (1985), a work of speculative fiction, or *Cat's Eye* (1988), which shifts between two semiotic modes.

*The Handmaid's Tale*, like the near-future fiction of Huxley or Orwell, is not to be read simply as a prophecy or cautionary tale, but as a reflexion on our contemporary political and social practices. But beyond even the social satire, through a metadiscursive enunciative act involving multiple producers and receivers (for there is a long framed narrative and a short framing one), Atwood problematizes the relationships between art and life, historical fact and experiential event, between public and private memory, between fiction and non-fiction, as well as between different categories of fiction such as the

From *Études Anglaises* 51, no. 4 (October–December 1998). © 1998 Didier Érudition.

novel and the (pseudo)autobiography, and she challenges our assumptions about authenticity and the processes of representation. In a blurring reminiscent of the photograph in *Surfacing*, *Handmaid* questions how literary texts and life writing are read and interpreted, and simultaneously highlights the fact that history too is an invention, a collage, a subjectively pieced-together text. As Arnold Davidson points out, the "very scantiness of the evidence" emphasized by the novel's epilogue "underscores how much history is the product of historians," and that "context itself is a construct." We effectively learn from the pseudo-documentary framing "Historical Notes" that the text is a multiple re-construction made even more fragile by double temporal distancing: it is the reassembling based on "*guesswork*" of an "*approximate*" transcription of "*un*numbered" tapes *assumed* to be genuine, arranged "in *no* particular order," containing a *non*-synchronous recording (albeit *pretending* to synchronicity) made two *centuries* previously (emphases mine unless otherwise indicated).

The epilogue of *Handmaid* thus reminds us that history, like fiction, is a discourse. But Atwood goes even further in problematizing the representations with which we try to make sense of the world. The self-conscious narrator of the dislocated embedded tale constantly calls attention to the fabricated nature of her story, insisting "This is a reconstruction. All of it is a reconstruction," and repeatedly discussing the procedures of her own narration:

> I made that up. It didn't happen that way. Here is what happened.
> . . . There wasn't any thunder though, I added that in.

The process of enunciation which foregrounds the code which governs its construction, along with the text's fractured time sequence, its embedding and doubling back, its gaps and blanks, its hesitations and multiple variants of the same event, signal that we are being invited to decode a *récit spéculaire* (Dällenbach) or specular fiction. To make sense of this self-reflexive story, all the receivers of her enunciative act (for the historians of the epilogue are in a way intratextual versions of the projected reader) would do well to take the advice the narrator gives in a passage that mirrors the above extract from *Surfacing*:

> What I need is perspective. The illusion of depth, created by a frame, the arrangement of shapes on a flat surface. Perspective is necessary. Otherwise there are only two dimensions. Otherwise you live with your face squashed against a wall, everything a huge foreground, of details, close-ups, hairs . . . the molecules of the

face. . . . Your own skin like a map . . . crisscrossed with tiny paths that lead nowhere.

This reflection on sub/objectivity is situated within the broader postmodern challenge, in both literature and painting, to traditional notions of perspective (as well as to notions of authority, conventional patterns, or constraints in general, such as linearity, causality or textual closure). As Linda Hutcheon points out, narrators in postmodern fiction "become either disconcertingly multiple and hard to locate . . . or resolutely provisional limited."

Like many of her Canadian contemporaries who refuse to limit themselves to one genre or even artistic field, Atwood is a poet and a novelist who plays with forms and genres, writing prose poems (*Murder in the Dark*) and "short fictions" (*Good Bones*) that defy the structured sphere of the short story. But Atwood is also a visual artist, and for the Canadian editions of her books, she has either commissioned, selected or adapted art for her covers, or designed the covers herself. She often uses her own collages or photographs to blend art and artefact, the representational and the functional, the factual and the fictional. Like her prose, the collages call attention to the manufactured reality of mass culture in the postmodern fashion that consists in contesting through subversion, through irony and parody, rather than through rejection.

Although postmodern texts share the fragmentation and self-reflexivity of modernist ones, critics such as Andreas Huyssen have remarked that postmodernists have distanced themselves from the modernists' rejection of dominant mass culture and their tendency to oppose high and low art. In the place of what has been termed in some circles as cultural élitism and hermeticism, postmodernists offer "cultural democratizing of high/low art distinctions" as well as "contextualizing theories of the discursive complexity of art," and the recognition that all perception and articulation are shaped by the social context. Marta Caminero-Santangelo points out that postmodernists, with their political questioning and social commitment, seek to reach a larger audience than a privileged few, and consequently situate their resistance to or criticism of the dominant culture from within.

Readers of Atwood cannot fail to notice how all the while satirizing mass culture, she works within its sphere, and how her textual fabric incorporates the common references of consumer society, particularly the mass media, the basis of popular entertainment. It is no coincidence that to express her sense of loss, Offred quotes the refrain of Elvis Presley's "Heartbreak Hotel," music now forbidden by the totalitarian theocratic regime of Gilead that has overthrown the American government, and no coincidence either that her tale is recorded/superscribed on and concealed within tapes containing ethnic folk songs fashionable in the 1980s or the biggest hits of pop and rock stars like Elvis Presley or Boy George, encompassing the tastes of successive generations. There are numerous references to pre- and post-Gilead activities involving the mass media that contemporary readers can relate to. These are sites not only of representation, but also of the production of ideology through the technologies of (institutionalized) discourse. The novel calls attention to how they generate political, social, and cultural control, and how they construct our perception, dictate how we see and how we value ourselves and the Other.

The verbal and pictorial discourse of the mass media brings into play diverse codes regulating the aesthetic, the ethical, the technological, and the communicational. We have but to examine the Commander's ironic claim as to how his dystopic fundamentalist regime has ameliorated the lives of women—double-edged irony in that it simultaneously satirizes the dystopic dimension of our contemporary society and its tendency to replace the genuine with the fake:

> Think of the trouble [women] had before. Don't you remember the singles bars, the indignity of high-school blind dates? The meat market. Don't you remember the terrible gap between the ones who could get a man easily and the ones who couldn't? Some of them were so desperate, they starved themselves thin or pumped their breasts full of silicone, had their noses cut off.

There are abundant references in *Handmaid*, as in her other fiction, to photographic image, camera, and frame. In the nightmarish future, Polaroid cameras still exist, and the historical in/significance of members of society are measured through their absence from or presence in photographs:

> there will be family albums, too, with all the children in them; no Handmaids though. From the point of view of future history, this kind, we'll be invisible.

The surrogate mother Handmaids, devoid of names and identities (they are given the first name of whichever man they currently "belong" to, preceded by the preposition signifying appurtenance: Of-fred, Of-glen, etc.), and absent from family portraits, leave no trace in history, which is as much a human construct as the family album is.

Pictures have power. After her daughter has been taken away from her, Offred is shown "a picture of her . . . her face a closed oval." The narrator later calls to mind "the ghost of a dead girl, a little girl who died when she was five." The little girl who did not die does not exist for the narrator (who wonders if she in turn has ceased to exist for her daughter or if she lives on as "a picture somewhere, in the dark at the back of her mind"). As Hutcheon formulates so well, "that past *was* real, but it *is* lost" (emphases in the text). Hutcheon adds that this lost or displaced past can be reinstated as "the referent of language, *the relic or trace of the real*" (emphasis mine). But in this story, in which the narrator has "lost time" and attempts to reconstruct it, sites of visual representation seem to vie with language to contain the relic or trace of the real, as well as the displaced past. When Offred tries to conjure up in her mind the image of her loved ones, she perceives them from a technical perspective, as a blending of different processes and stages of photographical production, such as the flat surface or screen of the *camera obscura* onto which the images are projected, or the paper support of the print itself:

> I try to hold them still behind my eyes, their faces, like pictures in an album. But they won't stay still for me, they move, there's a smile and it's gone, their features curl and bend as if the paper's burning, blackness eats them.

All these photographic images serve multiple functions. They arrest and displace time, for they freeze the moment of the subject photographed and place duration into the realm of the viewer. They signal the way that society constructs and conditions human identity: in an interview with Sharon Wilson, Atwood confesses her interest in a photograph's ability to freeze time and to "freeze characters in roles that are socially conditioned, desired or feared." Does the Commander not turn himself into a living, breathing photograph the first time Offred enters his study, in order to conform to some socially constructed image vehicled or even generated by popular magazines?

> The Commander is standing in front of the fireless fireplace, back to it, one elbow on the carved wooden overmantel, other hand in his pocket. It's such a studied pose, something of the country squire, some old come-on from a glossy men's mag. . . . When I knocked he probably rushed over to the fireplace and propped himself up.

Atwood shows that we see the world through what Coleridge termed the secondary Imagination, involving a structuring process, an elaboration, that "dissolves, diffuses, dissipates, in order to re-create." Atwood's characters do not merely re-activate images, they stage them. They reiterate, construct and represent the world, in the sense of a representation which is a *mise en scène*, a performance or production. Another of the multiple functions then, of the recurrent use of the visual image is to blur the borders between art and life, the natural and the artificial, the genuine and the imitation.

What is real/reel? Is our reality tangibly material or does it consist in mere images projected on our minds like the sun streaming through the fanlight of coloured glass, falling across the floor, "red and blue, purple," but impalpable, illusory, for Offred stretches out her hands, and "they *fill* with flowers of light." "The future is in your hands," repeats one of the agents of indoctrination called "Aunts," holding out her own hands. But Offred remarks,

> there was nothing in them. They were empty. It was [the Handmaids'] hands that were supposed to be full, of the future; which could be held but not seen.

By taking the metaphor literally, Atwood creates aporia with the isotopy *full/empty*. The future which can be held but not seen is the inverse image of the flowers of light that can be seen but not held. Atwood signals the illusory nature of reality with Offred's systematic play with language, but also by drawing attention to the powerful hallucination of the photograph that, as Barthes points out, entices us to grasp what was, but is no longer (*Chambre claire*). *Handmaid* illustrates Barthes's argument that by becoming commonplace, the photograph has taken over to the detriment of reality itself, to the extent that we make our behaviour conform to artificial stereotypes. In a stunning mirror inversion, the Commander who takes on the "studied pose" from a men's magazine, becomes what the magazine advertisements imitate: "he looks like a vodka ad in a glossy magazine." It is no longer a question of art imitating life, but of "life" imitating (commercial) art.

To aggravate the ontological confusion, images relating to the world of spectacle, the spheres of professional performance or popular representation abound. There are multiple references to actors, the theatre, movies, masquerade, circus and travesty, with all their different components, as in the descriptions of the (exemplary) prostitutes in the illicit brothel that, better than a film reel in which the audience cannot interact, spins the illusion of "walking into the past." The prostitutes, who are literally obliged to make a "spectacle" of themselves in their grotesque, variegated costumes (the ersatz Playboy Bunnies are "girls dressed for Easter, in rabbit suits"), remind the narrator of a "stage play, a musical comedy." The brothel is a stage on which the women are made to act out male fantasies, and where there is a privileged space behind the "curtain" where the masks can drop: in the washroom's "rest area," in a description loaded with terms belonging to the semantic field of the false, a woman

> in a cat suit with a tail made of orange fake fur is re-doing her make-up. This is like backstage: greasepaint, smoke, the materials of illusion.

Like Serena Joy's sitting room, in which some things "are authentic, some are not," in which the paintings are either genuine period portraits or canvasses that Serena Joy is "passing off as ancestors," but where "[t]here's no way of knowing," the narrative blurs the border between event and representation, between product and packaging, even inversing their roles. We have seen how Atwood subverts traditional patterns by likening the "flesh and blood" Commander to a figure in a vodka advertisement. In another sequence in which the Commander decides to play the role of a "casual" host, we learn that "[a]ll he needs is a toothpick in the corner of his mouth to be an *ad* for rural democracy; as in an *etching*. Flyspecked, some old burned *book*." And when the narrator and the other female employees are told it is now illegal for women to work, her colleague's protest, the trite formula "You can't just *do* that," sounds "false, improbable, like something you would say on television" (emphasis in the text). Such subversion/inversion is a systematic strategy in her fiction: "reality" becomes a bad film devoid of verisimilitude.

*Handmaid* is a novel meant for the same audiences that flock to Atom Egoyan films in which the characters' sole point of reference is television and video. Atwood targets contemporary readers who increasingly communicate with one another and the external world through electronic images and wavelengths, and whose contact with print culture is dominantly through magazines and other popular publications. Although the writer's stance is a critical one, and although she often mocks the popular taste of mass culture, in exemplary objects such as the store cushion with "an embroidered view of Niagara Falls" (*Surfacing*), Atwood places her novels firmly within this very culture. In this too, her work is resolutely postmodern, for "its critique coexists within an equally real and equally powerful *complicity* with the cultural dominants within which it inescapably exists" (Hutcheon).

On the one hand, she underscores and criticizes how the sites of visual representation generate and perpetuate ideology. The now-outlawed fashion magazines Offred leafs through, "infinitely discardable," are emblems of our throw-away consumer culture, for just as the magazine is discarded and forgotten, so is the current partner in favour of a new one, different and yet the same. The images in them are representations of a representation, catching the reader in a quasi-religious, infinite spiral propagating illusion and lies.

> What was in them was promise. They dealt in transformations; they suggested an endless series of possibilities, extending like the reflections in two mirrors set facing one another, stretching on, replica after replica, to the vanishing point. They suggested one adventure after another, one wardrobe after another, one improvement after another, one man after another. They suggested rejuvenation, pain overcome and transcended, endless love. The real promise in them was immortality.

On the other hand, as we have already glimpsed, Atwood operates within the very field of this popular culture, structuring her narrative along the same patterns of mirror images, doubles, replicas, imitations, variations, inversions. The text, like the mass media it describes, is a construct, like a (faked) photograph, like the moving pictures/movies, like a David Hockney collage with all its slippages. The self-reflexive narration makes use of the very conventions it parodies, to suggest that the conventions of representation generate our "reality." The subjunctive and the modals of the metanarrative distance us from the scene even as it unfolds under our eyes like a tentative film take:

> If there were a fire in the fireplace, its light would be twinkling on the polished surfaces, glimmering warmly on flesh. I add the firelight in.

Similarly, the multiple variants the narrator offers us of the same event, destroy the seamlessness of verisimilitude and call attention to the fabricated nature of the text. They do so partly through the self-conscious hesitations and revisions ("I'll have to revise that" or "there's a scar, no, a wound"), and partly through close assimilation with the visual arts of popular culture. The description of what we divine to be the lawns and façades of Boston revolves around a simile taking for granted that a magazine like *Better Homes and Gardens* is a cultural reference shared by all: "they're like the beautiful pictures they used to print in the magazines about homes and gardens and interior decoration" in which, the narrator aptly notes, "there are no children." What we have is a parodic representation of an already illusory representation of America. Juxtaposed like a collage are the three versions of what happened to Offred's husband Luke after their aborted attempt at flight: contrary but equivalent versions of death, captivity, or escape that create aporia, for the narrator believes "all three versions of Luke, at one and the same time." The scenes are flat surfaces on which the narrator rearranges the components. In one of them, she pictures his clothes in her mind, "bright as a lithograph or a full-colour advertisement, from an ancient magazine," and the brain the bullet passed through is described as "the place where all the pictures were." The parallel triple variants of the encounter with her lover Nick are presented like cinematic replays or second and third takes, with the camera moving back to the original point to begin its tracking:

> I reach the top of the stairs, knock on the door there. He opens it himself. . . . I made that up. It didn't happen that way. Here is what happened. I reach the top of the stairs, knock on the door.

These multiple tellings of the same event, with their parallel structures, series of duplications and repetitions, evoke the magazine "reflections in two mirrors set facing one another, stretching on, replica after replica, to the vanishing point," and questioning the authenticity of any one image, of any one "truth."

Atwood's recurrent recourse to intertextuality also works to create a network of resonances that it is up to the reader to piece together, like a puzzle or collage. The intertexts are pieced into the narrative rather like the mismatched body parts and different artistic periods fused together by Gail Geltner in the collage that Atwood commissioned for the first Canadian edition of *Handmaid*. Geltner's strategies of pasting the head of the Madonna onto the body of the infant Jesus, and of superimposing the eyes and arms of the male patron onto her face and body, reflect central patterns in the novel. They signal the infantilisation and de-powerment of women, and blur the borders between the mythical/mystical and the real. Similarly, Atwood's use of intertexts, as Wilson points out in *Fairy-Tale Sexual Politics*, foregrounds the composite nature of our cultural context and heritage, our entrapment in pre-existing patterns, all the while offering the possibility of transformation. Just as Geltner subverts Memling's painting with her collage, just so does Atwood playfully subvert our culture's mythic motifs (from *Genesis* to the Demeter/Persephone myths) and folk tales.

Among the fairy tale intertexts of *Handmaid* is the Grimms' "Little Red Riding Hood," which is already a rewriting of Perrault's "Petit Chaperon Rouge," which in turn is already a literary reconstruction of an oral folk tale. But encoded into the text are also indirect references to the Hans Christian Andersen tale "The Red Shoes," in which the heroine who puts on the shoes is doomed to dance herself to death, as well as to the 1948 film adaptation starring *Moira* Shearer as the ballerina. There are multiple bits of the narrative collage drawing attention to the narrator's red shoes, part of her colour-coded uniform, which she recurrently puts on and takes off, or exchanges for a lighter summer version. The very first description of the shoes in the collage creating a web of interconnections is proleptic, preparing us through the rhetoric of denial for the sinister dance of death that is to follow in the later executions of non-conformists. Offred's "red shoes, flat-heeled to save the spine and not for dancing," anticipate the description of the three women with sacks covering their heads hanged and left as examples on the Wall, a description that fuses the motif of violence and death with the motif of the industries of illusion and representation:

> Beneath the hems of the dresses the feet dangle, two pairs of red shoes, one pair of blue. If it weren't for the ropes and the sacks it could be a kind of dance, a ballet, caught by flash-camera: mid-air. They look arranged. The look like showbiz.

The name of Off-red suggests a stance of resistance to the relegated role of Handmaid, a stance that the narrator has adopted ever since her capture and stay in the re-education centre, and it suggests the ominous possibility that she too might end up like the other subversive elements of this repressive regime. The narrator ends up recapitulating, and her allusion to the death dance shows how she has off(e)red herself up to the dominant ideology: "I don't want to be a dancer, my feet in the air, my head a faceless oblong of white cloth."

Atwood's text is a complex collage of analeptic and proleptic elements glued together by reiterated fragments that recur like refrains and punctuate the narration with the intrusion of the "real" man-made time of "present" experience, albeit recollected, blended with the reconstituted "past" time of memory. There are numerous references to the bell chiming, the clock ticking, Cora knocking, the intercrossing of Aunt Lydia's platitudes and Moira's subversions, gestures such as the narrator wiping her face with her sleeve as she comes out of a dream or reverie. There are many recurrences as well of the narrator's repeated play with the polysemy of words, and of the hypnotic repetition of the (pseudo)Latin phrase *Nolite te bastardes carborundorum:* a symbol of resistance although it is originally an "empty" acoustic image, a signifier without a signified, before being identified as dog Latin, in other words inauthentic, and as distorted as Offred's image in the mirror. Many of the pieces of the collage are syncretic, fusing and connecting the novel with other works by writers ranging from Homer, Chaucer, Marlowe, Shakespeare and Hawthorne to Tennyson, Orwell, T.S. Eliot, Burgess, Freud and Marx. Their interplay sets up a web of resonances and incites the projected reader to become a co-creator, to explore and to interconnect in order to generate meaning.

One example of Atwood's use of intertext to compose her narrative collage is the recurrent reference to tulips:

> The tulips are opening their cups, spilling out colour. The tulips
> are red, a darker crimson towards the stem, as if they had been
> cut and are beginning to heal there.

The association with blood and violence that is immediately set up anticipates the description of the hanged man whose blood, seeping through the white bag that covers and erases his head, forms a small red mouth. Offred notes that

> [t]he red of the smile is the same as the red of the tulips in Serena
> Joy's garden, towards the base of the flowers where they are
> beginning to heal.

and later, when she reconstitutes one of the possible versions of her husband's fate, she imagines:

> there's a scar, no, a wound, it isn't healed yet, the colour of tulips,
> near the stem end, down the left side of his face where the flesh
> split recently.

The tulips thus evoke not only regeneration and rebirth, but also mutilation, blood, and death. But the intertextual reference to Sylvia Plath's poem "Tulips," which reinforces this connection through lines like "Their redness talks to my wound, it corresponds," produces additional resonances that foreground other leitmotivs of the novel: the effacement of identity, of memory and story, (self)destruction, the stripping of body and name, surveillance and power(lessness).

The weaving of intertextual elements into the textual fabric signals the interdependence of artistic production and cultural context or heritage. But Atwood's collage also contains fragments that allow the alert reader to participate in the creative process, to see the total picture of the design. Recurrent images like blood or flowers, associated simultaneously with pain and passion, death and fertility, create aporia. The blood of a wound, of a lipsticked mouth or a menstrual cycle, a tulip shedding its petals "like teeth," signal the composite, illusory nature of truth through the multiplicity of "tiny paths" that "crisscross" and "lead nowhere." But there are other images in the collage crucial to a more complete construction of meaning, a more total picture of the arrangement of shapes. If there are many teasing references to the moon, it is not just because it embodies the cosmic cyclical time of the seasons or the biological time of the body, but because it is an important clue, one of many scattered in the text as to the narrator's secret name. Like the buried treasure it is compared to, Offred's real name is encoded into the text, and the reader is challenged to dig it up as the key to the Chaucerian *sententia* or lesson of the tale. The scope of this essay does not allow me to develop this key aspect of Atwood's textual strategy, which I examine in another article. Suffice it to say for our purposes here that the pattern of hide-and-seek, of concealment and display, once again signals the writer's complicity with as well as questioning of the dominant mass culture within which it functions.

If *Handmaid* is an exploration of representation, perception and *ap*perception, it also illustrates Roland Barthes's definition of a text as an onion containing a multitude of surfaces:

> agencement superposé de pelures (de niveaux, de systèmes) dont le volume ne comporte finalement aucun cœur, aucun noyau, aucun secret, aucun principe irréductible, sinon l'infini même de ses enveloppes—qui n'enveloppent rien d'autre que l'ensemble même de ses surfaces.

The text self-reflexively calls attention to the fact that it is a mere "arrangement of shapes on a flat surface," exposing the illusion of depth as a mere question of framing. Atwood goes even further by equating the surface of the page with the surface of the also framed photographs. In other works like *Surfacing*, Atwood calls attention to the photograph's "borders of blank *paper*," site of liminality likened to "windows opening into a place" we can "no longer reach." In an earlier poem, "This Is a Photograph of Me," the speaker's disturbing description of a photograph taken the day after she was drowned, (con)fuses surface of the lake and surface of the printed picture. In "The Page," Atwood also exposes the page's illusion of depth by playing "literally" with its spatial dimension and encouraging us to look "beneath" the page where there is "another story":

> The page is not a pool but a skin. . . . You touch the page, it's as if you've drawn a knife across it, the page has been hurt now, a sinuous wound opens, a thin incision. Darkness wells through.

The playful advice addressed to the receiver who might decide to enter the page, to "take a knife and some matches, and something that will float," like the parodic interactive fiction of "Happy Endings," signals the co-dependence of production and reception in the spinning of illusion. The collage structure of *Handmaid*, like these other fictions, underscores the fact that an artistic work is not a fixed product that readers consume, but a process, an arrangement, in which they collaborate.

DOMINICK M. GRACE

# The Handmaid's Tale: *"Historical Notes" and Documentary Subversion*

Although only a dozen pages long, the "Historical Notes" appearing at the end of Margaret Atwood's *The Handmaid's Tale* have been the subject of repeated critical scrutiny. Commentaries on the "Historical Notes" consistently suggest that the world of 2195 depicted therein is far from an eutopian alternative to the dystopia of Gilead; indeed, commentators consistently note the sexism of Pieixoto and suggest, more or less explicitly, that the conditions that led to the founding of Gilead in the first place still exist in the world of 2195. Ken Norris, for instance, argues that "The desire of future scholars to dress up in period costumes and 'play' at the roles of Gileadean society, the sexism of Professor Pieixoto, and his failure to learn anything of the human equation in Offred's story, all suggest that the informing principles of Gilead have not entirely disappeared," and his is far from the strongest articulation of this position. The world of 2195 is one in which women once again assume positions of authority, in which Native North American peoples are evidently part of dominant North American culture, and in which there is a renewed respect for nature (which one could contrast with Serena Joy's gardening strategies). This future might appear, therefore, to be an eutopian alternative to Gilead, and perhaps even to the world of today, if we can accept at face value that the sexist and racist assumptions prevalent in Gilead (and today) have been eradicated; this,

From *Science-Fiction Studies* 25, part 3 (November 1998). © 1998 by SF-TH Inc. at DePauw University.

however, we cannot easily do. The dissatisfaction readers feel with the alternative to Gilead offered by the world of the "Historical Notes," and the discomfort readers feel when faced with Pieixoto's perpetuation of attitudes that the novel suggests helped create Gilead in the first place, are inconsistent with the expectations often aroused by dystopian fictions.

That the future world of the "Historical Notes" is far from ideal is one of the easily-recognized devices Atwood employs to undercut our traditional expectations; while the opposition between alternate societal models in utopian fiction often serves to provide a simple binary opposition between eutopian and dystopian possibilities, Atwood instead offers degrees of dystopia. Similarly (and less evidently, perhaps), whereas science fiction often uses such devices as the pseudo-documentary to create verisimilitude, to validate the tale as real or true—to encourage us, in effect, to suspend our disbelief and accept that we are reading history, not fiction—Atwood eschews the conventional function of the pseudo-documentary voice. In *The Handmaid's Tale*, Atwood invokes a model that, in its standard use, serves to validate, or support, the authority of the work, but she does so in ways that subvert the conventional function of pseudo-documentary devices in science fiction. David Ketterer notes that "The different realities of science fiction are generally located in what purports to be the real future," but Atwood ultimately denies her tale this purported historicity.

The seminal utopian text, Thomas More's *Utopia*, and the originary science-fiction text, Mary Shelley's *Frankenstein*, firmly establish the often-invoked pseudo-documentary convention in their narratorial claims to documentary evidence to validate the truth of the narrative (Walton claims to have even the letters exchanged between Felix and Safie, which were taken by the creature, passed on to Victor, and thence to him). The documentary gestures in such texts invite readers to accept the historicity of the primary narrative by providing witnesses to at least some of the events narrated and by providing putative documentary evidence, such as Walton's letters to his sister as well as the primary documents he claims to have seen. Of course, in such texts as *Utopia* and *Frankenstein*, the action occurs in the "past," Raphael Hythloday recounting his adventures to Thomas More and the internal chronology of *Frankenstein* dating the action at least two decades before the novel's publication in 1818.

*Frankenstein*'s pseudo-historicity is less developed than *Utopia*'s, consisting really only of the Walton frame narrative, which provides a fairly straightforward and believable context for the novel's more fantastic narrative. More makes use of rather more elaborate pseudo-documentary techniques, including pseudo-correspondence and extensive reference to real historical figures—himself included—as witness to Hythloday's account.

Hythloday is even represented as having "joined himself in company with Amerigo Vespucci, and in the three last voyages of those four that be now in print and abroad in every man's hands, he continued still in his company," thus neatly inscribing Hythloday in contemporary travel literature and thereby "historicizing" him.

Like *The Handmaid's Tale*, these texts are presented as oral performances recorded (or edited) by others; unlike *The Handmaid's Tale*, they represent actions which are historically anterior to the time at which the texts were published. As a text purporting to recount future history, Atwood's novel confronts a rather greater credibility gap than do texts such as those of Shelley or More. Nevertheless, the extension of pseudo-documentary devices to various kinds of sf narrative, including narratives set in the future, as a legitimation device is a logical enough application of this principle and one that has a long history in science fiction, whether written within the genre or outside it. Any number of texts provide purported documentary evidence of different kinds to enhance narrative verisimilitude. Even claims of editorial intervention in the text presented can serve to validate the text, by suggesting that the editor has devoted time and care to a careful representation of an "original" text. *In The Shape of Things to Come* (1933), for instance, H. G. Wells presents himself as a sedulous editor who has "had indeed to arrange and rearrange [the chapters] after several trials, because they do not seem to have been read and written down by Raven in their proper chronological sequence," while in *The Purple Cloud* (1930), M. P. Shiel more modestly claims merely to have translated a shorthand document and notes that "the title, division into paragraphs, &c., have been arbitrarily contrived . . . for convenience."

Such strategies conventionally serve to invite the reader's suspension of disbelief, and, on the face of it, Atwood's "Historical Notes" might seem to do the same. Patrick Murphy identifies several examples of such devices in his "Reducing the Dystopian Distance: Pseudo-Documentary Framing in Near-Future Fiction." Murphy considers Atwood's novel at some length in his discussion and, although he recognizes that Atwood does not use the "Historical Notes" section simply to suspend disbelief, he also asserts that the section "tells readers that it did happen and that the journal is being critically studied in 2195." Chinmoy Banerjee also sees the function of the "Historical Notes" as an attempt to contextualize Offred's narrative historically: "The main function of the notes is apparently to ground and explain the tale."

However, the extent to which the "Historical Notes" section provides any validation at all to the narrative that precedes it is open to considerable discussion. The section is radically disjunctive, leaping forward some 200 years, totally abandoning the characters and narrative perspective of the bulk of the novel, and in fact querying that perspective in several ways, including querying its status as text. Even the purely retrospective aspect of the notes disorients readers. While *The Handmaid's Tale* is often described as a frame narrative, in fact there is no analogue for the "Historical Notes" at the beginning of the text to signal to readers that Offred's narrative is unfolding within a different and larger context. The "Historical Notes" force a purely retrospective re-evaluation of the text, unlike the pseudo-documentary strategies in the vast bulk of such fictions, which almost invariably precede the text or are incorporated throughout it, to signal clearly to the reader their presence. Because there is no hint in the body of the text of the recontextualizing to come at its end, the "Historical Notes" are discontinuous and disjunctive; they invite us to question, rather than accept, the authenticity of what we have just read. They invite an active interrogation of the text.

The historical leap, and the re-evaluation it forces of our assumptions about the historicity of the action, are significant and serve as challenges to our view of the status of the text we have been reading; they destabilize the reader's sense of Offred's narrative as history. Two binary models of historical representation may be applied to *The Handmaid's Tale*. Jamie Dopp contrasts an essentialist view of history with a materialist view, and concludes that the novel is basically essentialist, asserting the inevitability of oppression. David Ketterer contrasts the linear model of history with the cyclical, suggesting that Atwood adopts the latter model—a position consistent, incidentally, with Robert H. Canary's discussion of far-future sf (the "Historical Notes" are placed 200 years in the future) as contrasted with near-future sf. What makes the "Historical Notes" so important, and indeed the question of history in the novel so important, however, is the abrupt shift required by the "Historical Notes" in both models, and the consequent damage to verisimilitude. For nearly 300 pages, we have been located in a near-future dystopia, vividly realized and recognizably derived from our own time (albeit with minimal attention to detailed extrapolation): the model seems linear. Similarly, we have for nearly 300 pages watched Offred become increasingly abject until she finally surrenders to forces beyond her control: this is what Dopp sees as the novel's essentialist position. However, in the "Historical Notes" we leap forward 200 years and discover a society much like our own pre-Gileadean society, which suggests a cyclical rather than a linear model of history, and we discover in that society that the extreme repression of Gilead has ended, so the apparently essentialist model is replaced by a materialist model, one that suggests that Gilead is neither inevitable nor permanent. We are thrown into disarray, explicitly invited to reinvestigate the text because of the revelations about its nature in the "Historical Notes." As we look back, we find that the apparently simple linear and essentialist historical model is deceptive. In short, we find that the application of a single, simple historical model to the action is impossible: *both* the linear/essentialist *and* the cyclical/materialist models are invoked because of the disjunction between Offred's narrative and Pieixoto's academic address.

Indeed, Atwood shows little interest in validation devices that create the illusion of historicity at all. Although the bulk of the novel is set in a very near future, for instance, there is virtually no explanation provided of how we got from "now" to "then"; the novel is a third of the way to completion before Offred offers a few paragraphs of the sort of expository extrapolation which we would expect to be essential and to appear early in the novel, and in fact the bulk of the contextualizing exposition occurs in the "Historical Notes" section, a curious narrative decision given the novel's repeated assertion that context is all, and the cause of numerous complaints that the novel does not provide a believable rationale for the rise of the Gileadeans—it does so only retrospectively, and in the voice of a highly questionable authority. As Jamie Dopp avers, "The novel offers no explanation of the larger political context of [the Gileadean] regime, nor any explanation for its resort to such extreme levels of terror"; indeed, Chinmoy Banerjee complains that "the critical force of Atwood's dystopia is . . . put into doubt by the historical superficiality of the fiction." However, such complaints approach the tale from Pieixoto's perspective. Far from providing a validating context, the "Historical Notes" serve to undercut our faith in the reliability—the historicity—of the tale because they demonstrate the limitations of a univocal, factual approach to understanding Offred's experiences.

But neither does the bulk of the text invite us to accept its voice as historically authoritative. Offred's voice itself does not encourage us to see her tale as history. She speaks in the present tense, a fact which in itself discourages us from seeing her narrative as fixed, final, and anterior; it is, instead, ongoing, and it unfolds for us as it does for her. We might note here, incidentally, that Atwood manages by the use of this device to echo the use of the journal prevalent in such seminal dystopian works as *We* and *1984*, the influence of which on *The Handmaid's Tale* is fairly evident. This device denies the idea of historicity by having the action, even the "past" action, unfold in an eternal "now," rather than in a closed and finished "then." When Offred does use the past tense, she uses it in relation to her life before the Gileadean regime—in our "now"; our present is Offred's past. Offred also repeatedly acknowledges the contingency of her own narrative, acknowledging that, despite her use of the present tense, she is not experiencing events but recounting them. "This is a reconstruction," she tells us; "All of it is a reconstruction." She acknowledges that she has silently expanded Moira's account of her attempted escape, although she asserts that "I've tried to make it sound as much like her as I can"; she provides multiple narratives of Luke's fate, claiming to believe them all: "The things I believe can't all be true, though one of them must be. But I believe in all of them." She provides multiple versions of her first sexual encounter with Nick, and finally concludes, "I'm not sure how it happened; not exactly." Even her final words provide no definitive truth: "And so I step up, into the darkness within; or else the light." That is, Offred's account is clearly experiential, a reflection of her own thoughts and perspectives, rather than an objective and historical report.

Offred's narrative strategies consistently stress the failure of any single reading of an event to be valid. Indeed, they challenge the very notion of a textually fixed, historical truth. Offred comments at various points, for instance, on the failure of texts to provide convincing pictures of reality or to account for female experience. "The newspaper stories were like bad dreams to us," she observes; "How awful, we would say, and they were, but they were awful without being believable." Such accounts of rape and mutilation, of women "interfered with as they used to say," are supposedly factual and objective, but nevertheless feel "melodramatic" and do not seem real in the context of the lives lived by Offred and her friends prior to the Gileadean takeover. The texts do not capture their experiences: "they were about other women, and the men who did such things were other men." Instead, Offred says, "We were the people who were not in the papers. We lived in the blank white spaces at the edges of print. . . . We lived in the gaps between the stories." That is, accounts of female experience are partial and limited, leaving much out, perhaps more than is included. The "reality," or a significant proportion of it, exists outside the texts, so the texts provide only stories, not the whole story.

Gilead represents perhaps the most extreme example of textual reductionism, for it reduces all experience to a single perspective, a single story, and not even an unadulterated one, for the scriptures that serve as the basis of Gileadean society are read selectively and even modified, as Offred recognizes at different times; one example is the version of the Beatitudes recited at lunch at the Red Centre: "*Blessed be the poor in spirit, for theirs is the kingdom of heaven. Blessed are the merciful. Blessed are the meek. Blessed are the silent.* I knew they made that up, I knew it was wrong, and they left things out too, but there was no way of checking." The Gileadeans combine a belief in the authoritative power of a text to determine truth with the power of those who control the text to alter it to suit their needs. That is, their practice points up the failure of text as text, free from the power of the interpreter, to determine or even reflect truth.

Offred, by contrast, attempts to find the truth in multiple, subjective perspectives. As David S. Hogsette suggests: "Offred gradually recognizes that she can manipulate language in order to create her own subjectivity, a subjectivity that can enable her to act as a subversive agent against the oppressive reality created by the Republic of Gilead." Offred's own litanies contrast with those imposed by the Gileadean regime, as we see in her reflections on the word "chair":

> I sit in the chair and think about the word *chair*. It can also mean the leader of a meeting. It can also mean a mode of execution. It is the first syllable in *charity*. It is the French word for flesh. None of these facts has any connection with the others.
>
> These are the kinds of litanies I use, to compose myself.

While Offred insists on the multiple yet distinct meanings the word carries, Pieixoto plays on the multiple meanings of the word "chair" to collapse them, thus making a sexual and sexist pun at the expense of Maryann Crescent Moon: "I am sure we all enjoyed our charming Arctic Char last night at dinner, and now we are enjoying an equally charming Arctic Chair. I use the word 'enjoy' in two distinct senses, precluding, of course, the obsolete third (*Laughter*)." For Pieixoto, and for his audience, as the laughter indicates, joking about Maryann Crescent Moon's sexual appeal—she's good enough to eat—is acceptable, and is indicative of his reductive and simplistic view. Unlike similar Gileadean litanies of singular, univocal conformity, Offred's litanies are personal, multivocal, and self-defining; they are her mode of self-composition.

Indeed, to some extent, Offred liberates herself from her oppressive reality by transforming it into a fiction:

> I would like to believe this is a story I'm telling. I need to believe it. I must believe it. Those who can believe that such stories are only stories have a better chance.
>
> If it's a story I'm telling, then I have control over the ending. Then there will be an ending, to the story, and real life will come after it. I can pick up where I left off.
>
> It isn't a story I'm telling.
>
> It's also a story I'm telling, in my head, as I go along.

By fictionalizing, by thinking of her experiences as those in a story, by inventing multiple possibilities, Offred can come to terms, to some extent, with what is happening to her. Her life is not a story, but a genuine sequence of experiences—but it is also a story, a sequence of experiences given meaning and context by her process of self-composition, and the truth resides more in the story Offred constructs (or reconstructs) than it does in the facts.

Offred's account is on its face, then, not a conventional singular, univocal expression of "truth," but a "contra-logical, hierarchy-resistant, circularly ambiguous narrative." The "Historical Notes" section further undermines the historical authority of Offred's account by revealing that the text of the novel is not the direct record made by Offred of her experiences, but is itself a construct, a transcript of tape-recorded commentaries, edited and structured, and interpreted by its twenty-second-century editors, who have, in a way, repeated the very process that Offred herself uses, but with a very different agenda. In effect, our entire experience of Offred's account has been deceptive, for we have been reading it, but it is not a document at all, but a series of recorded audiotapes. The text we have read is a documentary study, a transcription edited by male scholars, not an unmediated account of Offred's experiences; it is a retrospectively organized interpretation of that account. All that we have assumed about the text we have been reading, including the authority of the order in which the events are narrated, is violated by the "Historical Notes," and the voice we thought we were listening to is subsumed, even fictionalized, by Pieixoto.

Documentaries purport to record accurately a moment in history, but manifest in Atwood's "Historical Notes" is that in fact they do nothing of the kind. Far from adding to the authority of Offred's account by providing an objective, historical context for it, far from making her tale more believable, the "Historical Notes" section casts doubt on the validity of the entire documentary mode. It does so in several ways. One of those ways, of course, is by providing such a clay-footed figure as Pieixoto as the voice of authority; we can hardly accept that he could be the arbiter of truth. But there are more significant questions raised about the historicizing of Offred's account.

Pieixoto's acknowledgment that the tale we have read is an editorial construct "based on some guesswork . . . and to be regarded as approximate, pending further research" recalls Offred's own acknowledgments of her reconstruction of events, but whereas for Offred the possibilities opened up by reconstructions and the alternate possibilities they provide play a key role in the narrative, for Pieixoto such contingency is a blemish to be removed, he hopes, when further research provides the univocal, final, true account. Completely lacking in Pieixoto's commentary is any recognition that the very process of transcription and editing makes such a univocal truth impossible to find.

The *Canterbury Tales* analogy Pieixoto cites itself underscores this point. First, the fact that Professor Wade has labeled the account "The Handmaid's Tale" "in homage to the great Geoffrey Chaucer" undermines the claims he and Pieixoto make about the truth value of their transcription by likening that transcription to a work of fiction, "a literary creation" rather than a historical account. Second, and more significantly, Chaucer's works have themselves been shaped by editors; indeed, just as the order of Offred's tapes has been determined by Pieixoto and Wade, so has the order of the *Canterbury Tales* been the subject of considerable editorial speculation, so much so that there are two different ordering principles (by Fragment, based on the order of the Ellesmere manuscript, or by Group, based on the "Bradshaw Shift") followed in editions of the work: which *Canterbury Tales* one reads depends on which edition one reads. The Chaucer reference doubly underscores the impossibility of Pieixoto's desire to arrive at a single, true version of the tale Offred recounts by likening her tale to fiction and by pointing up the problems inherent in editing the account.

His concern with such a search, and the implications of such a search for the idea he has of history, are key to an understanding of the "Historical Notes" section. Pieixoto sees history in terms of observable fact, in terms of simple and unequivocal truths and ordered cause and effect relationships. Because Offred has not provided the facts, Pieixoto has cause to lament the gaps that remain because of Offred's limitations:

> She could have told us much about the workings of the Gileadean empire, had she had the instincts of a reporter or a spy. What would we not give, now, for even twenty pages or so of printout from Waterford's private computer! However, we must be grateful for any crumbs the Goddess of History has deigned to vouchsafe us.

Even in this passage, we see Pieixoto's privileging of text over Offred's oral account; he would prefer computer transcripts to tape recordings. As Sandra Tomc notes, "It is no accident that Offred's tapes are discovered among other tokens of popular passion and bad taste—Elvis Presely tunes, folk songs, Mantovani instrumentals, and the screams of Twisted Sister— nor that all of these are laughed at and dismissed by Professor Pieixoto." Waterford's computer printouts might no doubt provide useful data, but how much understanding might they provide? Offred notes that the Commander is "truly ignorant of the real conditions under which we lived." The value of his testimony to provide understanding of life in Gilead is therefore highly suspect.

Of course, the other factual records to have survived have provided enough information for Pieixoto to consider two likely candidates for Offred's Commander, and to conclude that the most likely one was Frederick R.

Waterford, but it has left no evidence of Offred's true name. Or so Pieixoto argues, at any rate, concluding that the names Offred uses in her account are "useless for the purposes of identification and authentication. 'Luke' and 'Nick' drew blanks, as did 'Moira' and 'Janine.' There is a high probability that these were, in any case, pseudonyms. . . ." He ignores the fact, noted by numerous readers from Harriet Bergmann onward, that of the names listed at the end of chapter one, only June is unaccounted for in the text. Whether June is in fact Offred's real name is probably immaterial (and Pieixoto's point that the names used on the tapes are probably pseudonyms should not be dismissed lightly), but Pieixoto's failure even to address the possibility helps underscore the extent to which Offred is really invisible to him and thereby helps point up the failure of his approach to Offred's account.

Commenting on the photograph she's shown of her daughter, an example of the sort of concrete physical evidence that can pass from age to age and that Pieixoto wishes he possessed, Offred notes, presciently, "From the point of view of future history, this kind, we'll be invisible." Her qualification—"this kind"—is crucial, for it implies alternate models of history, and those models are distinct from Pieixoto's. For Pieixoto, history is artifact; for Offred, it is experience.

Indeed, if Pieixoto resembles Offred in one respect, in his reconstruction of the past into a coherent narrative, he resembles the Gileadeans in others. We have already observed his sexism, a trait that the Commander explicitly relates to the Gileadean takeover. Pieixoto's attitude to history is Gileadean as well. Like Aunt Lydia, "who was in love with either/or," Pieixoto seeks for the wonderfully simple, easy answers that Gilead attempted to provide. "Did our narrator reach the outside world safely and build a new life for herself? *Or* was she discovered in her attic hiding place, arrested, sent to the colonies *or* to Jezebel's, *or* even executed?" he wonders (emphasis added). Was Fred Waterford or Judd, he wonders. Only one answer is possible, of course, and we as readers probably wonder also. However, the answers are really irrelevant, except as facts. As we have seen, one of Offred's comforts is considering possibilities, not facts, and leaving the truth unfixed and open; even in her litany, "chair" means several different things simultaneously, unbound by "either/or." Knowing the answers Pieixoto seeks will add nothing to our ability to understand Gilead or to evaluate it. But we can recognize the desire to ask such questions in the Gileadean mentality.

When commenting on why the revolution occurred, for instance, the Commander rejects the abstract in favor of the concrete: "We have the stats from that time," he asserts; "Men were turning off on sex, even. They were turning off on marriage." When Offred notes that the Gileadeans overlooked love—which, incidentally, Offred identifies as by definition incapable of reduction to the singular and known: "the way love feels is always approximate," she tells us—the Commander says, "But look at the stats, my dear. Was it really worth it, *falling in love?*" For the Gileadeans, truth is reducible to numbers, or stats—or to scripture. That such a reduction is manifestly inadequate is demonstrated amply by the novel—and that Pieixoto has not recognized this truth is equally manifest.

Pieixoto's search is for facts only. His desire for twenty pages of printout from Waterford's computer is unsettlingly reminiscent of the Commander's blithe assertion of the power of statistics over human experience. Pieixoto has a compelling record of a human experience, but he wants names and dates; because we don't know Offred's real name, we don't know much about her, according to Pieixoto. He wants history, but Offred gives him only her story, and he is hesitant to accept its validity. He is more concerned with the mechanics involved in transcribing, and validating the authenticity of, the tapes—even going so far as to state, "if the author is telling the truth, no machine or tapes would have been available to her"— than he is with their contents.

His attitude to the contents of the tapes, and to their implications, is revealing:

> If I may be permitted an editorial aside, allow me to say that in my opinion we must be cautious about passing moral judgement upon the Gileadeans. Surely we have learned by now that such judgements are of necessity culture-specific. Also, Gileadean society was under a good deal of pressure, demographic and otherwise, and was subject to factors from which we ourselves are happily more free. Our job is not to censure but to understand.

In assuming here the editorial role, Pieixoto is assuming his authoritative role in order to abdicate the very essence of that authority. The process of editorial reconstruction he claims will lead ultimately to a reclamation of the truth is nothing if not a process of judgment, but here he denies the necessity of judgment. Judgment and understanding cannot, of course, be separated. Tellingly, though, Pieixoto couples his apparent abdication of judgment with an excuse for the Gileadeans' behavior, an excuse completely unnecessary if all we are concerned with is the facts, and not judgment. One cannot excuse Gilead without at least implicitly judging it. Pieixoto's is not a reliable voice.

Attempts to create pseudo-documentary or historical status for science-fiction works usually function to invite our suspension of disbelief, to see the story as history, as "real." Such works may well offer powerful and compelling visions of what might come, in the hope of preventing such events, but, as Pieixoto's attitude here suggests, our judgment of what *has* happened is very easily colored by our belief that we live outside, and are superior to, the closed and finished world of that historical past; we tend to view history from "the clearer light of our own day," as Pieixoto claims. Atwood does not wish to create such a historicized world in *The Handmaid's Tale*.

The "Historical Notes" require us not to accept as valid and authoritative what we have read, nor to believe passively what we are told, as documentary requires, but rather these Notes invite us to reject Pieixoto's model of complacent historical understanding and instead to engage in the far more challenging, and far more important, task of using our judgment, a faculty which Pieixoto suggests we ought to abandon when he asserts, "Our job is not to censure but to understand." Pieixoto, the documentarian, wants us to suspend our judgment in favor of his own putatively non-judgmental judgment. The novel requires us to recognize the folly of such a surrender to the documentary. If history is fixed and final, as Pieixoto would have it, if facts are just data—stats—and the past (and therefore, by implication, the future as well) is unitary and unalterable, we can learn nothing here. Instead, the novel undermines this notion of history, requiring us to recognize that gleaning truth from this text requires accepting its fictionality as the medium for that truth. Stories describe what *might* happen, and what might happen remains susceptible to change. Atwood's foregrounding and subverting of devices of verisimilitude makes our recognition of the possibility, rather than the reality, of the story evident. We recognize that Pieixoto's historicizing will only justify, not prevent, Gilead, and one hopes, we are encouraged to adopt a different stance. The necessity of doing so is clear enough: as Atwood herself has pointed out—and so does Pieixoto, for that matter—this story is not really fiction at all, for all of the Gileadean atrocities have occurred, in reality, already. They will continue to do so as long as we contextualize, compartmentalize, and historicize them, in order to avoid judging them.

# Chronology

1939     Born on November 18 in Ottawa, Ontario, Canada, Margaret Eleanor Atwood is the second of three children of Carl Edmund Atwood and Margaret Killam Atwood.

1945     Writes juvenile poems, "Rhyming Cats," as well as plays, poems, comic books, and a novel. Moves with family to Sault Ste. Marie, Ontario.

1946–61     Family lives in Toronto, Ontario; spends spring, summer, and autumn in Canadian bush.

1952–57     Attends Leaside High School in Toronto, writes for literary magazine *Clan Call*.

1957     Enrolls at Victoria College, University of Toronto, with the intention of becoming a writer. Begins reading poetry in public at Bohemian Embassy.

1959     Works as counselor at Camp White Pine, Haliburton, Ontario. Has first poem, "Fruition," published in a major literary journal, *The Canadian Forum*.

1961     Receives bachelor's degree. Moves to Boston. *Double Persephone*, her first book of poetry, is published.

1961–62     Attends graduate school at Radcliffe College and Harvard University on Woodrow Wilson Fellowship.

1962        Receives master's degree in English from Radcliffe College.

1962–63     Continues graduate studies at Harvard; meets James Polk.

1963–64     Moves to Toronto; works for market research company; poems published in *Poesie/Poetry 64*.

1964–65     Moves to Vancouver; teaches literature at University of British Columbia.

1965–67     Returns to Harvard for doctoral studies with help of Canada Council grant.

1966        Publishes a collection of poems, *The Circle Game*.

1967        Marries James Polk.

1967–68     Teaches literature at Sir George Williams University, Montreal.

1968        *The Animals in That Country* is published.

1968–70     Resides in Edmonton, Alberta. Teaches creative writing at University of Alberta.

1969        *The Edible Woman* is published.

1970        *The Journals of Susanna Moodie* and *Procedures for Underground* are published.

1970–71     Travels to England, France, and Italy.

1971        *Power Politics* is published.

1971–72     *Surfacing* is published. Writer-in-residence at York University, Toronto. Editor and member of board of directors of House of Anansi Press.

1972        *Survival* published.

1972–73     Writer-in-residence at University of Toronto.

1973        Receives D.Litt. from Trent University. Divorced. Moves to Allison, Ontario, with novelist Graeme Gibson.

1974        *You Are Happy* is published.

1976        Daughter, Eleanor Jess Atwood Gibson, born in May. *Selected Poems* and *Lady Oracle* published.

1977        *Dancing Girls and Other Stories* and a children's book, *Days of the Rebels*, are published.

1978        *Two-Headed Poems* and a children's book, *Up in the Tree*, are published.

1979    *Life Before Man* is published.

1980    Returns to Toronto. Receives D.Litt. from Concordia University. A children's book, *Anna's Pet*, is published.

1981    *True Stories* and *Bodily Harm* are published; collaborates on a film, *Snowbird*.

1982    *Second Words: Selected Critical Prose*, is published.

1983    *Murder in the Dark* and *Bluebeard's Egg*, short story collections, are published.

1984–86 President of International P.E.N., Canadian Centre (English speaking).

1985    *The Handmaid's Tale* is published. Writer-in-residence at the University of Alabama, Tuscaloosa.

1987    *Poems: 1976-1986* and *The Can-Lit Foodbook: From Pen to Palate; A Collection of Tasty Literary Fare* are published. Writer-in-residence at Macquarie University, New South Wales, Australia. Writes script for drama *Heaven on Earth*, produced on CBC and BBC.

1988    *Cat's Eye* is published.

1989    Writer-in-residence at Trinity University, San Antonio, Texas.

1990    *For the Birds*, a children's book, is published.

1991    *Wilderness Tips*, a collection of short stories, is published.

1992    *Good Bones* is published. Returns to Toronto; becomes Lecturer of English at the University of British Columbia, Vancouver.

1993    *The Robber Bride* is published.

1994    *Good Bones and Simple Murders*, a collection of short stories, is published.

1995    *Strange Things: The Malevolent North in Canadian Literature*, a collection of lectures, is published; *Morning in the Burned House*, a book of poems, is published; *Princess Prunella and the Purple Peanut*, a children's book, is published.

1996    *Alias Grace* is published.

# Contributors

HAROLD BLOOM is Sterling Professor of the Humanities at Yale University and Henry W. and Albert A. Berg Professor of English at the New York University Graduate School. He is the author of over 20 books, including *Shelley's Mythmaking* (1959), *The Visionary Company* (1961), *Blake's Apocalypse* (1963), *Yeats* (1970), *A Map of Misreading* (1975), *Kabbalah and Criticism* (1975), *Agon: Toward a Theory of Revisionism* (1982), *The American Religion* (1992), *The Western Canon* (1994), and *Omens of Millennium: The Gnosis of Angels, Dreams, and Resurrection* (1996). *The Anxiety of Influence* (1973) sets forth Professor Bloom's provocative theory of the literary relationships between the great writers and their predecessors. His most recent books include *Shakespeare: The Invention of the Human*, a 1998 National Book Award finalist, and *How to Read and Why*, which was published in 2000. In 1999, Professor Bloom received the prestigious American Academy of Arts and Letters Gold Medal for Criticism.

AMIN MALAK has taught at the University of Alberta.

ROBERTA RUBENSTEIN has been Professor of Literature and Director of the Women's Studies Program at American University. She is the author of *Boundaries of the Self: Gender, Culture, Fiction*, and the co author of *Worlds of Fiction*.

MADONNE MINER is a professor at Texas Tech University. She is the author of *Insatiable Appetites: Twentieth-Century American Women's Bestsellers*.

171

J. BROOKS BOUSON has been associate professor of English at Loyola University. He is the author of *The Empathic Reader: A Study of the Narcissistic Character and the Drama of the Self*, and most recently *Quiet As It's Kept: Shame, Trauma, & Race in the Novels of Toni Morrison*.

SHARON ROSE WILSON teaches English at the University of Northern Colorado. She co-edited *Approaches to Teaching Atwood's* The Handmaid's Tale *& Other Works* and is past co-president of the Margaret Atwood Society.

SANDRA TOMC teaches at the University of British Columbia.

GLENN DEER teaches at the University of British Columbia.

HILDE STAELS has taught at the University of Antwerp. She is the author of *Margaret Atwood's Novels: A Study of Narrative Discourse*.

KAREN STEIN is Professor of English and Women's Studies at the University of Rhode Island; she also is director of Graduate Studies in English. She has written essays on Atwood, Toni Morrison, and other women writers, and is the author of *Margaret Atwood Revisited*.

MARTA DVORAK has taught at the Université de Rennes II.

DOMINICK M. GRACE is an associate professor of English at Algoma University College in Ontario. He has taught a variety of courses and researched Chaucer and Shakespeare as well as science fiction and other pouplar genres.

# Bibliography

Andriano, Joseph. "*The Handmaid's Tale* as Scrabble Game," *Essays on Canadian Writing* 18 (1992/93): 89–96.

Baccolini, Raffaella. "'What's in a Name?': Language and Self-Creation in Women's Writing." In The *Representation of the Self in Women's Autobiography*, Vita Fortunati and Gabriella Morisco, eds. Bologna: University of Bologna, 1993.

Banerjee, Chinmoy. "Alice in Disneyland: Criticism as Commodity in *The Handmaid's Tale*." *Essays in Canadian Writing* 41 (Summer 1990): 74–92.

Bergmann, Harriet F. "'Teaching Them to Read': A Fishing Expedition in *The Handmaid's Tale*," *College English* 51 (1989): 847–54.

Bignell, Jonathan. "The Handmaid's Tale: Novel and Film," *British Journal of Canadian Studies* 8, no. 1 (1993): 71–84.

Carminero-Santangelo, Marta. "Moving Beyond 'The Blank White Spaces': Atwood's Gilead, Postmodernism, and Strategic Resistance," *Studies in Canadian Literature* 19, no. 1 (1994): 20–42.

Carrington, Ildikó de Papp. *Canadian Writers and Their Works*, vol. 9. Toronto: ECW Press, 1987.

———. "A Swiftian Sermon." *Essays on Canadian Writing*, no. 34 (Spring 1987): 127–32.

Christ, Carol P. "Margaret Atwood: Surfacing of Women's Spiritual Quest and Vision." *Signs* 2 (Winter 1976): 316–30.

Davey, Frank. *Margaret Atwood: A Feminist Poetics.* Vancouver: Talonbooks, 1984.

Dopp, Jamie. "Subject-Position as Victim-Position in *The Handmaid's Tale*," *Studies in Canadian Literature* 19, no. 1 (1994): 43–57.

Felski, Rita. *Beyond Feminist Aesthetics: Feminist Literature and Social Change.* Cambridge, Mass.: Harvard University Press, 1989.

Filipczak, Dorota. "'Is There No Balm in Gilead?' Biblical Intertext in Margaret Atwood's *The Handmaid's Tale*." In *Literature and Theology at Century's End*, Gregory Salyer and Robert Detweiler, eds. Atlanta: Scholars, 1995.

Finnell, Susanna. "Unwriting the Quest: Margaret Atwood's Fiction and *The Handmaid's Tale*." In *Women and the Journey: The Female Travel Experience*,

Frederick Bonnie and Susan H. McLeod, eds. Pullman.: Washington State University Press, 1993.

Fitting, Peter. "The Turn from Utopia in Recent Feminist Fiction." In *Feminism, Utopia, and Narrative*, Libby Falk Jones and Sarah Webster Goodwin, eds. Knoxville: University of Tennessee Press, 1990.

Foley, Michael. "'Basic Victim Positions' and the Women in Margaret Atwood's *The Handmaid's Tale*," *Atlantis* 15, no. 2 (1990): 50–58.

———. "Satiric Intent in Margaret Atwood's *The Handmaid's Tale*," *Commonwealth Essays and Studies* 11, no. 2 (Spring 1989): 44–52.

Fullbrook, Kate. "Margaret Atwood: Colonisation and Responsibility." In *Free Women: Ethics and Aesthetics in Twentieth-Century Women's Fiction*. Philadelphia: Temple University Press, 1990.

Givner, Jessie. "Names, Faces and Signatures in Margaret Atwood's *Cat's Eye* and *The Handmaid's Tale*," *Canadian Literature* 133 (Summer 1992): 56–75.

Godard, Barbara. "Telling It Over Again: Atwood's Art of Parody," *Canadian Poetry* 21 (Fall–Winter 1987): 1–30.

Goldsmith, Elizabeth, ed. *Writing the Female Voice: Essays on Epistolary Literature*. Boston: Northeastern University Press, 1989.

Grace, Sherrill E. *Violent Duality: A Study of Margaret Atwood*. Montreal: Vehicule Press, 1980.

Grace, Sherrill E., and Lorraine Weir, eds. *Margaret Atwood: Language, Text and System*. Vancouver: UBC, 1983.

Gray, Francine du Plessix. "Margaret Atwood: Nature as the Nunnery." In *Adam and Eve and the City: Selected Nonfiction*. New York: Simon and Schuster, 1987.

Hales, Leslie-Ann. "Genesis Revisited: The Darkening Vision of Margaret Atwood," *Month* 20, no. 7 (July 1987): 257–62.

Halliday, David. "On Atwood." *Waves* 15, no. 4 (Spring 1987): 51–54.

Hammer, Stephanie Barbe. "The World As It Will Be? Female Satire and the Technology of Power in *The Handmaid's Tale*," *Modern Language Studies* 20, no. 2 (Spring 1990): 39–49.

Hengen, Shannon. *Margaret Atwood's Power: Mirrors, Reflections and Images in Select Fiction and Poetry*. Toronto: Second Story Press, 1993, pp. 110–16.

Hogsette, David S. "Margaret Atwood's Rhetorical Epilogue in *The Handmaid's Tale*: The Reader's Role in Empowering Offred's Speech Act," *Critique* 38 (1997): 262–78.

Howells, Coral Ann. *Margaret Atwood*. New York: St. Martin's Press, 1996.

———. "Margaret Atwood: *Bodily Harm, The Handmaid's Tale*," In *Private and Fictional Words: Canadian Women Novelists of the 1970s and 1980s*. London and New York: Methuen, 1987.

———, and Lynette Hunter, eds. *Narrative Strategies in Canadian Literature*. Buckingham: Open University Press, 1991.

Ingersoll, Earl G., ed. *Margaret Atwood: Conversations*. London: Virago, 1992.

———. "Margaret Atwood's *The Handmaid's Tale* as a Self-Subverting Text." In *Cultural Identities in Canadian Literature*, Bénédicte Mauguière, ed. New York: Peter Lang, 1998.

Jacobus, Lee A., and Regina Barreca. "Margaret Atwood Issue." *Lit: Literature Interpretation Theory* 6 (December 1995).

Keith, W. J. "Apocalyptic Imaginations: Notes on Atwood's *The Handmaid's Tale* and Findley's *Not Wanted on the Voyage*." *Essays on Canadian Writing* no. 35 (Winter 1987): 123–34.

Kolodny, Annette. "Margaret Atwood and the Politics of Narrative." In *Studies on Canadian Literature: Introductory and Critical Essays*, Arnold E. Davidson, ed. New York: Modern Language Association of America, 1991.

Lacombe, Michele. "The Writing on the Wall: Amputated Speech in Margaret Atwood's *The Handmaid's Tale*," *Wascana Review* 21, no. 2 (Fall 1986): 3–20.

Lecker, Robert, Jack David, and Ellen Quigley, eds. *Canadian Writers and Their Works: Essays on Form, Context, and Development.* Toronto: ECW Press, 1987.

McCombs, Judith, ed. *Critical Essays on Margaret Atwood.* Boston: G. K. Hall, 1988.

———. *Margaret Atwood: A Reference Guide.* Boston: G. K. Hall, 1991.

Mendez-Egle, Beatrice, ed. *Margaret Atwood: Reflection and Reality.* Edinburg, Texas: Pan American University, 1988.

Montelaro, Janet J. "Maternity and the Ideology of Sexual Difference in *The Handmaid's Tale*," *Lit: Literature Interpretation Theory* 6, nos. 3–4 (December 1995): 233–56.

Murray, Heather. "'Its Image in the Mirror': Canada, Canonicity, the Uncanny," *Essays in Canadian Writing* 42 (Winter 1990): 102–30.

Mycak, Sonia. *In Search of the Split Subject: Psychoanalysis, Phenomenology, and the Novels of Margaret Atwood.* Toronto: ECW, 1996.

Myhal, Bob. "Boundaries, Centers, and Circles: The Postmodern Geometry of *The Handmaid's Tale*," *Lit: Literature, Interpretation, Theory* 6 (1995): 213–31.

Nicholson, Colin, ed. *Margaret Atwood: Writing and Subjectivity.* London: Macmillan, 1994.

Nicholson, Mervyn. "Food and Power: Homer, Carroll, Atwood and Others," *Mosaic* 20, no. 3 (Summer 1987): 37–55.

Nilsen, Helge Normann. "Four Feminist Novels by Margaret Atwood," *American Studies in Scandinavia* 26, no. 2 (1994): 126–39.

Norris, Ken. "'The University of Denay, Nunavit': The 'Historical Notes' in Margaret Atwood's *The Handmaid's Tale*," *American Review of Canadian Studies* 20, no. 3 (1990): 357–64.

Palmer, Carole L. "Current Atwood Checklist, 1988." *Newsletter of the Margaret Atwood Society* no. 5 (1988): 5–11.

Parker, Emma. "You Are What You Eat: The Politics of Eating in the Novels of Margaret Atwood," *Twentieth Century Literature* 41, no. 3 (Fall 1995): 349–68.

Pearlman, Mickey, ed. *Canadian Women Writing Fiction.* Jackson: University Press of Mississippi, 1993.

Perrakis, Phyllis Sternberg. "The Female Gothic and the (M)other in Atwood and Lessing," *Doris Lessing Newsletter* 17, no. 1 (1995): 1, 11–15.

Rao, Eleonora. *Strategies for Identity: The Fiction of Margaret Atwood. Writing About Women: Feminist Literary Studies* 9. New York: Peter Lang, 1993.

Raschke, Debrah. "Margaret Atwood's *The Handmaid's Tale*: False Borders and Subtle Subversions," *Lit: Literature Interpretation Theory* 6, nos. 3–4 (December 1995): 257–68.

Reesman, Jeanne Campbell. "Dark Knowledge in *The Handmaid's Tale*." *CEA Critic: An Official Journal of the College English Association* 53, no. 3 (Spring–Summer 1991): 6–22.

Rigney, Barbara Hill. *Margaret Atwood.* Eva Figes and Adele King, eds. Totowa, N. J.: Barnes and Noble. 1987.

Rubenstein, Roberta. "Escape Artist and Split Personalities: Margaret Atwood," *Boundaries of the Self: Gender, Culture, Fiction.* Urbana: University of Illinois Press, 1987.

Slonczewski, Joan L. "A Tale of Two Handmaids." *Kenyon Review* 8, no. 4 (Fall 1986): 120–24.

Sparrow, Fiona. "'This Place Is Some Kind of a Garden': Clearings in the Bush in the Works of Susanna Moodie, Catharine Parr Traill, Margaret Atwood and Margaret Laurence," *The Journal of Commonwealth Literature* 25, no. 1 (1990): 24–41.

Staels, Hilde. *Margaret Atwood's Novels: A Study of Narrative Discourse.* Tübingen, Germany: Francke, 1995.

Stein, Karen F. "Margaret Atwood's *The Handmaid's Tale*: Scheherezade in Dystopia,"
        *University of Toronto Quarterly* 61 (1991/92): 269–79.
St. Pierre, P. Matthew. "Envisioning Atwood." *Cross Currents* 36, no. 3 (Fall 1986):
        371–73.
Suarez, Isable Carrera. "'Yet I Speak, Yet I Exist': Affirmation of the Subject in
        Atwood's Short Stories." In *Margaret Atwood: Writing and Subjectivity*, Colin
        Nicholson, ed. London: Macmillan Press and New York, St. Martin's Press,
        1994. 230–47.
Templin, Charlotte. "Atwood's *The Handmaid's Tale*," *Explicator* 49, no. 4 (Summer
        1991): 255–56.
Updike, John. "Expeditions to Gilead and Seegard." *New Yorker* 62, no. 12 (May 12,
        1986): 118, 121–23.
Van Spanckeren, Kathryn, Jan Garden Castro, and Sandra M. Gilbert, eds. *Margaret
        Atwood: Vision and Forms*. Carbondale: Southern Illinois University Press,
        1988.
Verwaayen, Kimberly. "Re-examining the Gaze in *The Handmaid's Tale*," *Open Letter*
        9, no. 4 (1995): 44–54.
Wagner-Martin, Linda. "Epigraphs to Atwood's *The Handmaid's Tale*," *Notes on
        Contemporary Literature* 17, no. 2 (1987): 4.
Wall, Kathleen. *The Callisto Myth from Ovid to Atwood: Initiation and Rape in Literature*.
        Montreal: McGill-Queen's University Press, 1988.
White, Roberta. "Margaret Atwood: Reflections in a Convex Mirror." In *Canadian
        Women Writing Fiction*, Mickey Pearlman, ed. Jackson: University Press of
        Mississippi, 1993.
Wilson, Sharon R., Thomas B. Friedman, and Shannon Hengen. *Approaches to
        Teaching Atwood's* The Handmaid's Tale *and Other Works*. New York:
        Modern Language Association of America, 1996.
Workman, Nancy V. "Sufi Mysticism in Margaret Atwood's *The Handmaid's Tale*,"
        *Studies in Canadian Literature* 14, no. 2 (1989): 10–26.
York, Lorraine M. "The Habits of Language: Uniform(ity), Transgression and
        Margaret Atwood." *Canadian Literature* 126 (Autumn 1990): 6–19.
———, ed. *Various Atwoods: Essays on the Later Poems, Short Fiction, and Novels*.
        Concord, Ontario: Anansi, 1995.

# *Acknowledgments*

"Margaret Atwood's *The Handmaid's Tale* and the Dystopian Tradition" by Amin Malak from *Canadian Literature* 112 (Spring 1987): 9–15. © 1987 by the University of British Columbia, Vancouver. Reprinted by permission.

"Nature and Nurture in Dystopia: *The Handmaid's Tale*" by Roberta Rubenstein from *Margaret Atwood: Vision and Forms*, edited by Kathryn VanSpanckeren and Jan Garden Castro. © 1988 by the Board of Trustees of Southern Illinois University. Reprinted by permission of the publisher.

"'Trust Me'. Reading the Romance Plot in Margaret Atwood's *The Handmaid's Tale*" by Madonne Miner from *Twentieth Century Literature* 37, no. 2 (Summer 1991): 148–67. © 1991 by Hofstra University. Reprinted by permission.

"The Misogyny of Patriarchal Culture in *The Handmaid's Tale*" by J. Brooks Bouson from *Brutal Choreographies: Oppositional Strategies and Narrative Design in the Novels of Margaret Atwood*, by J. Brook Bouson. © 1993 by the University of Massachusetts Press. Reprinted by permission.

"Off the Path to Grandma's House in *The Handmaid's Tale*: 'Little Red Cap'" by Sharon Rose Wilson from *Margaret Atwood's Fairy-Tale Sexual Politics* by Sharon Rose Wilson. © 1993 by the University Press of Mississippi. Reprinted by permission.

"'The Missionary Position': Feminism and Nationalism in Margaret Atwood's *The Handmaid's Tale*" by Sandra Tomc from *Canadian*

*Literature* 138/139 (Fall/Winter 1993): 73–85. © 1993 by the University of British Columbia, Vancouver. Reprinted by permission.

"*The Handmaid's Tale*: Dystopia and the Paradoxes of Power" by Glenn Deer from *Postmodern Canadian Fiction and the Rhetoric of Authority*, by Glenn Deer. © 1994 by McGill-Queen's University Press. Reprinted by permission.

"Margaret Atwood's *The Handmaid's Tale*: Resistance through Narrating" by Hilde Staels from *English Studies* 76, no. 5 (September 1995): 455–67. © 1995 by Swets & Zeitlinger. Reprinted by permission.

"Margaret Atwood's Modest Proposal: *The Handmaid's Tale*" by Karen Stein from *Canadian Literature* 148 (Spring 1996): 57–71. © 1996 by the University of British Columbia, Vancouver. Reprinted by permission.

"What Is Real/Reel? Margaret Atwood's 'Rearrangement of Shapes on a Flat Surface,' or Narrative as Collage" by Marta Dvorak from *Études Anglaises* 51, no. 4 (October–December 1998): 448–460. © 1998 Didier Érudition. Reprinted by permission.

"*The Handmaid's Tale*: 'Historical Notes'and Documentary Subversion" by Dominick M. Grace from *Science-Fiction Studies* 25, part 3 (November 1998): 481–94. © 1998 by SF-TH Inc. at DePauw University. Reprinted by permission.

# Index

Abortion, 17, 113
Afghanistan, 1, 69
American Puritanism, 2, 65–66, 87–90,
    113, 128, 129–31
Andersen, Hans Christian, 69, 149 50
Angels, 16, 51
*Animal Farm* (Orwell), 15
Animals, 15–16, 17, 109
Aphrodite, 64, 69
Atwood, Margaret
  concept of dystopian fiction, 1, 2, 9,
    22–23, 93–112, 125–26
  food and, 135
  nationalism of, 82–91
  poetry of, 108–9, 143, 152–53
  as visual artist, 143
Aunts, 43
  described, 6–7
  Elizabeth, 55
  as indoctrinators of handmaids, 14,
    46–47, 53, 56, 70, 114, 117
  Lydia, 7, 14, 46–47, 53, 56, 117, 121
Austen, Jane, 77–78, 108


Bad mother, Serena Joy as, 47, 49, 64
Banerjee, Chinmoy, 87, 96, 109, 157,
    159
Barthes, Roland, 146, 152
Beaumont, Charles, 134

Beauvoir, Simone de, 6
Bergmann, Harriet, 61, 93–95, 164
Bilhah, 49–50, 64, 66, 76, 78, 113
Binary oppositions, in dystopian
    fiction, 5
Birds, 15
Birth control, 17
Birthing ceremony, 18, 47, 48, 101–2
Blood
  color of, 24, 46, 105, 122, 151–52
  of Corn Mother, 64
  menstrual, 48
  in sacrifice, 68
  violence and, 52
  and Wall in Gilead, 24–25, 54, 103,
    104
Bloom, Harold, 1–2
Bluebeard, 74, 75
*Bluebeard's Egg*, 68, 74
*Bodily Harm*, 12, 13, 14, 41, 42, 45, 46,
    58, 63, 74, 75, 93
Bouson, J. Brooks, 41–62
*Brave New World* (Huxley), 1, 4
Brontës, 2, 69
Burgess, Anthony, 1


Caminero-Santangelo, Marta, 143
Canada
  literature of, 8, 82, 83, 88, 135

as metaphorical colony, 8
and nationalism of Atwood, 82–91
native populations of, 20, 77, 91,
    122–23
Canary, Robert H., 158
*CanLit Foodbook, The: From Pen to
    Plate—A Collection of Tasty Literary
    Fare*, 135
Cannibalism, 134–36
*Canterbury Tales* (Chaucer), 162–63
Carter, Angela, 67
*Cat's Eye*, 47, 58, 68, 70, 93, 141
Cattle, 15, 68–69
Cattle prods, 15, 70, 98
Chairs, 25–26, 54, 77, 101, 161, 164
Change, in dystopian fiction, 5–6
Characterization
  in dystopian fiction, 5
  in *The Handmaid's Tale*, 26–27
Chase, Richard, 88
Chatterjee, Gopal, 77
Chaucer, Geoffrey, 162–63
Children
  absence of, 17
  cannibalism and, 134–36
  as commodities, 12, 134–36
  deformed, 12–13, 17, 48, 134–36
Christian Coalition, 1
Christianity, 65–66
Cixous, Hélène, 67
*Clockwork Orange, A* (Burgess), 1
Coleridge, Samuel Taylor, 145–46
Colonies, 4, 22, 47, 118
Commander, The
  attitudes toward women, 29–30
  interest in language, 27–28
  old things and, 28–29
  probable name, 163–64
  relationship with Offred, 19, 21–22,
    26, 27–35, 48–52, 56
  Scrabble games with Offred, 19,
    21–22, 37–38, 70–71, 74, 120

Commanders of the Faith
  lack of freedom, 8, 109
  names of handmaids and, 6, 144
  ritual insemination ceremony, 3–4,
    16, 22, 46–48, 49–50, 52, 70, 113
"Company of Wolves, The" (Carter),
    67
Corn Mother, 64
Cowart, David, 61
Crone Goddess, 64, 71


Davey, Frank, 96, 108–9
Davidson, Arnold, 59, 60, 78, 89,
    93–94, 128, 142
Davidson, Cathy, 87–88
Death, 101–2. *See also* Wall in Gilead
Dedications
  as framing device, 138
  to Perry Miller, 87–89, 129–30
  to Mary Webster, 68–69, 87, 89–90,
    129–30
Deer, Glenn, 85, 93–112, 128, 137
Demeter, 64–65, 66, 67, 73, 76
Denay, Nunavit, 59, 76–77, 91,
    122–23, 128
Dene, 77, 91, 122–23
Diana, 64, 67, 71, 77
Disembodiment, 13–14
Dismemberment, 13–14, 69, 117
Dog, Johnny Running, 20, 77
Dopp, Jamie, 87, 158, 159
Dostoyevsky, Fyodor, 7–8
*Double Persephone*, 64, 72
Douglas, Ann, 88
Dream-nightmares, in dystopian
    fiction, 4–5
Dvorak, Marta, 141–51
Dystopian fiction
  Atwood's concept of, 1, 2, 9, 22–23,
    93–112, 125–26
  characteristics of, 4–6

examples of dystopia in, 1, 4, 159
irony in, 9–10


Econowives, 43
Eden, 64
*Edible Woman, The*, 11, 135
Egg, 56, 101, 102, 122, 136–37
Egoyan, Atom, 147
Ehrenreich, Barbara, 22–23, 37, 85
Epigraphs
  as framing devices, 127, 130–40
  from *Genesis*, 49–50, 131–32
  "A Modest Proposal" (Swift), 132–40
  Sufi proverb, 127, 128, 130–31
Essentialism, 158–59
Eucharist, 65
Eurydice, 125
Evangelical fundamentalist right, 22,
  41, 66, 81
Eve, 67
Extramarital affairs, 31–33
Eyes (spies), 14, 27, 46, 58, 109, 111


Fairy tales
  "Red Riding Hood" (Little Red Cap),
    63, 64–79, 149
  "The Red Shoes," 44–45, 69, 149–50
  "The Robber Bridegroom," 76
*Fairy-Tale Sexual Politics* (Wilson), 149
Faludi, Susan, 41
Falwell, Jerry, 41
Fascism, clerical, 2
Fashion magazines, 147–48
Feet, mutilation of women's, 14, 45,
  55, 69
Feminism
  antifeminist backlash and, 41–42, 61
  irony and, 9–10
  as politics of liberation, 85, 90–91. *See
    also* Nationalism

Fiedler, Leslie, 88
Flowers
  symbolism of, 15, 24–25, 52, 56,
    64–65, 72–73, 75, 134, 151–52
  tulips, 15, 24–25, 54, 71–72, 105, 151
Foley, Michael, 61
Food
  cannibalism, 134–36
  odors of, 18
  sacrifice and, 18
Foucault, Michel, 3, 6
Fowler, Roger, 114, 115
Framing
  dedications in, 68–69, 87–90, 129–30,
    138
  epigraphs in, 49–50, 127, 128, 130–40
  in "Historical Notes" (to *The
    Handmaid's Tale*), 128–29, 142. *See
    also* "Historical Notes" (to *The
    Handmaid's Tale*)
  nature of, 127–29, 158
*Frankenstein* (Shelley), 156–57
Freibert, Lucy M., 33–34, 56–57,
  60–61, 94, 128, 131
Froula, Christine, 52
Frye, Northrop, 65


Garrett-Petts, W. F., 55, 61, 89, 94
Geltner, Gail, 149
*Genesis*
  epigraphs from, 49–50, 131–32
  Jacob, Rachel, and Leah in, 4, 49–50,
    63, 64–66, 113
Gilbert, Sandra, 53
Gilead, 66, 117. *See also* Republic of
  Gilead
Glendenning, Victoria, 37
*Good Bones*, 143
Grace, Dominick M., 155–66
Great Britain
  Canadian nationalism and, 90

Ireland and, 132–40
Great Goddess, 70, 121
Greene, Gayle, 37
Grimm Brothers, 63, 64–79, 149
Gubar, Susan, 53


Hades, 64–65, 74
Hagar, 66
Hales, Leslie-Ann, 59, 60
Handmaids
  birthing ceremony, 17, 47, 48, 101–2
  as breeders, 3–4, 6, 13–14, 15, 22, 43,
    44–45, 46, 47–48, 69, 116, 133–34
  clothing of, 15, 46, 67, 71, 127
  Commanders of the Faith and, 4
  described, 3–4
  infantilization of, 44
  maternity as wish and fear of, 12–13,
    48
  naming of, 6, 13, 68–69, 144
  nurture and, 12–13
  Particicution ceremony, 52, 56, 74,
    75, 131
  password of, 15
  Prayvaganza, 39, 46, 131
  reading and, 19, 53, 66
  re-education of, 14, 47
  ritual insemination ceremony, 3–4,
    16, 22, 46–48, 49–50, 52, 70, 113
  Salvaging ceremonies, 18, 19, 45, 75,
    107, 131
  suicide as escape for, 57–58
  See also Offred
Handmaid's Tale, The
  authoritative voice of victim in,
    96–100
  characterization in, 26–27
  controlling observer in, 109–12
  dedications, 68–69, 87–90, 129–30, 138
  as dystopian fiction, 1, 2, 9
  epigraphs, 49–50, 127, 128, 130–40

epilogue. See "Historical Notes" (to
    The Handmaid's Tale)
  film version, 52, 56, 93
  irony in, 9–10, 20, 122–26
  orchestrations of horror, 95, 100–108
  as parody of American society, 82–91
  reactions to, 81, 93
  as sadomasochistic fantasy, 43, 45, 85
  silenced voices in, 116–22
  skill of narrator, 95–100
"Happy Endings," 153
Harems, 47
Hawthorne, Nathaniel, 2, 89–90
Hecate, 64, 71
"Historical Notes" (to The Handmaid's
    Tale), 155–66
  critical responses to, 60–62, 93–96
  function of, 60, 129, 142, 157
  irony in, 9–10, 20, 122–26
  narrative strategy in, 42–43, 58–62,
    106–12, 115, 116–22
  origins of, 20, 42–43, 54–55, 89, 99,
    162–65
  parody in, 76–79, 88–89, 108–9
  patriarchy in, 20, 26, 59–60, 76–78,
    76–79, 88–90, 123–26, 137, 155,
    161–62
  satire in, 10, 43, 109, 128–29, 139–40
  setting for, 20, 59, 77, 78–79, 122–23
  women controlling women and, 47
History of Sexuality, The (Foucault), 3
Hitchcock, Alfred, 104
Hogsette, David S., 161
Howells, Coral Ann, 22, 59
Hutcheon, Linda, 130, 137, 143, 145,
    147
Huxley, Aldous, 1, 4, 93, 141
Huyssen, Andreas, 143


Incest, 49, 50–51
Inside Enderby (Burgess), 1

Intertext, 149–53
  Jacob, Rachel, and Leah story, 49–50,
    63, 64–66, 113
  "A Modest Proposal" (Swift), 65,
    132–40
  "Red Riding Hood" (Little Red Cap),
    63, 64–79, 149
  "Red Shoes" (Andersen), 44–45, 69,
    149–50
Inuit, 20, 77, 91, 122–23
Iran, 1, 69
Ireland, 132–40
Irony
  in dystopian fiction, 9–10
  frames in, 138–39
  in "Historical Notes," 9–10, 20,
    122–26
  purpose of, 130
Islam, 65–66

Jacob, 49–50, 63, 64–66, 69, 71, 74,
    113, 131
Jameson, Fredrick, 6
Jane Eyre (Brontë), 69
Janine
  incest and, 50
  pregnancy and childbirth, 17, 18, 48,
    101–2
Jeremiah, 65
Jesus, 149
Jezebels, 6, 71
Jezebel's
  described, 19
  Offred visits, 28–29, 34, 46, 51
Journals of Susanna Moodie, The, 75

Kafka, Franz, 19, 93
Kauffman, Linda, 60
Keith, W. J., 61
Ketterer, David, 156, 158

Khomaini, Ayatollah, 69
Kristeva, Julia, 115, 122

Laban, 66, 113
Lacombe, Michele, 61, 71, 94, 128
Lady Oracle, 12, 64, 69, 74, 78, 86, 93,
    108
Leah, 49–50, 63, 64–66
LeBihan, Jill, 128, 138
Levin, Harry, 88
Life Before Man, 12
Linguistic Criticism (Fowler), 114
Linguistics and the Novel (Fowler), 114
Little Red Cap, 63, 64–79, 149
"Little Red Readinghood" (Holland), 78
Livestock, 15
Logocentrism, 116, 123–26
Lolita (Nabokov), 107
Love
  effect of falling/being in love, 35–38,
    56
  lack of, 13–14, 19, 164–65
  reliance on traditional grammars of,
    36–37
  as subversive force, 22–23, 57, 121
Lucifer, 76
Luke, 76
  attitudes toward women, 29–33
  interest in language, 27–28
  old things and, 28–29
  relationship with Offred, 7, 17, 26,
    27–35, 38, 84

Macdonald, Larry, 96
MacKinnon, Catherine, 51
Madonna (Virgin Mary), 66, 70, 71,
    72, 121, 149
Malak, Amin, 3–10, 23, 37, 60, 93–94
Margaret Atwood: A Feminist Poetics
    (Davey), 108–9

Marthas, 17, 43, 44, 46, 47

Mary Magdalene, 71

Materialism, 116, 158–59

Matriarchy, "Red Riding Hood" (Little Red Cap) and, 67–68

"Matrix," 20, 78, 123

Mayday
  resistance movement, 15, 52–53, 58
  as word, 27, 75

McCarthy, Mary, 26–27, 126

Miller, Perry, 87–89, 129–30

Miner, Madonne, 21–39

Mirrors, 70, 116

Misogyny, 41–62
  of Professor Pieixoto, 20, 26, 59–60, 77–78, 88–91, 108, 123–26
  of Republic of Gilead, 6–10, 43, 129–30

"Modest Proposal, A" (Swift), 6, 43, 65, 127, 132–40

Moira
  foot torture of, 14, 45, 55, 69
  as goddess, 67
  as prostitute, 71
  relationship of Offred with Luke and, 31–32, 33
  as renegade, 17, 69, 83–84, 86, 110, 159–60

Moon, 122, 152

Moon, Maryann Crescent, 20, 59, 76–78, 91, 161

Moral Majority, 128

More, Thomas, 156–57

Mormonism, 2, 65–66

Murder in the Dark, 143

Murphy, Patrick D., 128, 129, 132, 157


Nabokov, Vladimir, 107

Narrator
  discursive law of theocracy and, 114–17

mind-style and, 114, 115, 117–22, 124–26

Offred's role as, 3, 8, 43–44, 95–112, 137, 142–45

self-reflexive, 42–43, 142–45, 148, 152–53

variations of same event, 36–37, 57, 148–49, 160–62

Nationalism, 82–91

Nature, 12–20

Nazism, 18, 35, 135–36

New Puritans, 1, 113

New Right, 41–42, 43, 62, 113

Nick
  as fairy-tale prince, 34, 36–39, 86
  relationship with Offred, 7, 17, 26, 33–37, 38–39, 56–57, 59, 73–75, 76, 85–86, 119, 133, 149
  and underground network, 7, 35, 58

1984 (Orwell), 1, 4, 7, 23, 63, 71, 74, 77, 78, 94, 159

Norris, Ken, 155

Northanger Abbey (Austen), 108

Northern Gothic, 2

Nothing Like the Sun (Burgess), 1

Nunavit, 20, 59

Nurture
  deformed infants and, 12–13, 17, 48, 134–36
  pregnancy and childbirth, 11–13, 17, 18, 48, 101–2
  ritual insemination ceremony, 3–4, 16, 22, 46–48, 49–50, 52, 70, 113


Objectification, 13, 46, 51, 60

Objectivity, 10, 20, 42, 108

Odors, 17–19, 118–19

Oedipal fantasy, 48–51

Offred
  chain of chairs, 25–26, 54, 101, 161, 164

compared with Red Riding Hood
(Little Red Cap), 68–79
escape of, 22–23, 39, 56, 75, 76–78,
108
former life of, 13, 14, 17, 18, 23–24,
30–32, 44, 45, 54, 74, 94–95,
97–98, 119, 164
hidden name ( June), 44, 94, 110–11,
118, 124, 152, 164
lack of freedom, 7–8
mother of, 47, 53–54
naming of, 6, 13, 43–44, 68, 84, 150
reading and, 19, 53
recovery of senses, 72–75, 119
relationship to Serena Joy, 33, 44, 46,
48–49, 52
relationship with the Commander,
19, 21–22, 26, 27–35, 48–52, 56
relationship with Luke, 7, 17, 26,
27–35, 38, 84
relationship with Nick, 7, 17, 26,
33–37, 38–39, 56–57, 59, 73–75,
76, 85–86, 119, 133, 149
relationship with Ofglen, 24–25, 27,
35, 39, 46, 52–53, 74, 120
ritual insemination ceremony, 16,
46–48, 49–50, 52, 70, 113
role as narrator, 3, 8, 43–44, 95–112,
137, 142–45
Scrabble games with the Commander,
19, 21–22, 37–38, 70–71, 74, 120
speech patterns of, 119–22
victimization of, 7–8, 96–100
visit to Jezebel's, 28–29, 34, 46, 51
Ofglen
name of, 6
relationship with Offred, 24–25, 27,
35, 39, 46, 52–53, 74, 120
Ofwarren, 6
Ofwayne, 6
Old Testament
Genesis, 4, 49–50, 63, 64–66, 113

Jacob, Rachel, and Leah story, 49–50,
63, 64–66, 113
Orwell, George, 1, 4, 7, 15, 93, 94,
126, 141
Other, women as, 6


"Page, The," 152
Pamela (Richardson), 106–7
Parody
of American society, 82–91
of Gothic form, 49–50, 108–9
in "Historical Notes" (to The
Handmaid's Tale), 76–79, 88–89,
108–9
of nature, 20
of patriarchy, 76–79, 87–89, 108
Particicution ceremony, 52, 56, 74, 75,
131
Patriarchy, 41–62
ambivalence about childbearing in, 12
antifeminist backlash and, 41–42, 61
biblical, 49–50, 63, 64–66
in "Historical Notes" (to The
Handmaid's Tale), 20, 26, 59–60,
76–78, 88–90, 123–26, 137, 155,
161–62
misogyny of, 43
parody of, 76–79, 87–89, 108
women to control women in, 46–47
Pearls, 53
Pen, 53, 97
Penis symbolism, 16, 51, 53, 75, 84,
133–34
Perrault, Charles, 67, 68, 149
Persephone, 64–65, 66, 67, 70, 72, 75,
76, 78
Phillips, Howard, 41
Photographs, 144–46, 152, 164
Pieixoto, James Darcy, 58–60, 76–78,
128–29, 137, 139–40, 155–56,
161–66

misogyny of, 20, 26, 59–60, 77–78,
    88–91, 108, 123–26
Pigs, 15, 47, 133
Plath, Sylvia, 151–52
Politics
  of autonomy, 85–87
  of liberation, 85, 90–91
  nationalism of Atwood and, 82–91
  power and, 12
  of sexual control, 8, 109–12
Polygamy
  Mormon, 2
  Old Testament, 4, 49–50, 63, 64–66,
    113
Pornography, 14, 45, 46
*Possessed, The* (Dostoyevsky), 7–8
Postfeminism, 62
Postmodernism, 2, 55, 61, 93, 143
Powe, B. W., 94
Power
  oppression, 111–12
  paradoxes of, 100–108
  politics and, 12
  sexuality and, 3–4, 6, 10, 109–12
  totalitarianism and, 4
Prayvaganza, 39, 46, 131
Presley, Elvis, 89, 143–44, 163
*Pride and Prejudice* (Austen), 77–78
Probyn, Clive T., 138–39
Pro-choice ideology, 12
Pro-family activism, 41
Pro-life ideology, 12
Prostitution, 6, 19, 34, 55–56, 71,
    146–47
Pullen, Charles, 136–37
Puritanism, 2, 65–66, 87–90, 113, 128,
    129–31


*Quill & Quire*, 133


Rachel, 49–50, 63, 64–66, 71, 113, 131

Rachel and Leah Center, 23, 38–39,
    97–98
Rape, 18, 46, 50, 51, 52, 64–65, 82
Rats, 15, 133
Reagan, Ronald, 91
Red (color), 88, 111
  of blood, 24, 46, 105, 122, 151–52
  of clothing, 67, 71
  of flowers, 15, 24, 71–72, 105
Red Center, 42, 45, 53, 55, 69, 70, 73,
    110, 160
"Red Riding Hood" (Grimms), 63,
    64–79, 149
"Red Shoes, The" (Andersen), 44–45,
    69, 149–50
"Reducing the Dystopian Distance:
    Pseudo-Documentary Framing in
    Near-Future Fiction" (Murphy),
    157
Religious Right, 22, 41, 66, 81
Republican Party, 1, 2
Republic of Gilead, 1
  and American fundamentalism of
    1980s, 87–88
  control of female rage, 52, 75
  misogyny in, 6–10, 43, 129–30
  natural world in, 12–20
  ritual insemination ceremony, 3–4,
    16, 22, 46–48, 49–50, 52, 70, 113
  roles of women in, 43
  sexuality and power in, 3–4
  totalitarianism of, 7–8, 10, 60, 115–17
  *See also* Handmaids
Richardson, Samuel, 106–7
Right-to-Life movement, 2
Rigney, Barbara, 59
"Robber Bridegroom, The" (Grimms),
    76
Robertson, Pat, 66
Romance, as anomaly, 19
Romance plot, 21–39, 81
  colonial autonomy and, 85–87, 90–91

in costume gothic, 86–87
implied author in, 111–12
in Offred's relationship with Nick,
    36–39, 56–57, 73–75, 85–86, 133,
    149
*See also* Love
Romania, 75
Rooke, Constance, 94
Rubenstein, Roberta, 11–20, 60, 94,
    128, 134

Sage, Lorna, 7
St. Nicholas, 73–74
Saint Paul, 76
Salmon, 16, 51, 133–34
Salvaging ceremonies, 18, 19, 45, 75,
    107, 131
Satire
    in "Historical Notes" (to *The
        Handmaid's Tale*), 10, 43, 109,
        128–29, 139–40
    in "A Modest Proposal" (Swift),
        132–40
Saul, 76
*Scarlet Letter, The* (Hawthorne), 89–90
Schlondorff, Volker, 93
Scrabble games, 19, 21–22, 37–38,
    70–71, 74, 120
*Second Sex, The* (de Beauvoir), 6
"Sense and Conscience" (Tennyson),
    72
Serena Joy
    as bad mother, 47, 49, 64
    flowers and, 15, 24–25, 52, 56, 105
    garden of, 24–25, 56, 70, 71–73, 105,
        121
    name of, 70
    Offred's secret relationship with
        Commander and, 58, 70–71
    relationship of Offred to, 33, 44, 46,
        48–49, 52

sitting room of, 147
Sexuality
    Commanders of the Faith and, 4, 8,
        16, 46–48, 49–50, 52, 70, 113
    degradation and violence in, 45, 46
    flowers and, 15, 24–25, 52, 134,
        151–52
    incest, 49, 50–51
    male sexual dominance, 19
    power and, 3–4, 6, 10, 109–12
    prostitution, 6, 19, 34, 55–56, 71,
        146–47
    as saleable commodity, 4
    Scrabble as, 21–22
*Shape of Things to Come, The* (Wells),
    157
Shearer, Moira, 69, 150
Shelley, Mary, 2, 156–57
Shiel, M. P., 157
Smells, 17–19, 118–19
Smith, Joseph, 2
Snow White, 66
Sons of Jacob Think Tank, 59–60, 113
Staels, Hilde, 113–26
Stein, Karen, 127–40
Sterilization, 113
Stimpson, Catherine, 82–83
Sufi proverbs, 127, 128, 130–31
*Surfacing*, 11–12, 64, 74, 75, 76, 78, 82,
    83, 141, 142–43, 147, 152
*Survival: A Thematic Guide to Canadian
    Literature*, 8, 82, 83, 88
Swift, Jonathan, 6, 43, 127, 128, 129,
    130, 132–40

Tennyson, Alfred, 72, 73, 78
Theocracy
    American Puritanism, 2, 65–66,
        87–90, 113, 128, 129–31
    as current menace, 1
    Mormonism, 2, 65–66

*See also* Republic of Gilead
"This Is a Photograph of Me," 152
*Through the Looking Glass* (Carroll), 78
*Times Literary Supplement*, 7
Tome, Sandra, 81–91, 128, 129–30,
    133, 163
Totalitarianism
  in dystopian fiction, 4
  Republic of Gilead and, 7–8, 10, 60,
    115–17
Touch, 56, 74, 119
Tree of Life, 70, 71
Triple Fates, 69
Triple Goddess myth, 63, 64, 67, 68,
    69, 71, 77
Triple Marys, 64, 68, 77
Truth, 165
Tulips, 15, 24–25, 54, 71–72, 105, 151
"Tulips" (Plath), 151–52
Turner, Alden, 87–88
Twisted Sister, 89, 163

Unbabies, 12–13, 17, 48, 134–36
Underground Femaleroad, 58, 59, 76,
    90, 114, 117
Unwoman, 4, 22, 47, 69
*Utopia* (More), 156–57

Venus, 64, 67, 71
Virgin Mary, 66, 70, 71, 72, 121, 149
Vision motifs, 109–12
  Eyes (spies), 14, 27, 46, 58, 109, 111
  mirrors, 70, 116
  photographs, 144–46, 152, 164

Wade, Professor, 123–24, 162–63
Wagner-Martin, Linda, 128
Wall in Gilead, 14, 24–25, 54, 59, 87,
    102–6, 120, 134, 150
*We* (Zamyatin), 4, 5, 99, 159
Webster, Mary, 68–69, 87, 89–90,
    129–30
Wells, H. G., 157
Wilson, Sharon Rose, 63–79, 145, 149
Wives, 4, 43, 113–14
Workman, Nancy V., 128, 130–31
Worms, 16, 134
Wyatt, Jean, 49

Young, Brigham, 2

Zamyatin, Yevgeny, 4, 5, 93, 99
Zelpha, 66